A LOOK AT CECIL·ALDIN'S DOGS AND HOUNDS

THE LAMBOURN PRESS

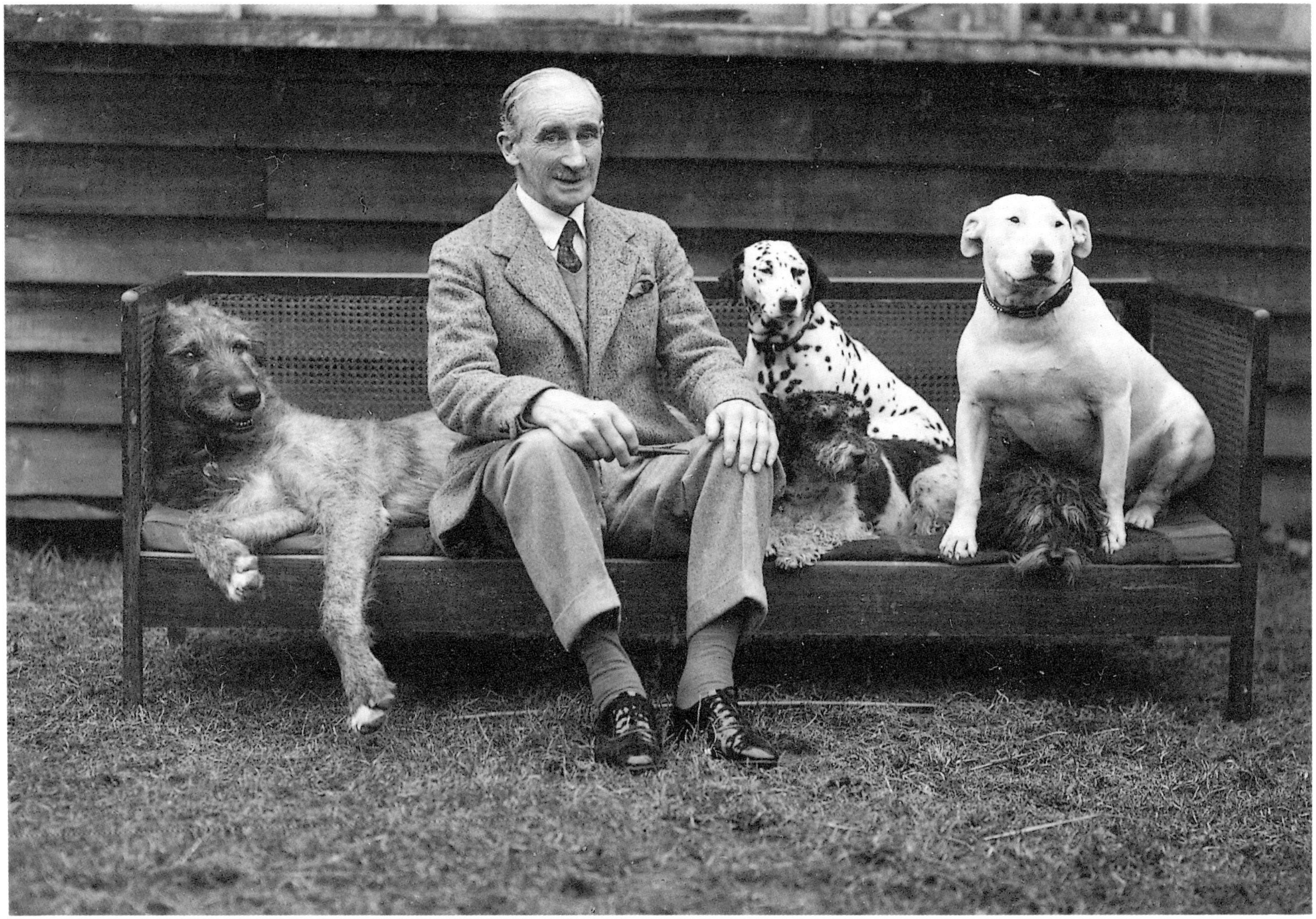

The Board of Directors, 1928.
Left to Right: Micky the wolfhound, Cecil Aldin, Loopy the dalmatian, Bogie the terrier, Cracker the bull-terrier and Turps the rough-haired dachshund.

The entire board was to accompany Cecil Aldin to Majorca in 1930.
In 1929 Aldin acquired a rough-haired sealyham by the name of Susan who was also to join the board on their foreign expedition.

A LOOK AT CECIL·ALDIN'S DOGS AND HOUNDS

by Rupert Collens

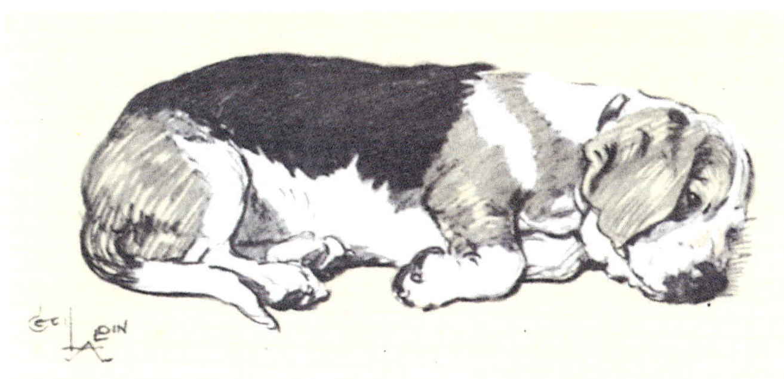

THE LAMBOURN PRESS
London · Dublin · Melbourne

THE LAMBOURN PRESS LTD
The Old Forge, 7 Caledonian Road,
London, N1 9DX, England
28 Molesworth Street, Dublin 2, Eire
9 Queen Street, Melbourne 3000, Victoria, Australia

First published 1990

A limited edition of 275 signed and specially bound copies is published
by
The Marlborough Bookshop and Sporting Gallery
6 Kingsbury Street, Marlborough, Wiltshire

Typeset in Stone Informal
DTP conversion and typesetting by Typographical Services

PRINTED BY
BAS PRINTERS LIMITED, OVER WALLOP, HAMPSHIRE

ISBN Limited Edition 1-872708-01-3
Trade Edition 1-872708-00-5

Dedication

I dedicate this book with much love to Charlie, an old-fashioned, bad tempered chow chow, the type which Cecil Aldin so beautifully depicted in his books *Just Among Friends* and *The Cecil Aldin Book,* and in whose office I wrote much of the book.

Contents

Acknowledgements

First and foremost I wish to express my deepest thanks and appreciation to Cecil Aldin's family, in particular his grandchildren and great-grandchildren, for their help and hospitality over many years. I would particularly like to thank them for the loan of an unpublished manuscript by Cecil Aldin's daughter, Gwen. I must also thank them for profuse loans from their lovely family collection including unique scrapbooks and photograph albums.

I would also like to put on record my gratitude to Roy Heron for writing the first serious book on Cecil Aldin *Cecil Aldin – The Story of a Sporting Artist* back in 1981. All lovers of Aldin's work owe Roy a vote of thanks for his pioneering research.

My fellow dealers, in particular Nick Potter of the Burlington Gallery, Mark Flower of the Court Gallery, John Yates of the Heale Gallery and Les Wilson of Halson Books, have rallied round wonderfully and sold me some good examples of Cecil Aldin's work for this book at most favourable prices, or lent me works to illustrate the book. No acknowledgements would be complete without a word of thanks to Pam Turnbull of The Countrymans Gallery (Kibworth Harcourt) for her vocal support and encouragement to make certain I completed my task; while to Barrie Marks I must acknowledge more than normal gratitude, not only as a supplier of Cecil Aldin's works over the years, but for his willingness to share his discerning knowledge of Aldin's work with me.

Lastly, but not least, I would like to thank the many collectors, most of whom wish to remain anonymous, for lending me material, in particular the Thurston and Biggs' families for loans from their collection, Viv Scott for letting me denude the Lamb Inn, Marlborough of decoration and Graham Goodwin for being kind enough to bring a lovely etching into me at short notice.

I would like to thank Jeannine Alexander very much for her patience in the production of this book, for typing the manuscript and for filing all the transparencies.

Introduction

This book is a celebration of Cecil Aldin both as a dog artist and as an endearing personality.

For me personally, and for hundreds of thousands, if not millions, of his other fans all around the world, he is the greatest and most enjoyable dog artist of all time.

To understand Aldin's work, it is necessary to know something about the enchanting and much-loved man he was which is why I say this book is intended as a 'celebration of Aldin'. He loved life and seemed to see the world through rose-tinted spectacles. Admittedly Aldin came from a reasonably prosperous background, had unlimited talent as an artist, and from a very early age was making a substantial income. However he did suffer from ill-health from his late teens onwards, his works were widely pirated in France and America (which must have been very annoying), but not once in all the books I have read, or in the many private letters, have I ever found him even complaining, let alone whingeing or whining.

There is absolutely no doubt at all that Aldin had a magical way, not only with brush and pen, but with animals and children.

Odd as it may seem, canine drawings or pictures *per se* accounted for less than one-third of Aldin's total output actually sold during his lifetime, so the reader must not think that dog pictures or drawings entirely dominated his working life. In fact it was not until after World War I, when Aldin was nearly fifty, and arthritis, a weak heart and general ill-health were slowing up his artistic output, that canine subjects accounted for more than half of his output.

When I say Aldin's 'output', I am in fact talking about the work he did for commercial reward. Throughout the whole of his life dogs were a dominant theme in his sketches and he built up a tremendous collection of these which he greatly valued and constantly referred to.

The reader may well ask why Aldin has received so little recognition by the artistic establishment and in the museum world and I will try to answer that question. Firstly, he was English and when I went to University in the late fifties/early sixties the idea that English art was anything but second-best would have been laughable. The artistic establishment would concede that Stubbs, Romney and Gainsborough were satisfactory artists but, of course, very parochial and provincial, being English. There was, and perhaps still is, a feeling amongst the so-called art intelligentsia that things foreign are better than things English, for no logical reason.

If, in the fifties and sixties, one had put forward the theory in an University exam paper that Twentieth Century artists, such as Sir Alfred Munnings, P.R.A., Lionel Edwards or Cecil Aldin were anything better than 'chocolate box' artists, one would have failed spectacularly and been the laughing stock of one's professors. I am pleased to say that more and more people in the artistic world now accept the fact, perhaps reluctantly, that Munnings was a great painter, not far behind the very best of the Twentieth Century painters on an international scale, and that Lionel Edwards and Cecil Aldin were very much better than mere 'chocolate box' painters.

There is another annoying trait to be found amongst British museum curators and that is 'Nanny knows best'. Cecil Aldin was immensely popular with all classes of society in the fifteen years leading up to World War I. Lord Lonsdale, one of the great 'grandees', whose style of living rivalled even that of the Royal Family, had a large number of Aldin's originals and prints throughout all his residences and was happy to have Aldin to stay as a guest at Barleythorpe. In fact Aldin's work was also represented in the private collections of the

Royal Family and one of his prints still graces, in miniature, the walls of Queen Mary's Doll's House.

At the same time as Aldin's work was to be found in the Royal collections and in most of the great houses of the country, his prints, especially the series such as the 'The Fallowfield Hunt' and 'The Bluemarket Races', were popular and common decorations in pubs throughout the length and breadth of the British Isles. In short Aldin was immensely popular with all the various strata of society and making a comparatively large income. For some reason those who run museums regard 'popular art', especially when the artist is financially highly successful in his own lifetime, as poor quality. It is, as Aldin would have said, "not art with a capital A", and therefore not suitable for exhibition in their hallowed halls. I personally believe that a modern day artist who suffers from the same problems with the "artistic and museum establishment" as Aldin did is David Shepherd, best known for his elephant portraiture. He is popular with "the man in the street" and financially highly successful, but we do not find his work in the Tate Gallery or the Walker Gallery in Liverpool. He has the wrong image, as did Aldin, and they both had the infuriating ability, as far as the art establishment is concerned, of being able to laugh at themselves and, even worse, at "art with a capital A".

It was indirectly thanks to the Royal Family that I first became acquainted with Aldin's work. In 1960 or 1961 I was in King Edward VII's Hospital for Officers (Sister Agnes) in the same ward as the late Lord (Tommy) Graves. I was there as I had stupidly gone out the back door of a horse during the Irish Grand National Meeting at Fairyhouse and I think Tommy was there merely due to old age. Amongst the large number of presents he received was a parcel from H.R.H. The Duke of Windsor and The Duchess of Windsor which contained a copy of Cecil Aldin's autobiography *Time I Was Dead*. This had been inscribed to Tommy by the Duchess with words to the effect of "this will bring back memories of the fun you and David had together hunting in Leicestershire". It also contained a photograph, signed by The Duke, taken from an Aldin painting. This large painting of The Duke of Windsor out with the Pytchley was the Duchess' favourite portrait of him and had a central position in their Paris home.

Lord Graves kindly lent me the book and then kept me amused for hours with tales of his derring-do on the hunting field and the turf. He was one of the few peers of the realm to become a bookmaker. He had been a close friend of Cecil Aldin and The Duke of Windsor and regularly hunted with them both.

In this book I will attempt to show the reader as much as possible of Cecil Aldin's canine work in the years between 1887 and 1934. For me one of the most important aspects of Aldin's work is its wide variety and I have noticed over the years how different aspects appeal to different people.

I make no apology for devoting so much of the second chapter to childrens' books. I personally think the illustrations and text, both by Aldin, for books such as *Rough and Tumble* and *Farmyard Puppies* are superb. Their high-class production, which was clearly overseen by Aldin, greatly enhances them.

Aldin's ability to do these wonderful illustrations for children was one of his great strengths as an artist, although I know they are simplistic and do not endear his work to the art establishment. Here I think the art establishment is wrong, as, for instance, no literary critic thinks less of Graham Greene for his ability to write childrens' books, as well as novels and travel books.

In this book I haven't necessarily selected what I consider to be Aldin's best work, or that which I personally like most. What I have tried to do is to give a balanced portfolio of images to demonstrate the range of his works and how, throughout his career, Aldin constantly changed his style. I believe this continual change of technique and the use of different media - from pen and ink drawings to poster paint, to pastel, to watercolours, to ivorine - was to prove one of Aldin's greatest assets. As a result at no time did his style ever become repetitive and I can honestly say that his work when aged sixty-four in 1934 was as fresh as that in 1900, when he was only thirty. This is fairly unusual for an artist as most of them have a 'golden period' after which their work tends to decline.

Finally I would like to comment on my dating of pictures and photographs. I believe if I quote an actual year that I am correct to within one year on either side. For instance, if I say 1925 I am fairly certain the painting or photograph was taken in the years 1924, 1925 or 1926. At the same time, after a period varying between fifty-five and one hundred years, it is very hard to say if Aldin acquired, shall we say, Susan, his sealyham, in late 1929 or early 1930.

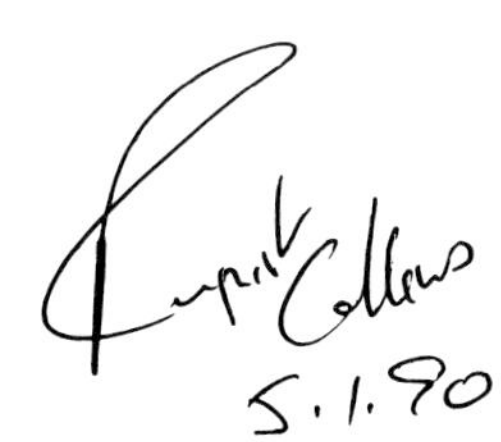

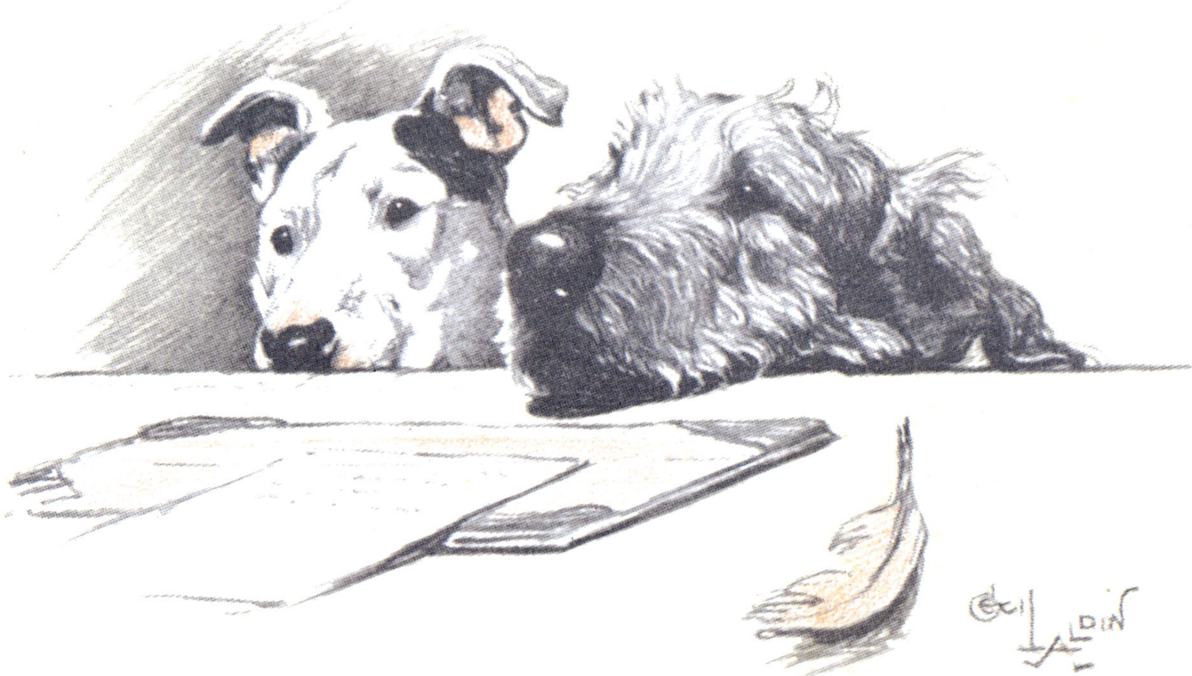

"Remember this is a book about dogs."
This is the caption used by Aldin in his book
Dogs of Character.

Chapter One
The First 30 Years (1870 to 1900)

The two dogs opposite, Micky and Cracker, entered Cecil Aldin's life soon after the end of World War I. They are probably the two most famous dogs in British art or literature and we shall meet them again later in this book.

This book is about Cecil Aldin's dogs and hounds, but I will start at the beginning and will try to present his life and works in a rough chronological order. The book is not a biography and I shall therefore keep my general comments to the barest minimum as I know the reader will wish to view Cecil Aldin's work, which is a far more eloquent testament to his ability and character, than anything I, or anyone else, could possibly write.

Cecil Aldin was born in Slough in 1870, the eldest of a family of four children. He had two brothers and a sister. At the time of his birth, the family had been prosperous builders for over thirty years, responsible for building much of Pimlico in the 1830's and, later on, much of South Kensington. When Cecil Aldin was a year old, his grandfather died and the family moved to London, living just off Kensington High Street in what is now Phillimore Place.

From an early age Cecil Aldin was fascinated by dogs, horses and, for some inexplicable reason, hunting. He tells us that his first memory of drawing from nature was "as a red-headed child sitting at a nursery window waiting for tradesmen's carts to pull up so he could 'dror' the ponies pulling them".

The most popular illustrators of the time were John Leech and Randolph Caldecott and their amusing and gay hunting and coaching scenes were to have an ever-lasting effect on Aldin. It is almost certain that he got this fascination with hunting from books, as there is no other logical explanation as to how a young child living in the centre of London, coming from a non-hunting family could have got his interest in the chase. One must put this near obsession down to a freak of heredity. Likewise there was nothing in his background to indicate to the world that Aldin would end up as a world-class artist although, like so many Victorians, his father was a keen amateur artist.

At the age of nine, Cecil Aldin was sent as a boarder to Eastbourne School, but his father's business took a downturn and Eastbourne proved too expensive. So Cecil and his two younger brothers went to Solihull Grammar School in Warwickshire, once again as boarders.

There is no doubt that Aldin was not an academic success at Solihull. Drawing or doodling pictures of horses, hunting scenes and dogs, rather than paying attention to class, regularly got him into trouble. He left school as soon as he decently could at the age of sixteen.

His mother had a series of what the Victorians called 'lap dogs' including a pug, a Scottish terrier and a pomeranian, none of which made any lasting impression on Cecil and one suspects they preferred the company of their mistress rather than a budding canine artist. As soon as he left school Cecil acquired his first dog model, a mongrel with a good dash of greyhound or lurcher in him, by the name of Gyp, and for the rest of his life dogs were to be his constant companions, both working and during his leisure hours. Gyp became a particularly adept model and would hold poses for hours. Gyp was quickly followed by two pedigree bulldogs, and a short-lived bloodhound.

On leaving school, a family conference was held to decide Cecil's future. His mother favoured a career in the Church but, he says, his father, a keen amateur artist himself, swayed the day in favour of an artistic career. The probable truth is that a career in the church was impractical, as in Victorian days a young man with pillar-box red hair and poor academic qualifications would not have gone far.

Cecil was therefore sent literally around the corner from Phillimore Gardens to the Melbury Road studio of the distinguished R.A., Albert Moore. Albert Moore was not interested in any way in animal or sporting painting and Cecil Aldin was equally uninterested in painting Grecian ladies sitting on cold, uncomfortable marble slabs. There was a mutual parting of the ways after a few weeks.

Aldin's next place of learning was only a few hundred yards further up Kensington High Street at the South Kensington Art School, now the Royal College of Art, where he went to study animal anatomy. His fellow students, who included such distinguished people as Edward Lutyens, remember him well for two reasons; firstly his youthfulness, as he was three or four years younger than the average student, and secondly for the fact that when he was in a general class, rather than an animal/anatomy class, how he used to cover his sketchbook with excellent imaginary studies of animals, showing virtually no interest in the subject he should have been studying.

Aldin certainly lasted longer at the South Kensington Art School than he did with Albert Moore, but there must be considerable doubt about his ability to have stuck the course there. However, salvation was at hand in the shape of Emily Moore (no relation to Albert), a spinster, who ran the Swan Inn at Leatherhead. Miss Moore must have been an unusual publican, as she strongly disapproved of people getting drunk, or even slightly inebriated, and only allowed smoking in one room in the whole building. She was clearly wealthy, having other businesses and farming interests in the locality, so was in an ideal position to further Aldin's embryonic career.

Miss Moore asked him to come down to Leatherhead to paint a picture of her Skye terrier. She took a great liking to Aldin and converted an old coach-house into a studio for him. He spent an idyllic nine months there, making a living from painting all types of animals for the locals. Certainly this boded well for the future as he had not yet attained his eighteenth birthday, but had managed to support himself from his own pen and brush.

Aldin's father then sent him as a pupil to the greatest ever teacher of animal painting, certainly in England if not the world, Frank Calderon. Amongst the highly successful artists Calderon was also to teach were Alfred Munnings, later Sir Alfred, President of the Royal Academy, and Lionel Edwards.

Calderon was then teaching at Midhurst in Sussex and Aldin moved down there, into a studio next to some buildings where the local butcher kept a scratch pack of harriers. Aldin became an avid follower of this pack, sometimes on foot, but more often on a butcher's pony lent to him by the harriers' owner and Master.

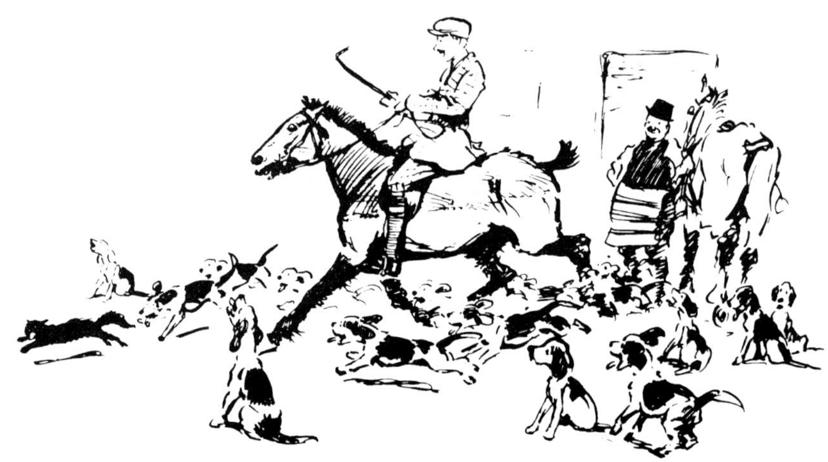

Continued on page 19

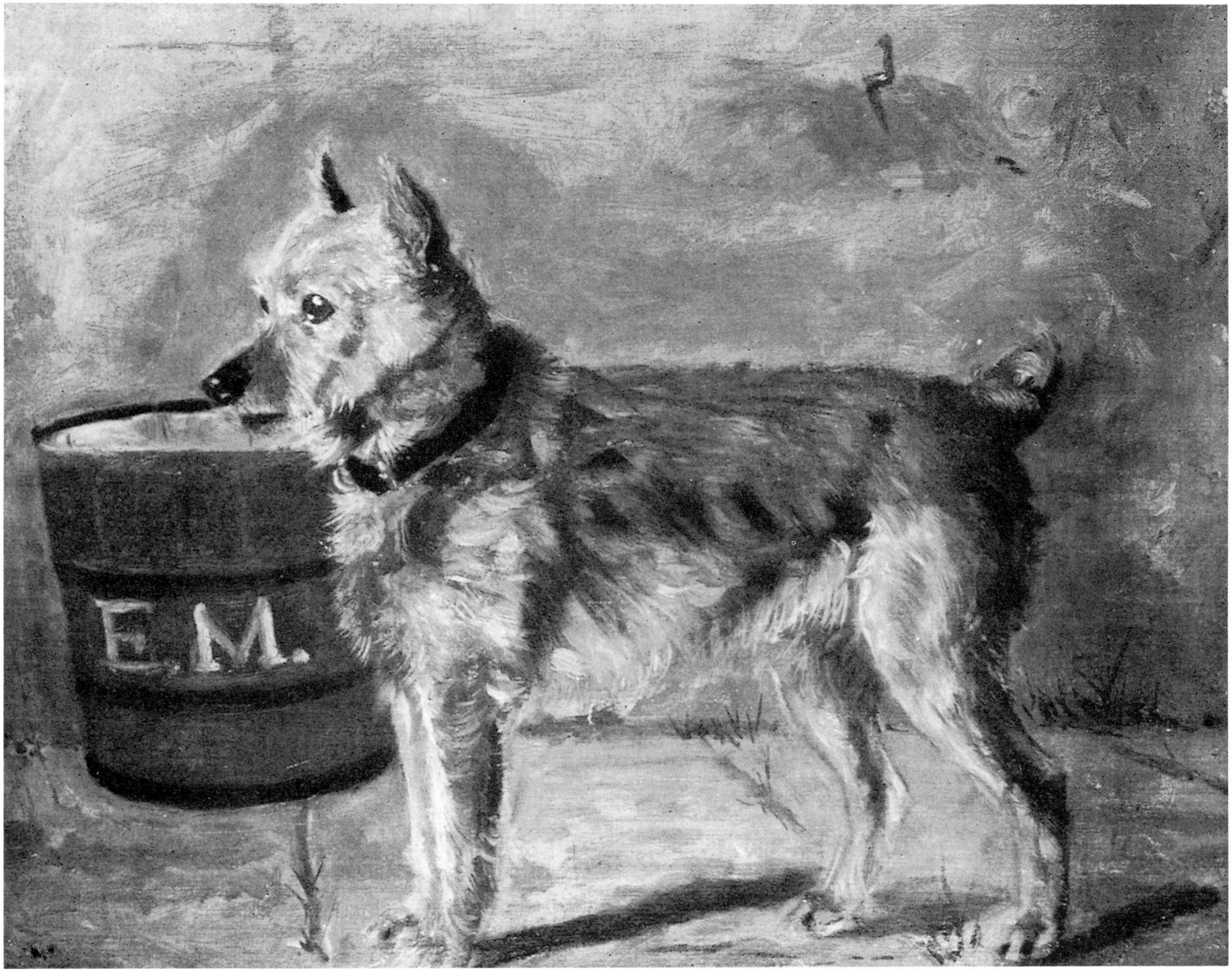

Cecil Aldin's first commission; he was aged seventeen.

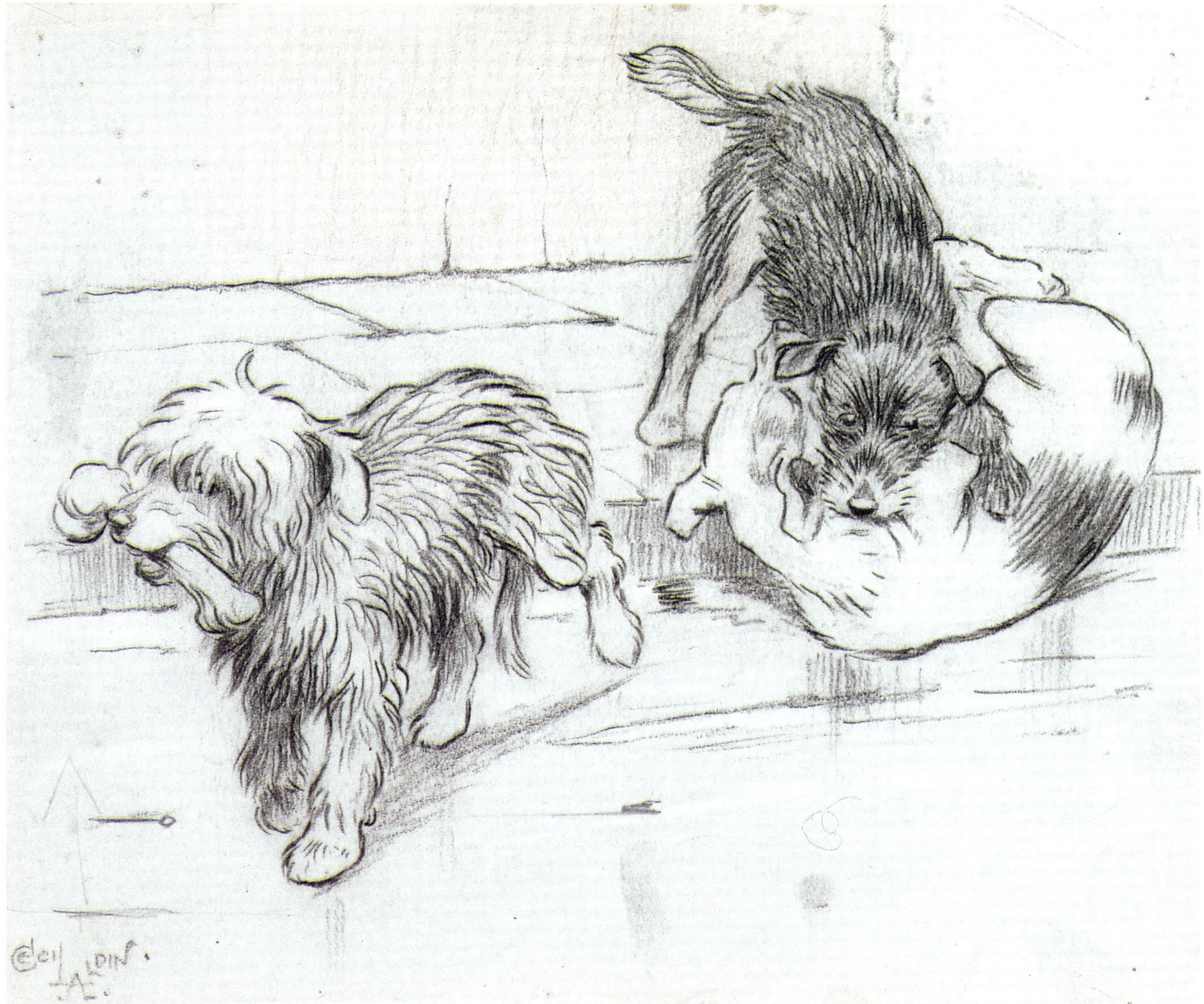

The drawing above is one of Aldin's early professional works, dating from around 1891. The two pictures on the right were both executed in 1893 and entitled 'Stop Thief' and 'A Serenade' and appeared in *The Sketch*.

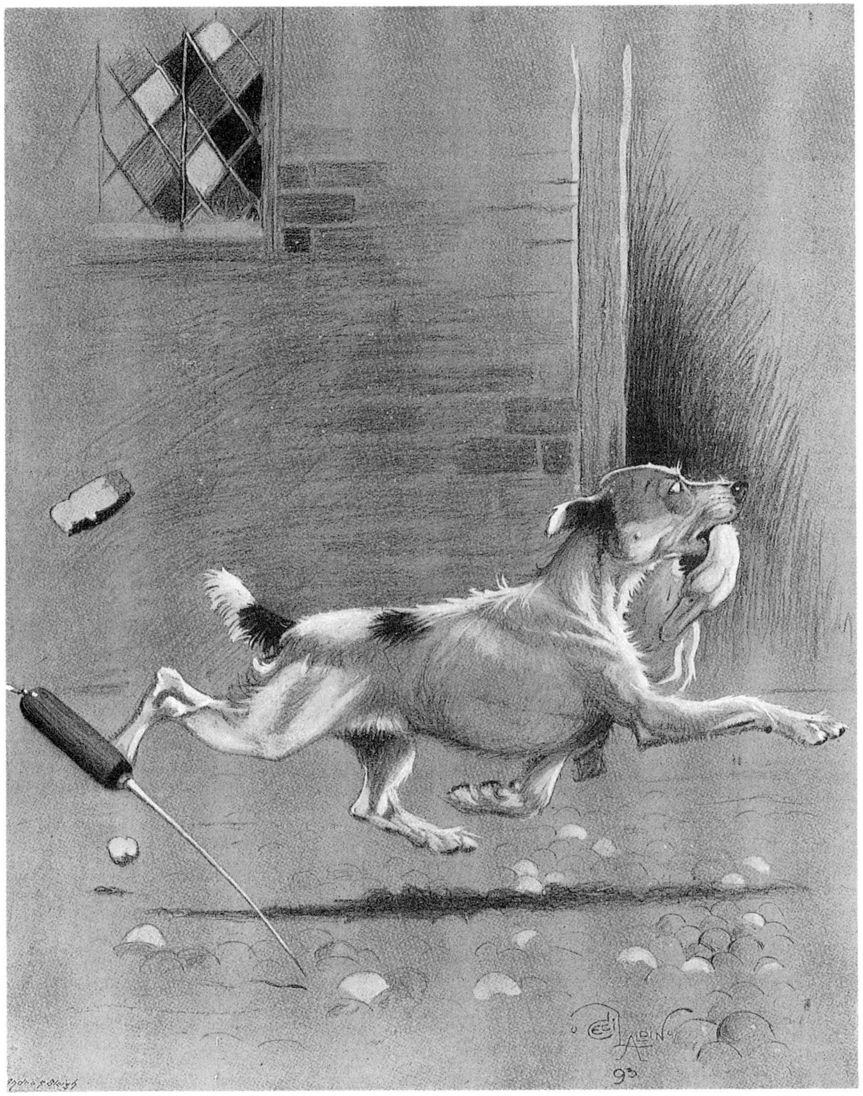

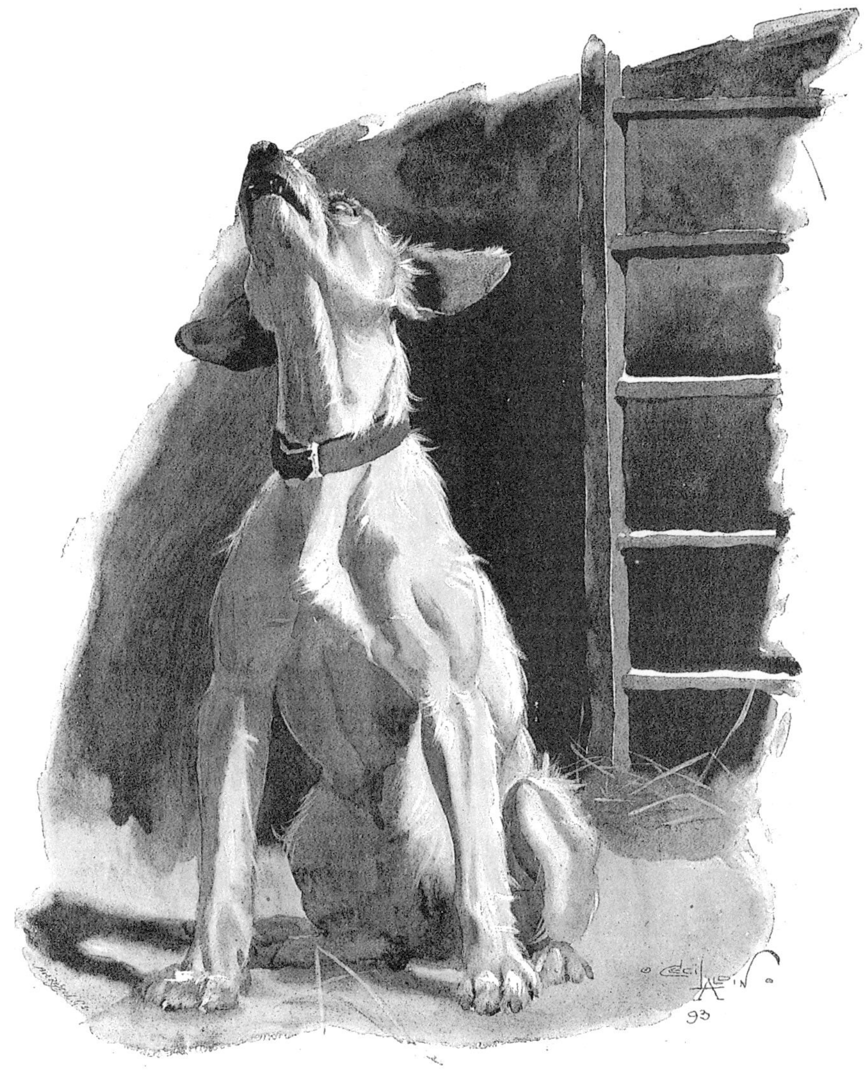

Like most of Aldin's illustrations, they were drawn in black and white, mainly pen and ink work, but with quite a bit of wash applied with a brush and the odd highlight which was applied with chalk after the drawing had otherwise been finished.

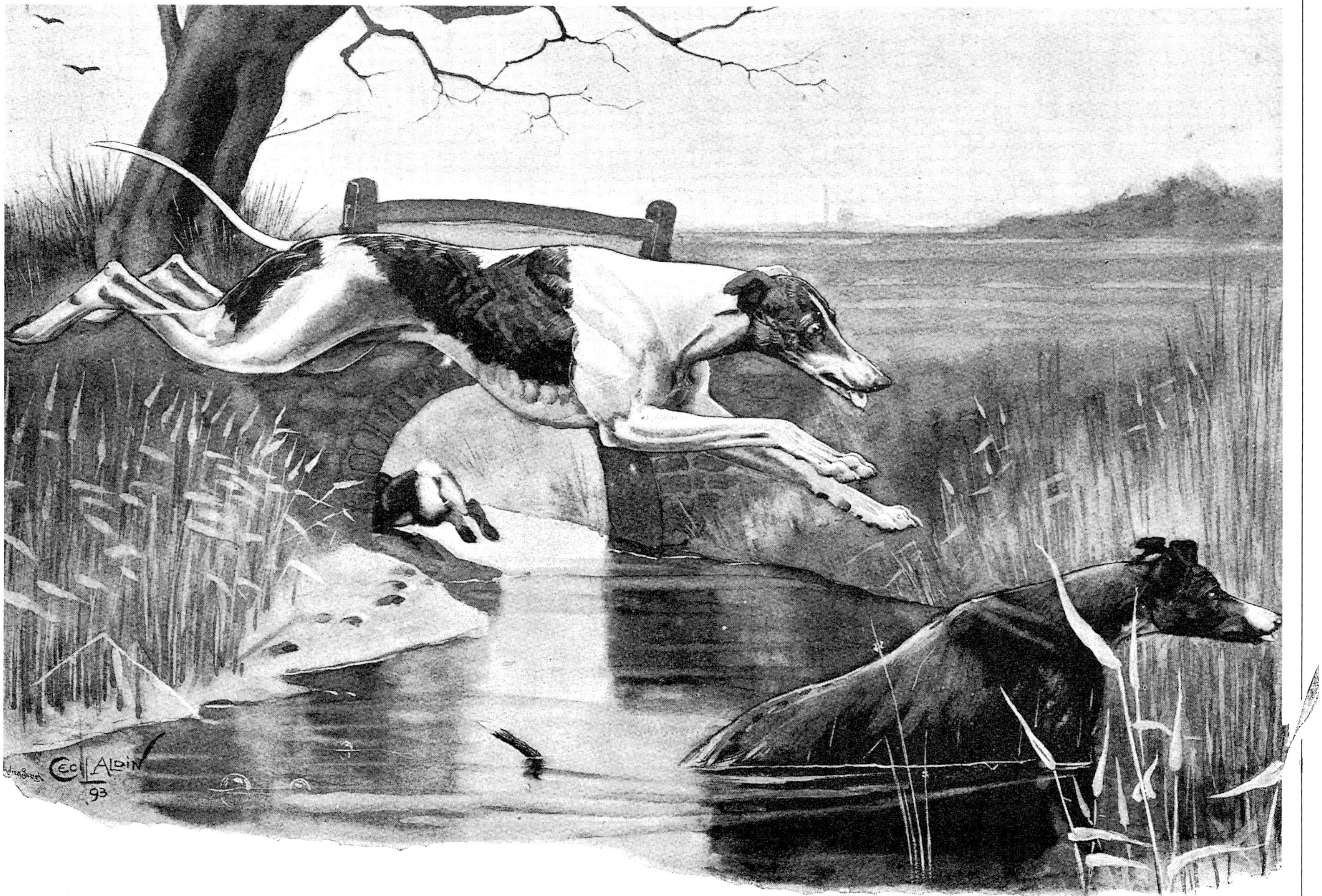

The drawing above appeared with two others in *A Year of Sport and Natural History* by Oswald Crawfurd, first published in 1895. This was one of the first times Aldin's work was to appear in a book. For me personally the ability to draw greyhounds is one of the best measures of an artist, as although elegant and finely boned, these dogs have tremendous strength.

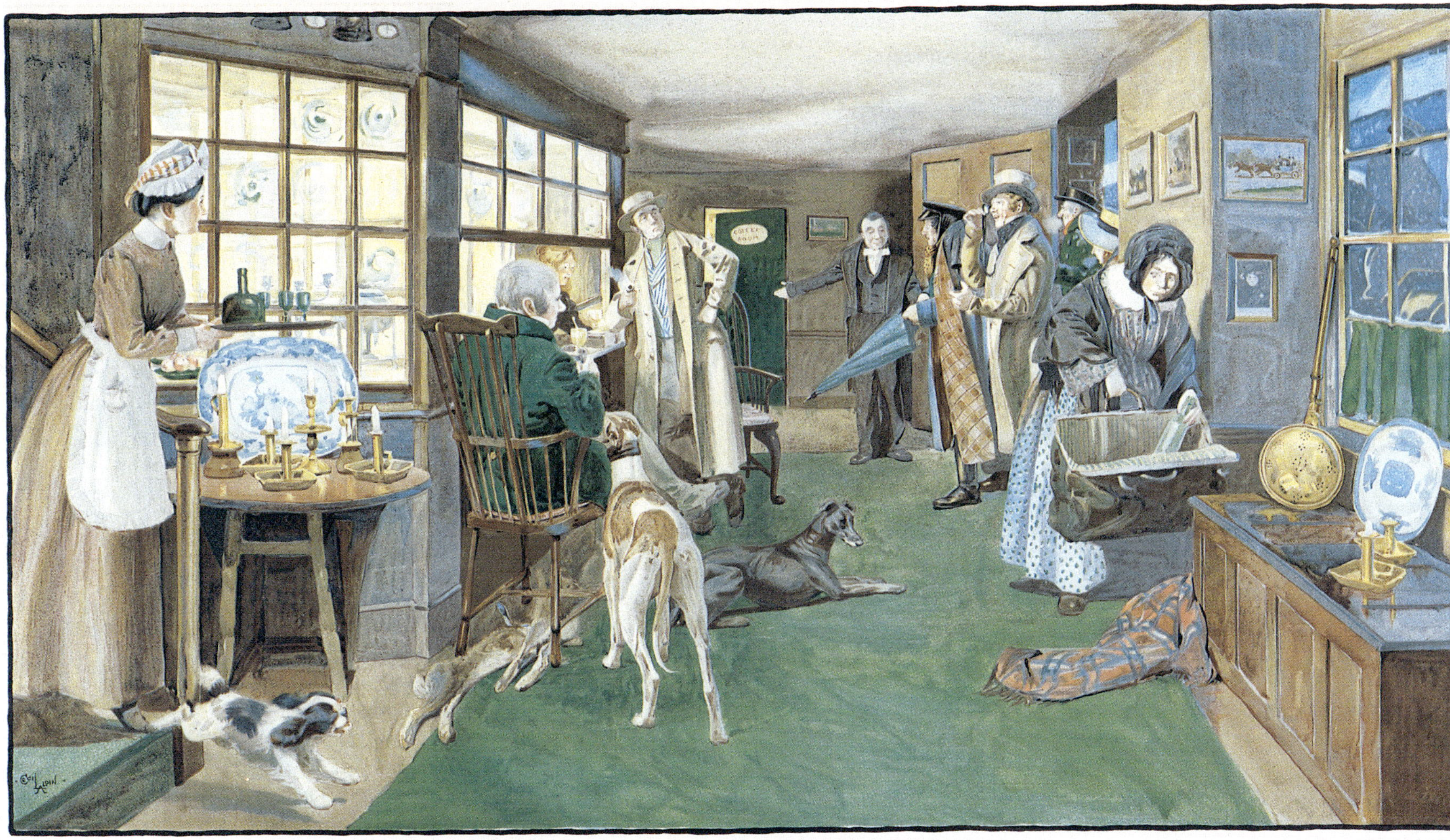

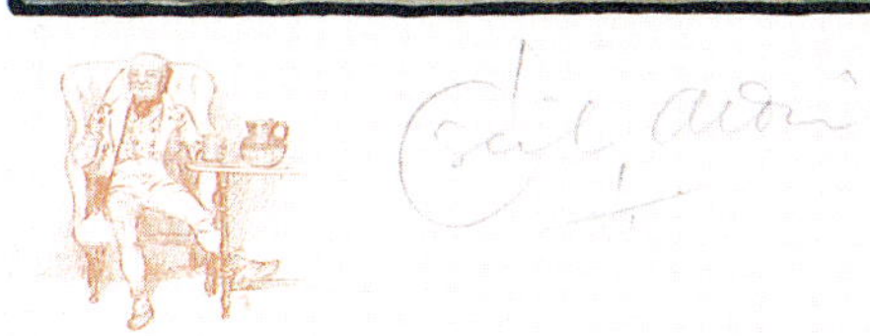

Cecil Aldin mastered the drawing of them in the 1890's and although the picture on the right is one of his large 'Inn' series executed between 1898 and 1905, it is dominated by the two greyhounds and the King Charles spaniel dashing in from the left. Aldin painted the King Charles loosely to give the impression of speed. Incidentally, this series of prints were all reproduced from landscape watercolours whereas the 1920 series of Inns were all reproduced from pastel drawings and were mainly portrait.

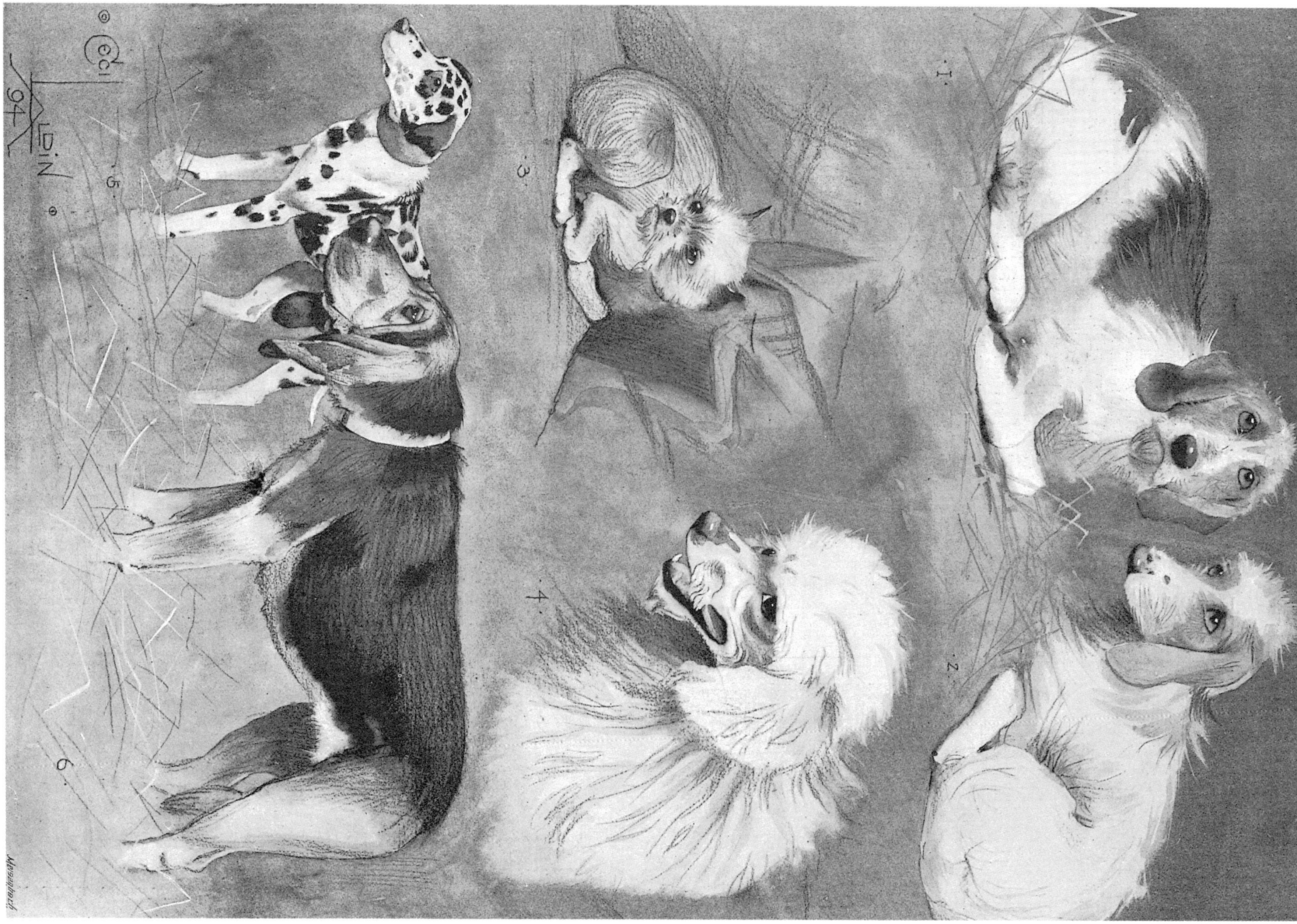

1. The Prince of Wales's rough-coated basset-hound, Beauty II.
2. The Prince of Wales's basset-hound, Bonnie II.
3. Mr. C.C. Haldenby's foreign dog, Fanica.
4. Mr. O.C. Thompson's poodle, King II.
5. Mr. George R. Sim's dalmation, Samson
6. Mr. Brough's bloodhound, Brunhilda.

THE KENNEL CLUB DOG SHOW AT THE CRYSTAL PALACE

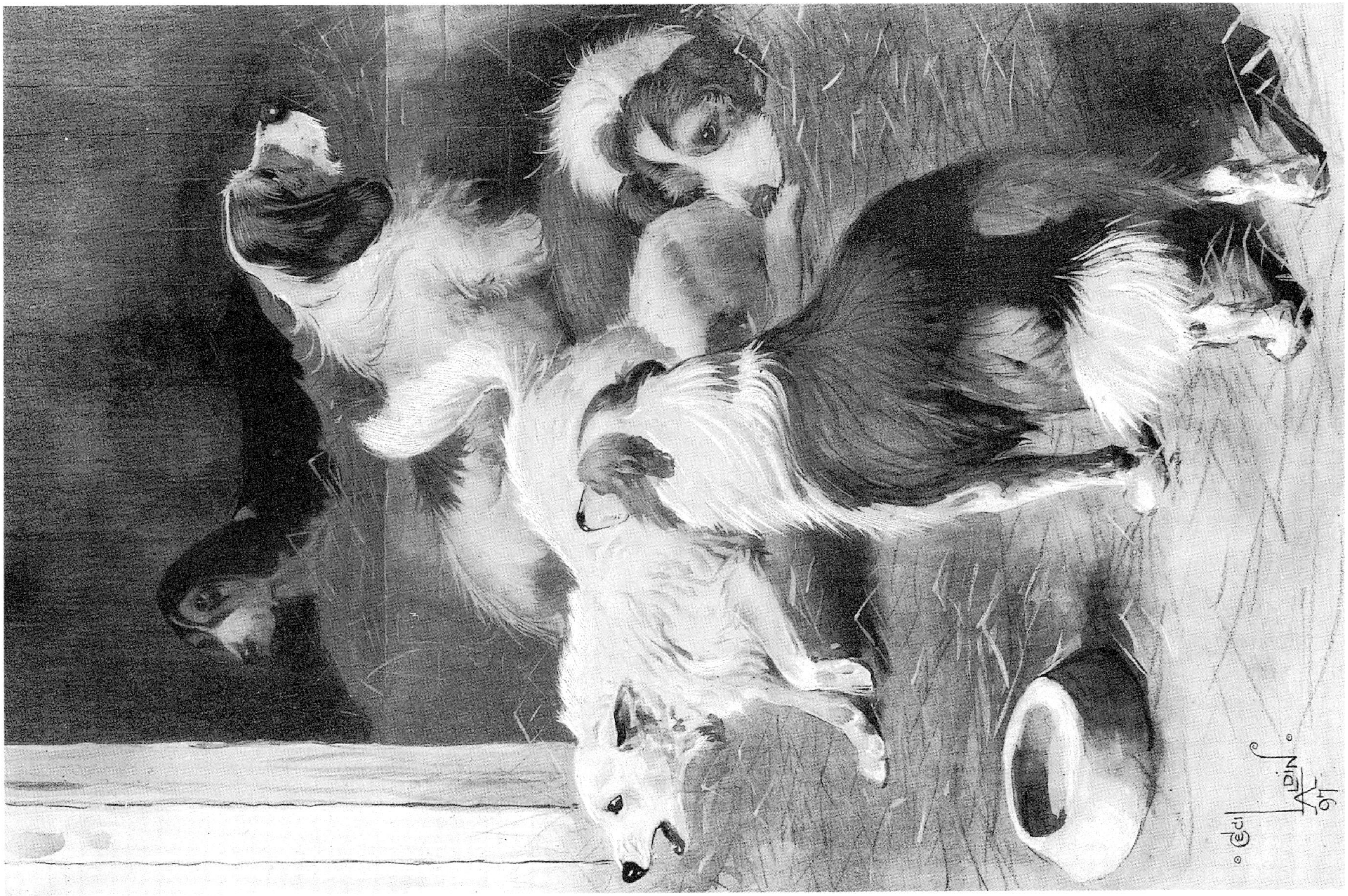

Dogs belonging to the Prince of Wales, exhibited at Cruft's dog-show at the Agricultural Hall.

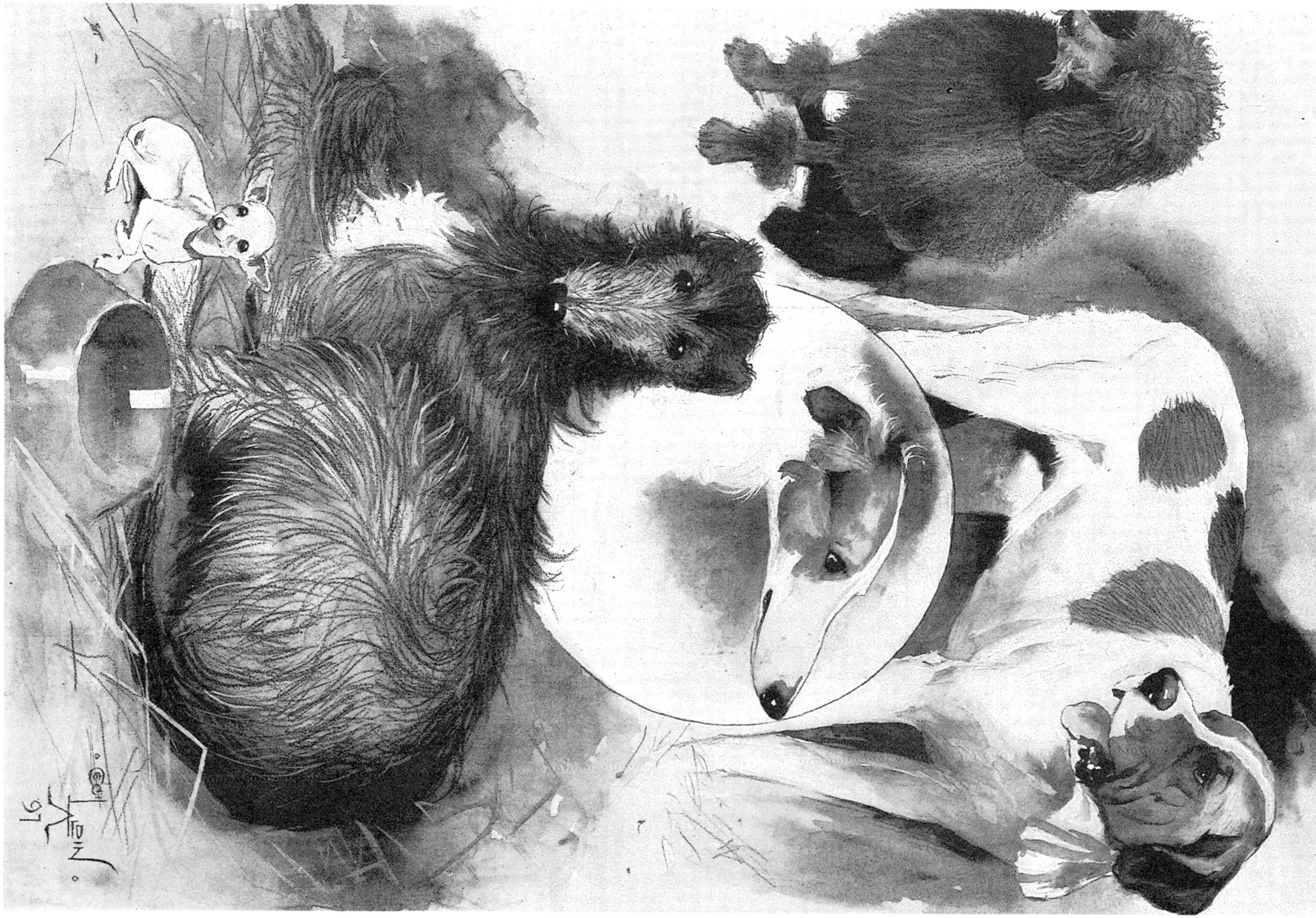

Mrs. Long's poodle, Black Satin
The Hon. Mrs. Algernon Bourke's, Mousie (chihuahua)
Miss Kate Stephens' St. Bernard, Trafalgar
The Princess of Wales's Borzoi, Alex
Mrs. Hood-Wright's deerhound, Selwood Fealer
PREMIERSHIP PRIZE-WINNERS AT THE LADIES' KENNEL ASSOCIATION'S SHOW
AT THE BOTANICAL GARDENS.

Midhurst was a great success. The Aldin family fortunes were on one of their upturns so his father could give him sufficient funds to live comfortably. He didn't have to worry about selling pictures or, for that matter, as he said, "no income and no income-tax returns to be filled up". He made considerable artistic progress and most importantly, although Calderon was a great teacher of animal anatomy and drawing, he also taught Aldin to draw architecture and other non-animal subjects successfully.

Aldin loved the life at Midhurst - plenty of hunting, not only with harriers, but also with the local foxhounds and otter-hounds, comfortable 'digs' which were visited often by his younger brothers or friends, and he was making satisfactory progress as an artist under the tuition of someone he admired.

All good things have to come to an end however, and in mid 1890 Aldin was removed back to London to live at Phillimore Place by his parents as he had suffered a serious attack of rheumatic fever, an illness of which he had a history, and which left him with a jumpy heart. By the end of the year, he had had his first two drawings accepted for publication which earned him £3.10s. and in early 1891, around the time of his twenty-first birthday, he took a studio in Chelsea.

The years 1891 to 1893 must have been a struggle for Cecil Aldin, like any other young artist trying to be accepted in Fleet Street, and one assumes that for the first year or two anyway, he was still supported by his father. However, as time went by, more and more illustrated papers such as *The Illustrated London News* and *The Graphic* started to take his work more and more regularly and economics improved. His father's business took another downturn in the early 1890's so it was essential that Cecil stood on his own two feet financially.

His first great breakthrough came in 1894 when Sir Douglas Straight, having seen some sketches he had made at London Zoo, commissioned Aldin to illustrate Rudyard Kipling's *Jungle Stories* for his magazine *The Pall Mall Budget*. This commission was very much the seal of acceptance and 1894 was a highly successful year for Cecil Aldin, both artistically and, equally important, financially. He tells us that he made the princely

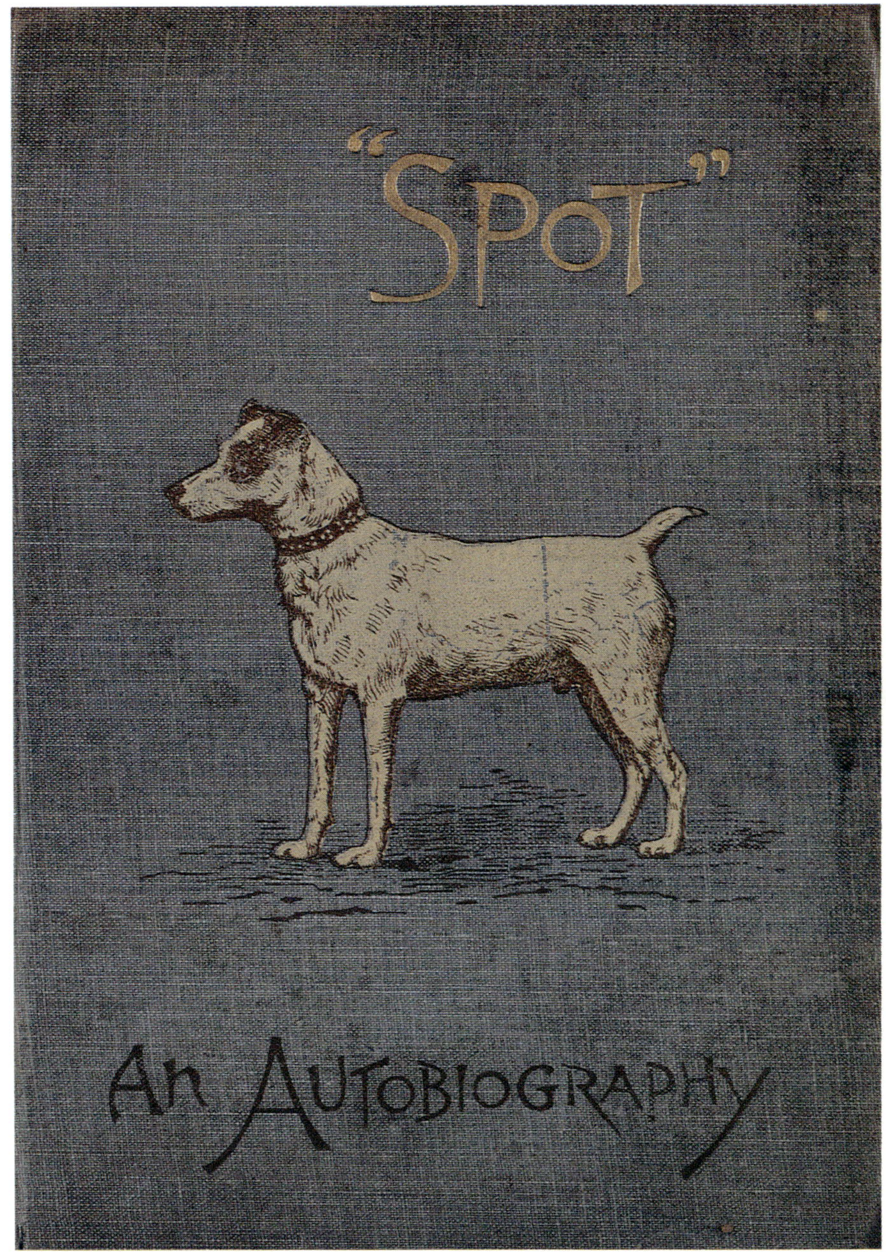

The first book Aldin illustrated was *Spot* in 1893.

sum of over £400 that year and on the strength of it got married in 1895.

Cecil Aldin, his new wife and three dogs set up home in Chiswick and he was to term the next nine years, until 1904, his 'Bohemian Days'. Certainly throughout the whole of these nine years he moved freely in leading artistic and theatrical circles. As soon as Aldin had his own house and garden his kennel of dogs rapidly increased and at one time he had thirteen dogs, mainly bulldogs, bull-terriers, bob-tails and terriers; but he also had, at various times, more than one poodle, a particularly beautiful white borzoi and the odd dalmatian.

Aldin's career continued to flourish during the first four or five years of his married life. He started doing illustrations for books. The first of these was *Spot* in 1893, and in 1895 he contributed illustrations to The Reverend John Isabell's *Wonderful Wonders* and to Oswald Crawfurd's *A Year of Sport and Natural History*. Also around this time, he started to report on, as well as illustrate, racing, hunting and coursing for various periodicals.

In 1897, Louis Meyer commissioned a pair of driving prints, featuring Aldin's wife, Rita. These were to be followed quickly by a number of dog prints. Some of these early dog prints were rather loosely drawn and lacking in colour and probably the first two to be any real success were the beautiful pair of prints showing 'westie puppies' playing and at rest, which I estimate were produced in the last two years of the nineteenth century. They are certainly rare and one can therefore deduce that they were produced early in his career before print runs had increased. Once Aldin had got the colouring of his prints right, lovely canine print after lovely canine print flowed from various publishers' offices. The most successful of his single dog studies was the charming print of a large mongrel entitled 'A Gentleman of Character'. I always think that this 'Gentleman' would have been an ideal playmate for T.S. Eliot's cats in his superb book *Old Possums Book of Practical Cats.* At this time Aldin was also producing very simplified prints aimed at the juvenile market such as 'Hunt the Slipper'.

Artists such as Aldin who made the majority of their income from periodicals were not unlike Fleet Street photographers of the current day. They were out and about attending events on a day-to-day basis and Dog Shows were Aldin's favourite haunts throughout the whole of the nineties. The then Prince and Princess of Wales, later King Edward VII and Queen Alexandra, kept an important kennel of dogs at Windsor which were regularly exhibited at shows, where Aldin drew them, as well as at Windsor itself.

In 1898 Aldin was elected a member of the Royal Society of British Artists and by the turn of the century Cecil and Rita had two much adored children, Dudley and Gwen.

The years 1899 and 1900 were to see the change from Aldin being a successful artist to becoming what I suppose nowadays one would call 'a mini-megastar'. Both he and his daughter Gwen always attributed the sudden upturn in his fortunes to the publication of the large set of six prints entitled 'The Fallowfield Hunt'.

These prints were an absolute sensation and sold and sold and sold. Suddenly Aldin had developed a completely unique style. These prints depicted idealised, late eighteenth century imaginary scenes, which I can only describe as Cecil Aldin's own make-believe Camelot.

Roy Heron, Aldin's distinguished biographer, says that Aldin had finally thrown off the influence of Caldecott in this series. I think the reverse. I believe Aldin went back to Caldecott's gay and colourful hunting scenes and modified, refined and made them more sophisticated. In doing so, Aldin perfected what could loosely be called 'The Caldecott School'. 'The Fallowfield Hunt' series was a natural progression from Caldecott's naivety.

Aldin followed 'The Fallowfield Hunt' with three other similar sets of six large prints - 'The Bluemarket Races' in 1901, 'The Harefield Harriers' in 1908 and 'The Cottesbrooke Hunt' in 1914.

These prints, of which space only allows me to illustrate two of 'The Bluemarket' series, are all still highly collected. Dogs and hounds, as such, play only a supporting role in them so I must reluctantly pass on.

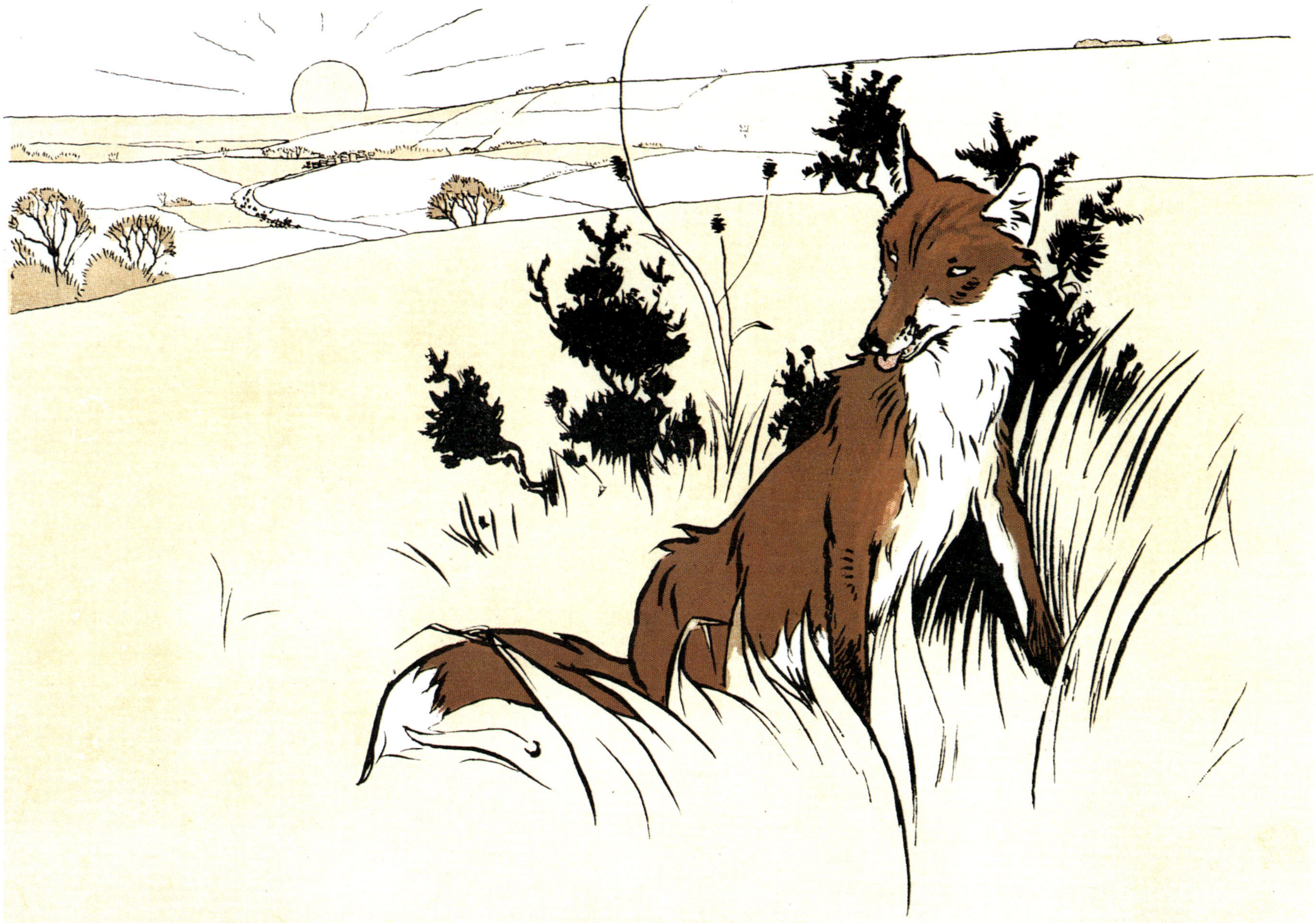

Pages 21 – 29 are all from *A Sporting Garland.*

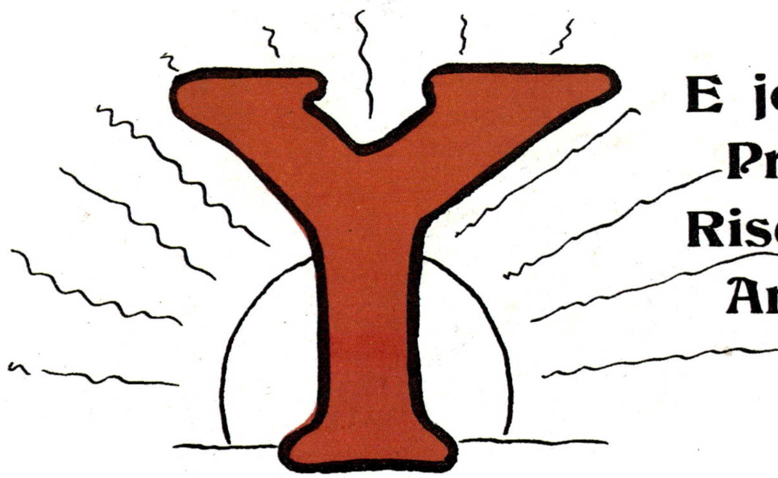

YE jovial hunters, in the morn
Prepare then for the chase;
Rise at the sounding of the horn,
And health with sport embrace.

When a-hunting we do go.

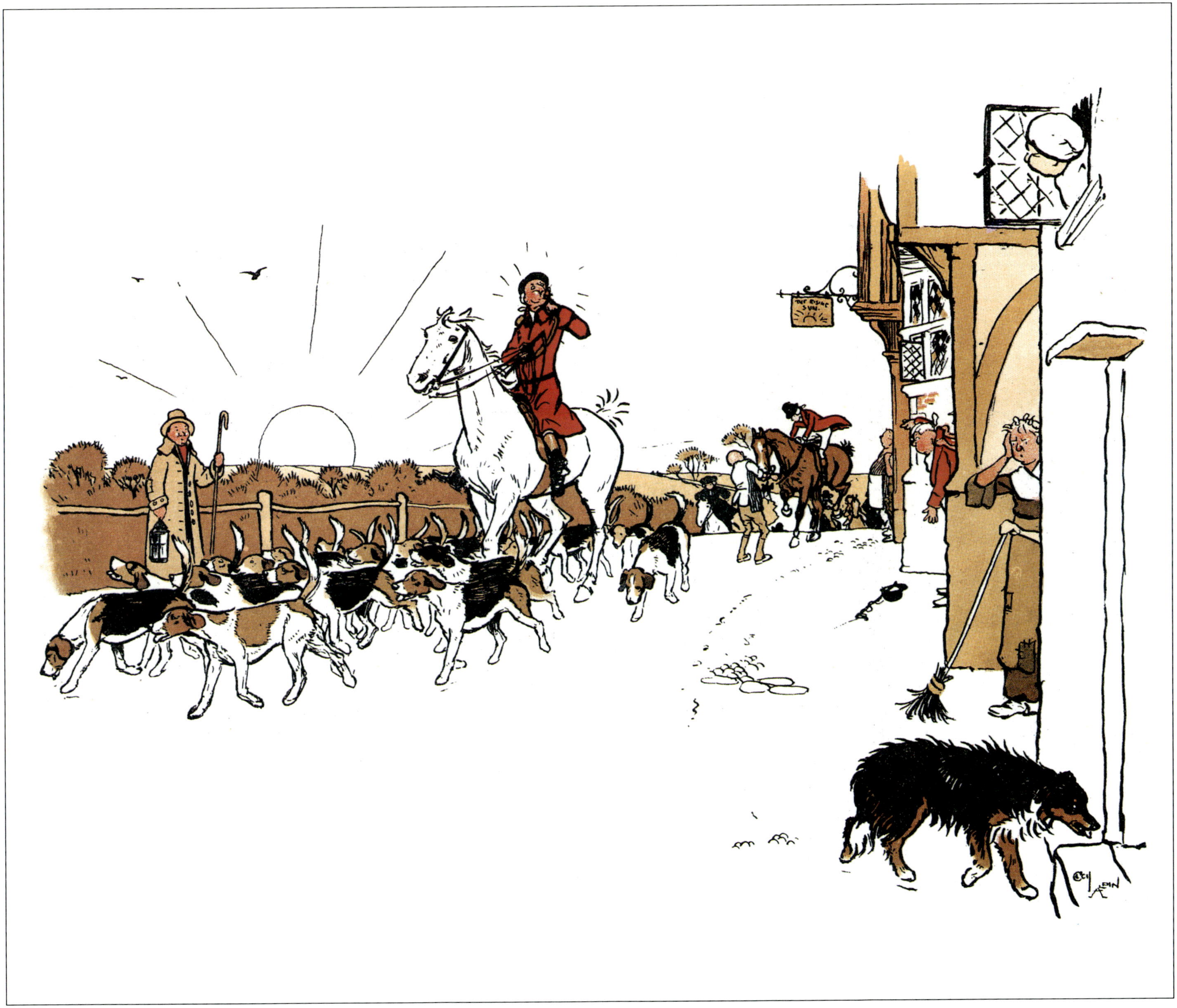
THE RISING
SUN.

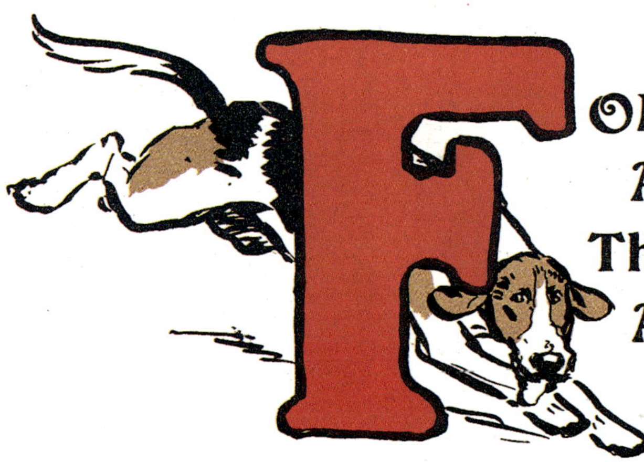

FOND Echo seems to like the sport,
And join the jovial cry;
The woods, the hills, the sound retort,
And music fills the sky.

When a-hunting we do go.

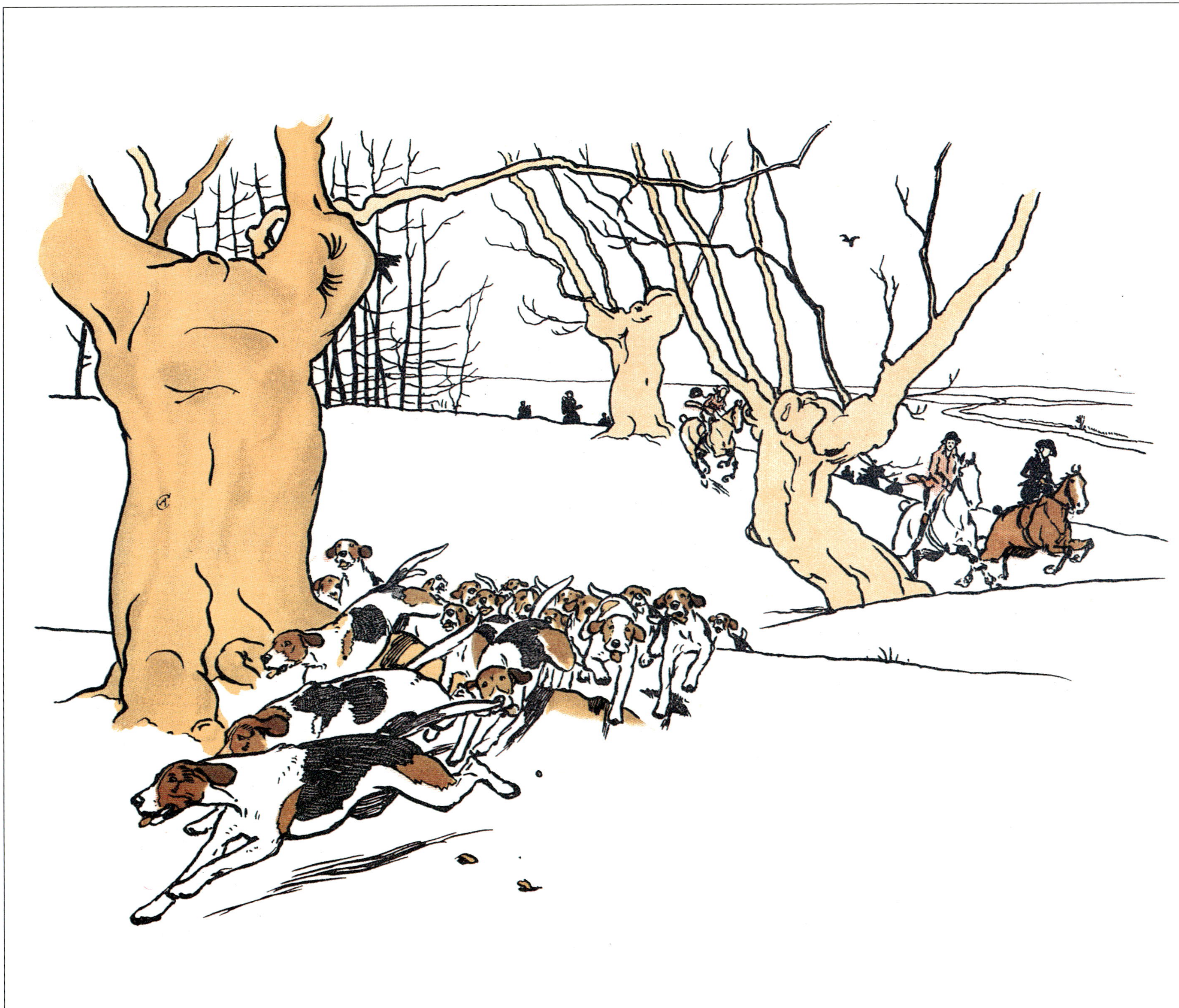

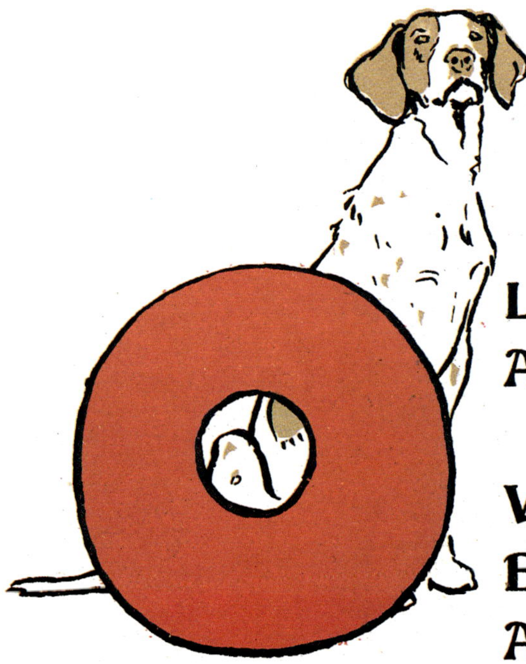

OLD Ponto makes a famous point,
As marble stiff, in ev'ry joint.
I cautiously proceed,
When quickly up the covey fly–
Bang, Bang–both barrels then I try–
And lo! a brace before me die,
The shooter's richest mead.

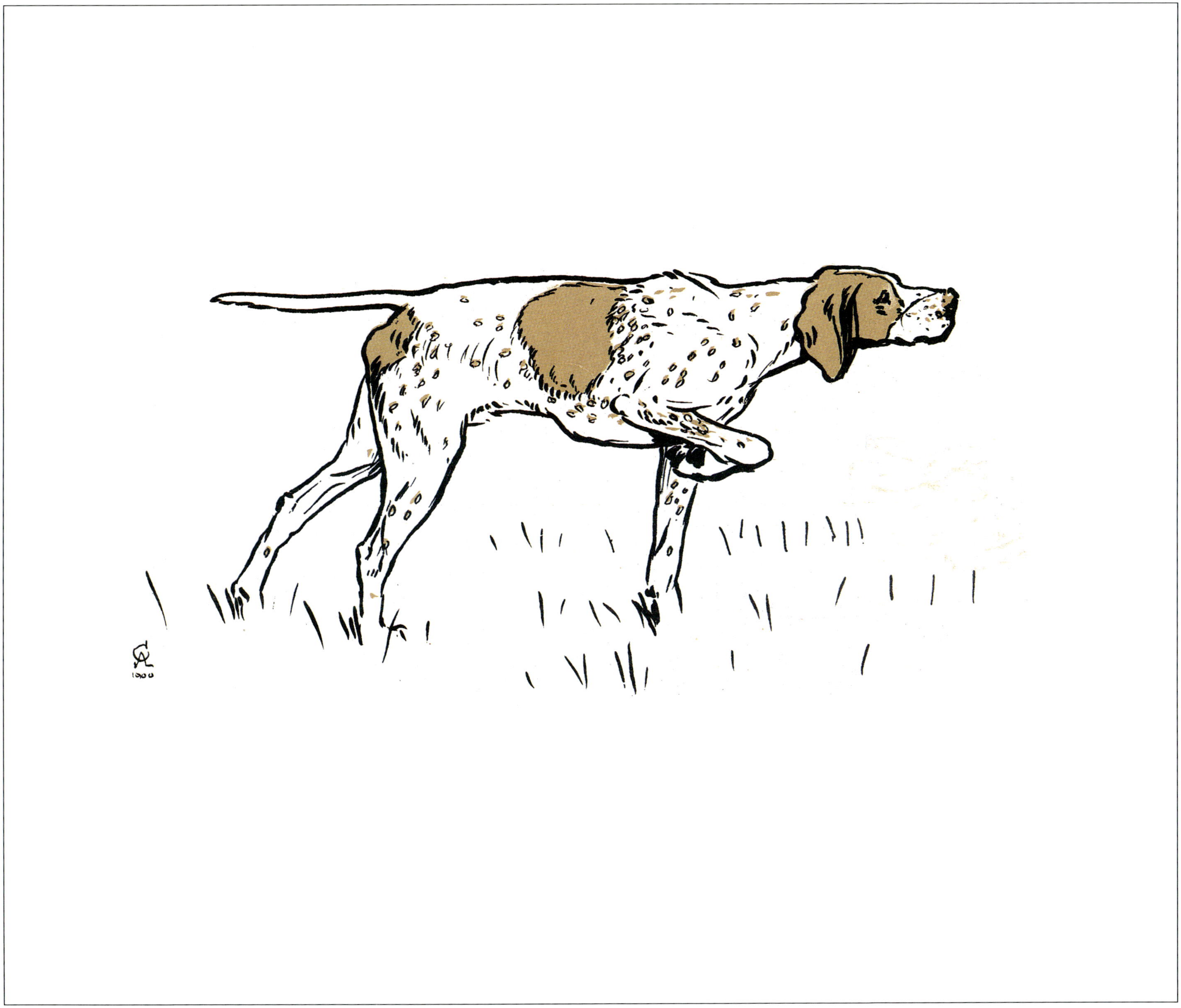

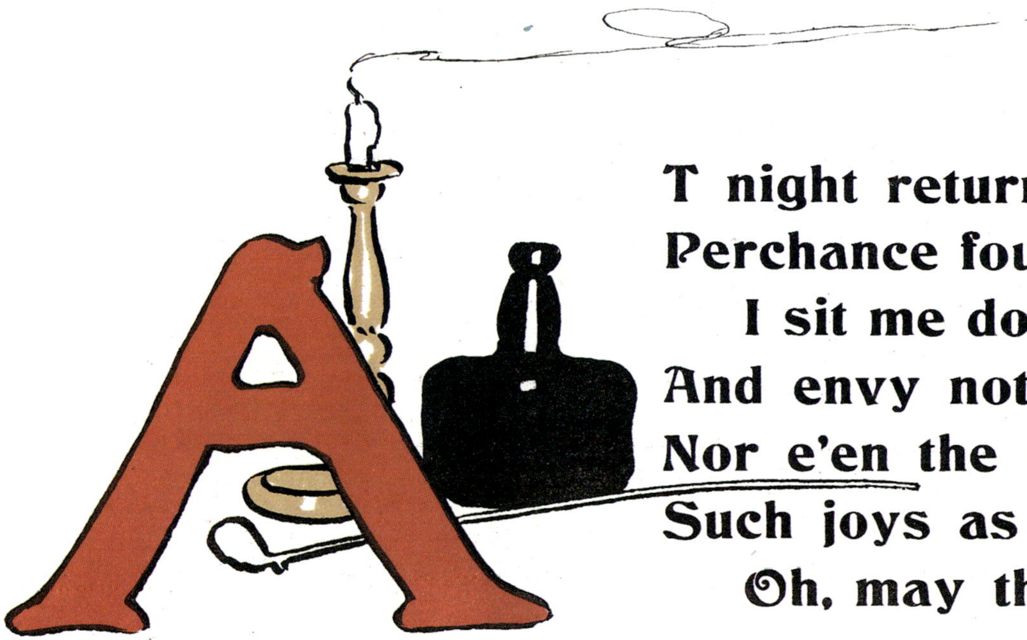

AT night return'd, my bag well fill'd,
Perchance four brace of pheasants kill'd,
I sit me down in peace,
And envy not ambition's cares,
Nor e'en the crown a monarch wears,
Such joys as mine he seldom shares
Oh, may that joy ne'er cease.

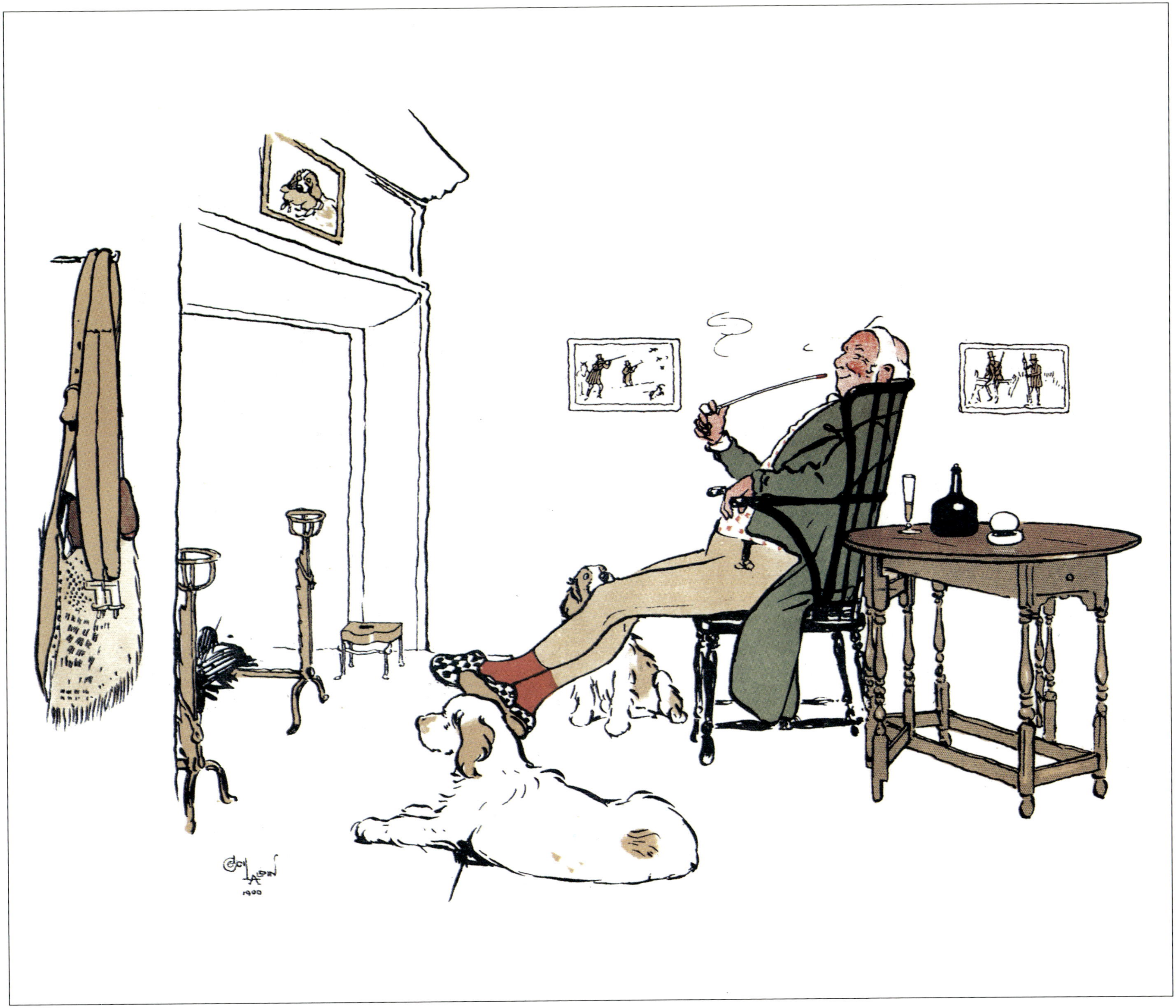
1900

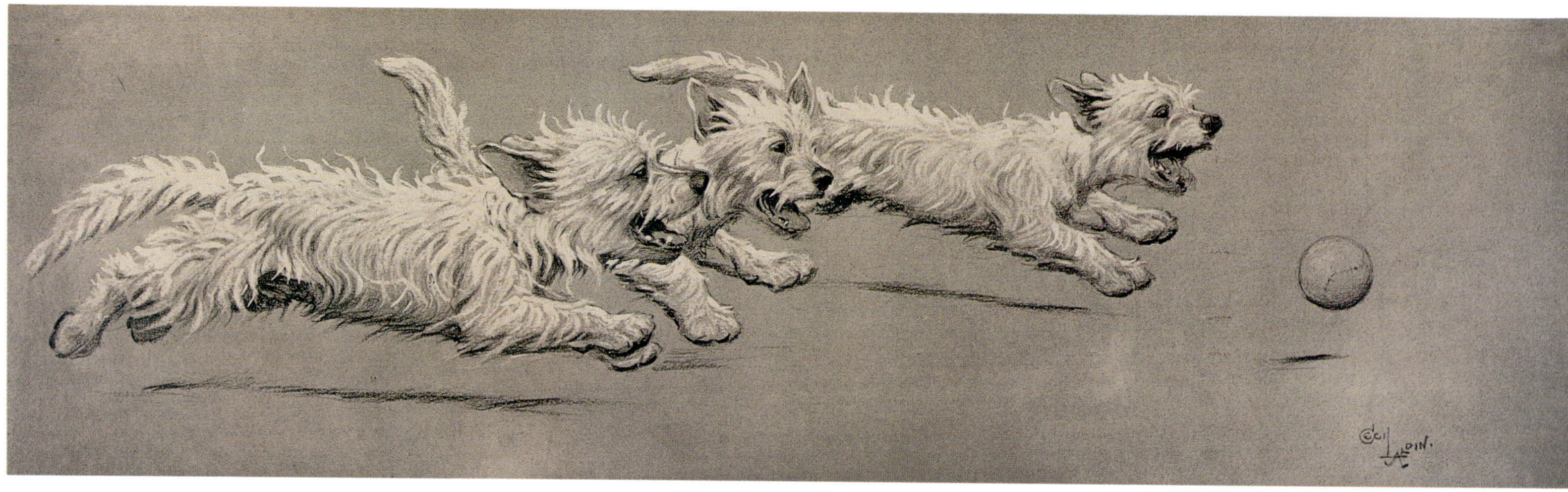

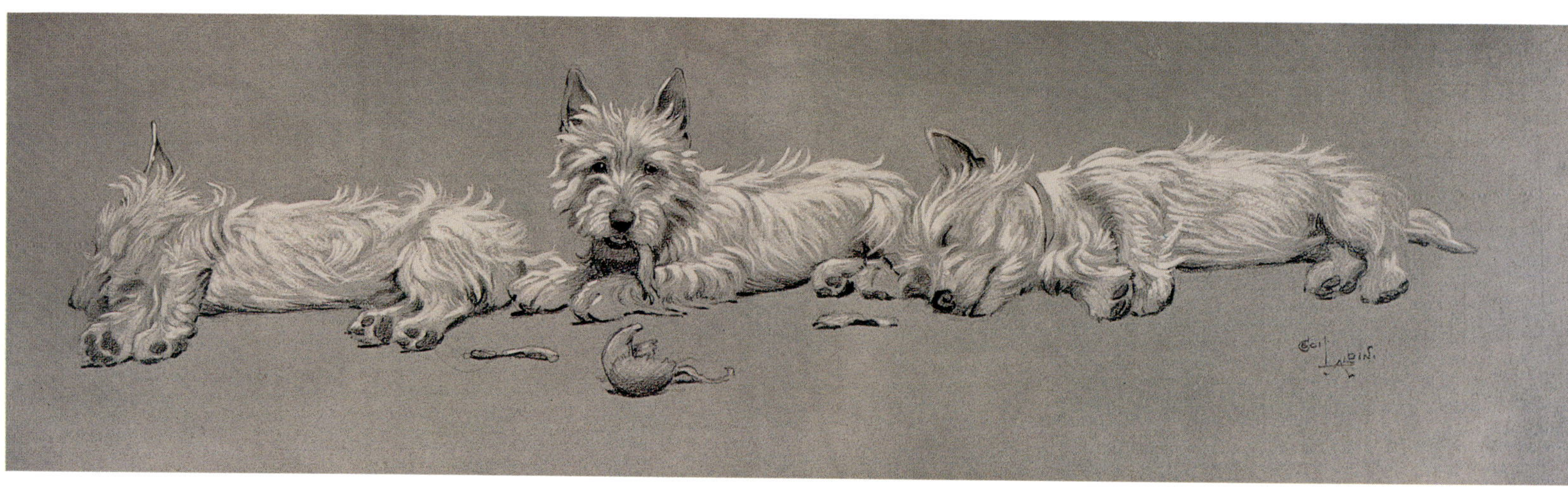

These prints date from the last two years of the nineteenth century.

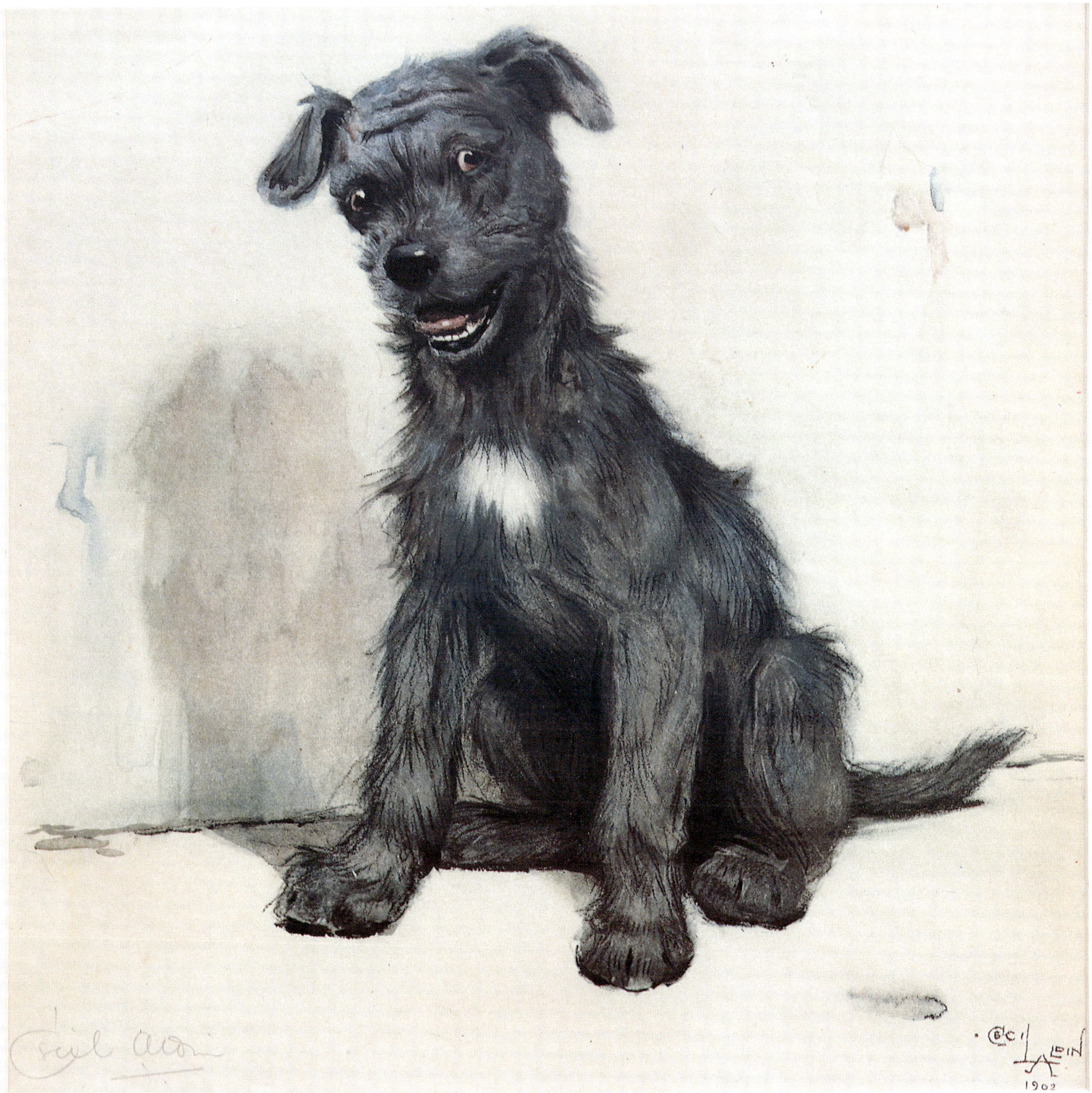

'A Gentleman of Character', although made into a print in 1902 was very reminiscent of his dog prints of the late 1890s but stronger and more competent.

'The Senses'

This set of five cards first appeared in *The Sketch* on five consecutive weeks during August to September 1899 as full page black and white illustrations. Within a few months they were reissued in postcard form.

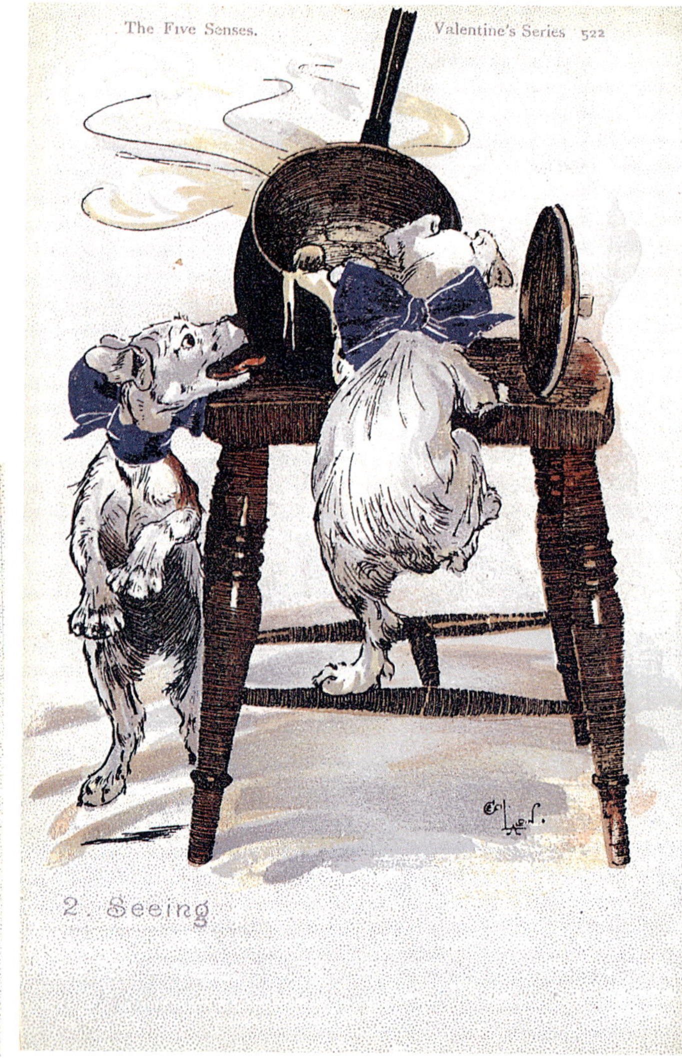

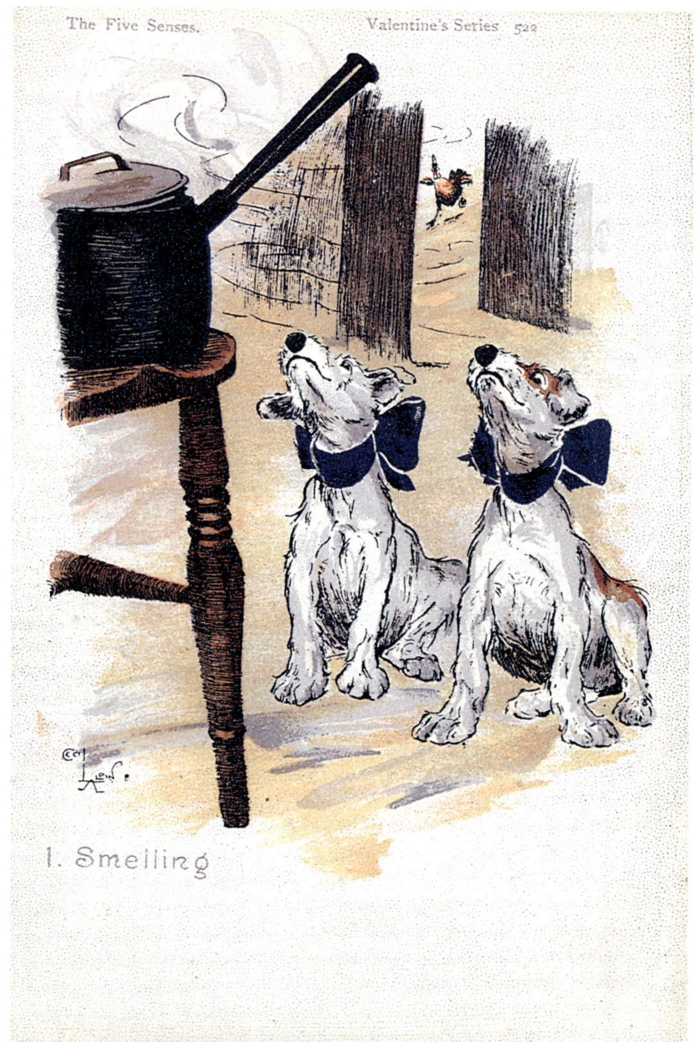

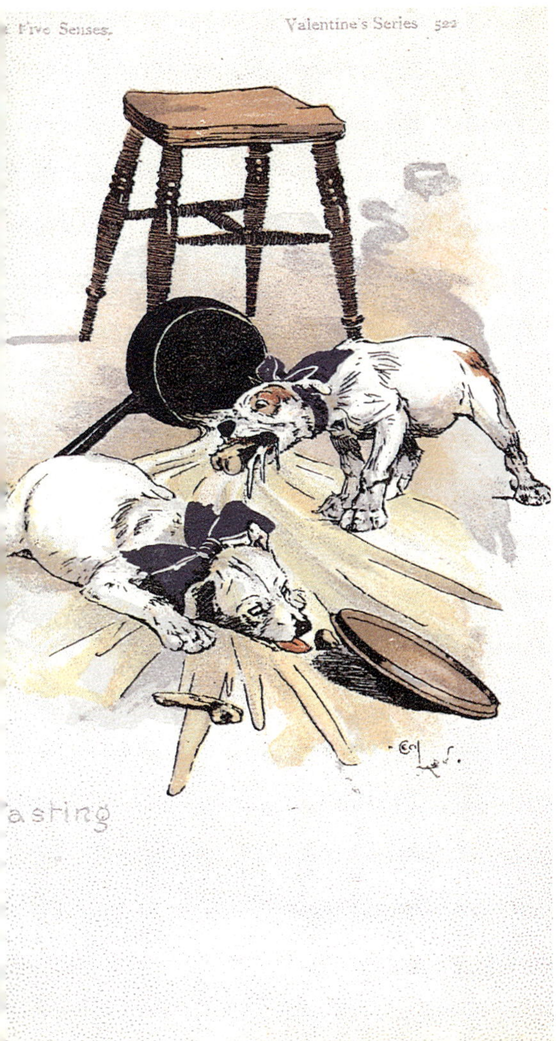
Five Senses.
Valentine's Series 522
asting

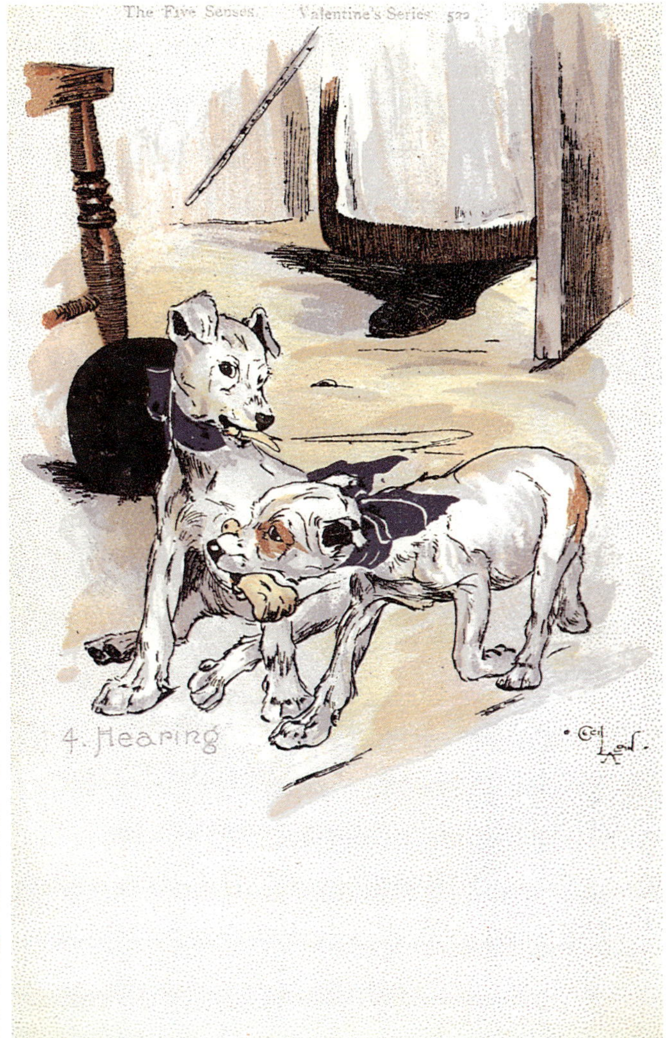
The Five Senses.
Valentine's Series 522
4. Hearing

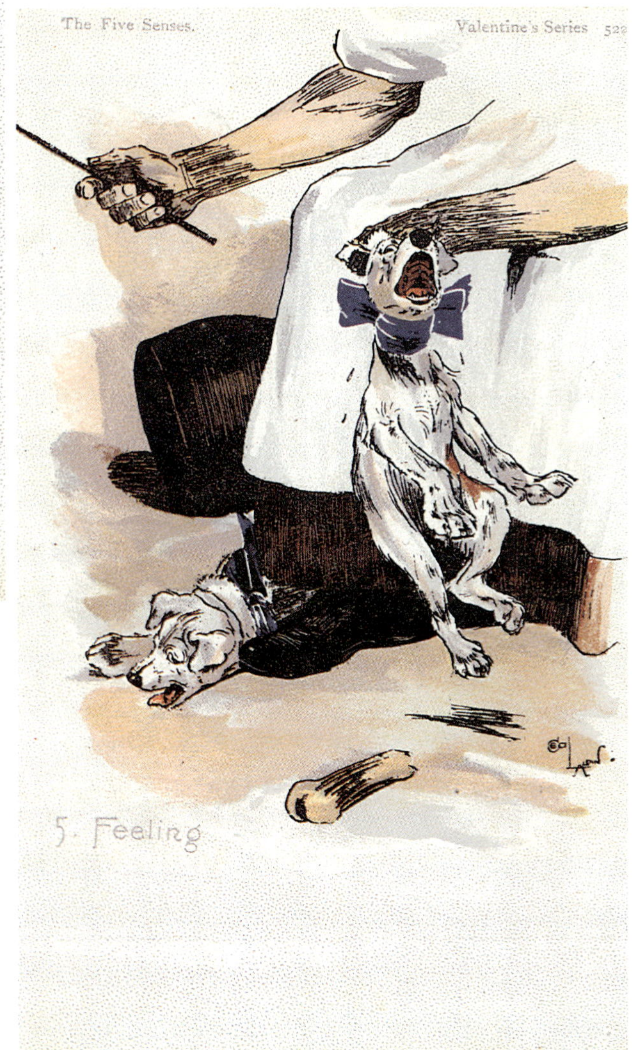
The Five Senses.
Valentine's Series 522
5. Feeling

'Bulldogs'

Bulldogs were Cecil Aldin's favourite pedigree breed from around the mid 1880's until well into the twentieth century. He purchased his first bulldog while still a pupil at South Kensington within a year of acquiring Gyp. They were also his favourite canine models in the 1890's and early 1900's. At one time, while living in Bedford Park in London, he had three or four of them, but after his move to Henley in 1904 they seemed to disappear from his kennel and appeared less frequently in his work.

These lovely watercolours were executed around 1912 and first appeared in public as illustrations for Maurice Maeterlinck's book *My Dog* which was first issued in England in an edition with Aldin's illustrations in 1913. They are typical of the work he was doing with bulldogs during the 1890's although by 1913 his style and his execution was, not unnaturally, very much more polished than his work of some twenty years earlier. For me these watercolours are good, if not great, quality canine paintings and although two of them may be slightly humorous, the third shows considerable pathos and they still demonstrate, quite clearly, Aldin's complete mastery of this subject by the time he had reached his early forties.

My research has thrown no light on the disappearance of bulldogs from Aldin's kennel in the early 1900's. I can only assume that he did not approve of the way the breed was being developed. Aldin's bulldogs, to my mind, were much more attractive and healthy than those one sees at Cruft's nowadays and I feel certain Aldin would probably have advocated the "Alternative Bulldog Club", with straighter legs and less squashed-in faces, rather like he used to advocate "Mongrel Dog Shows".

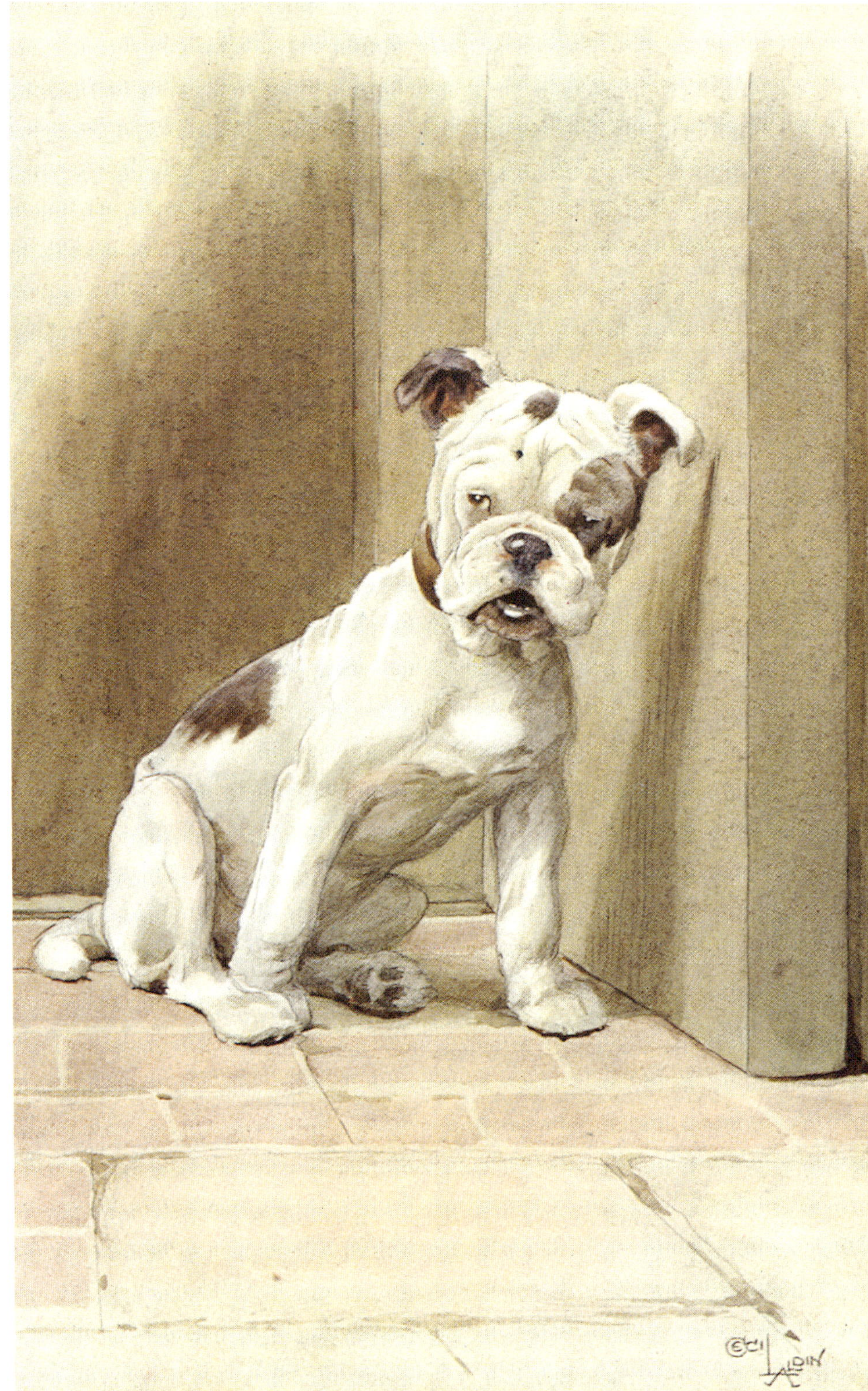

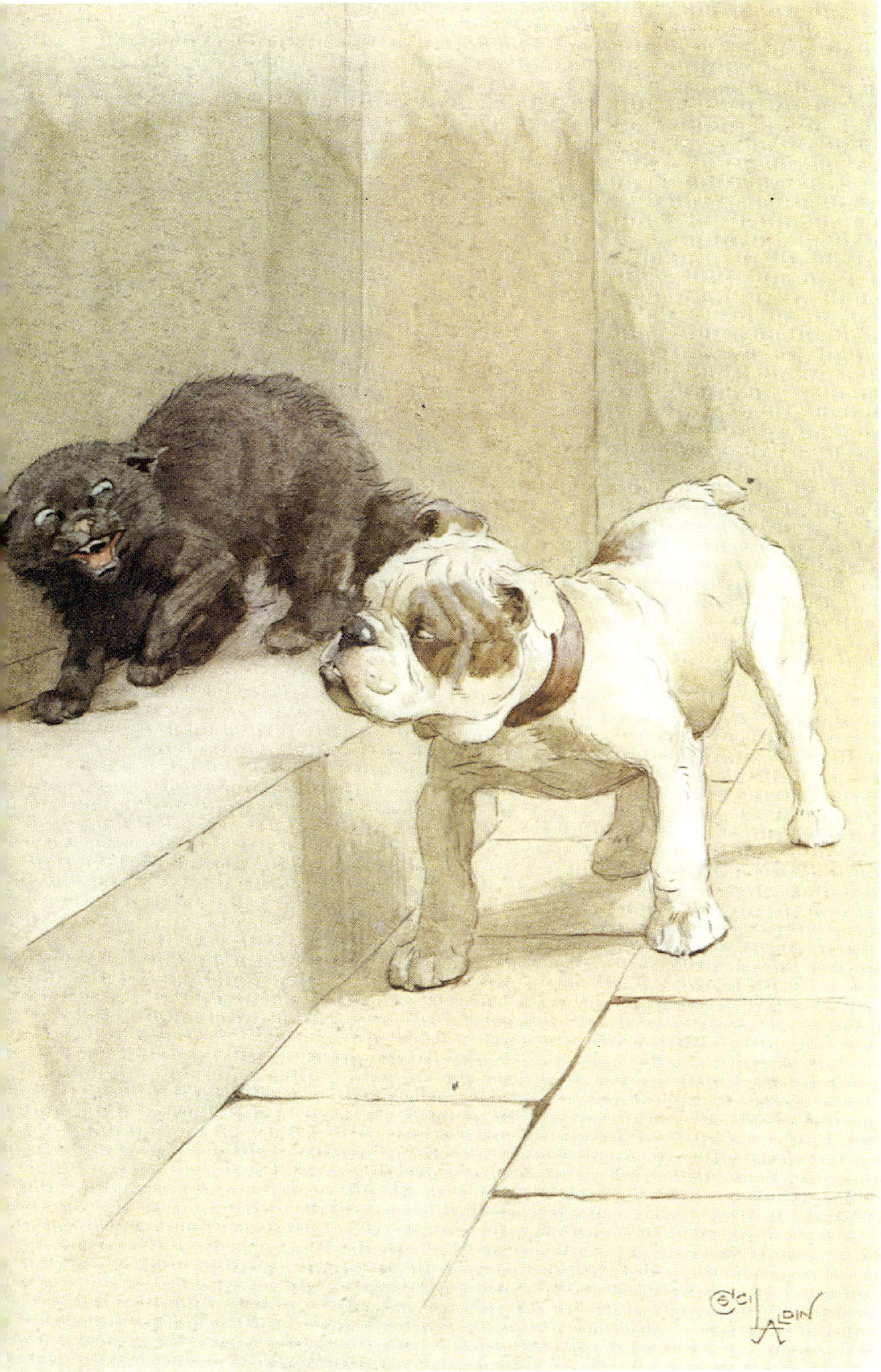

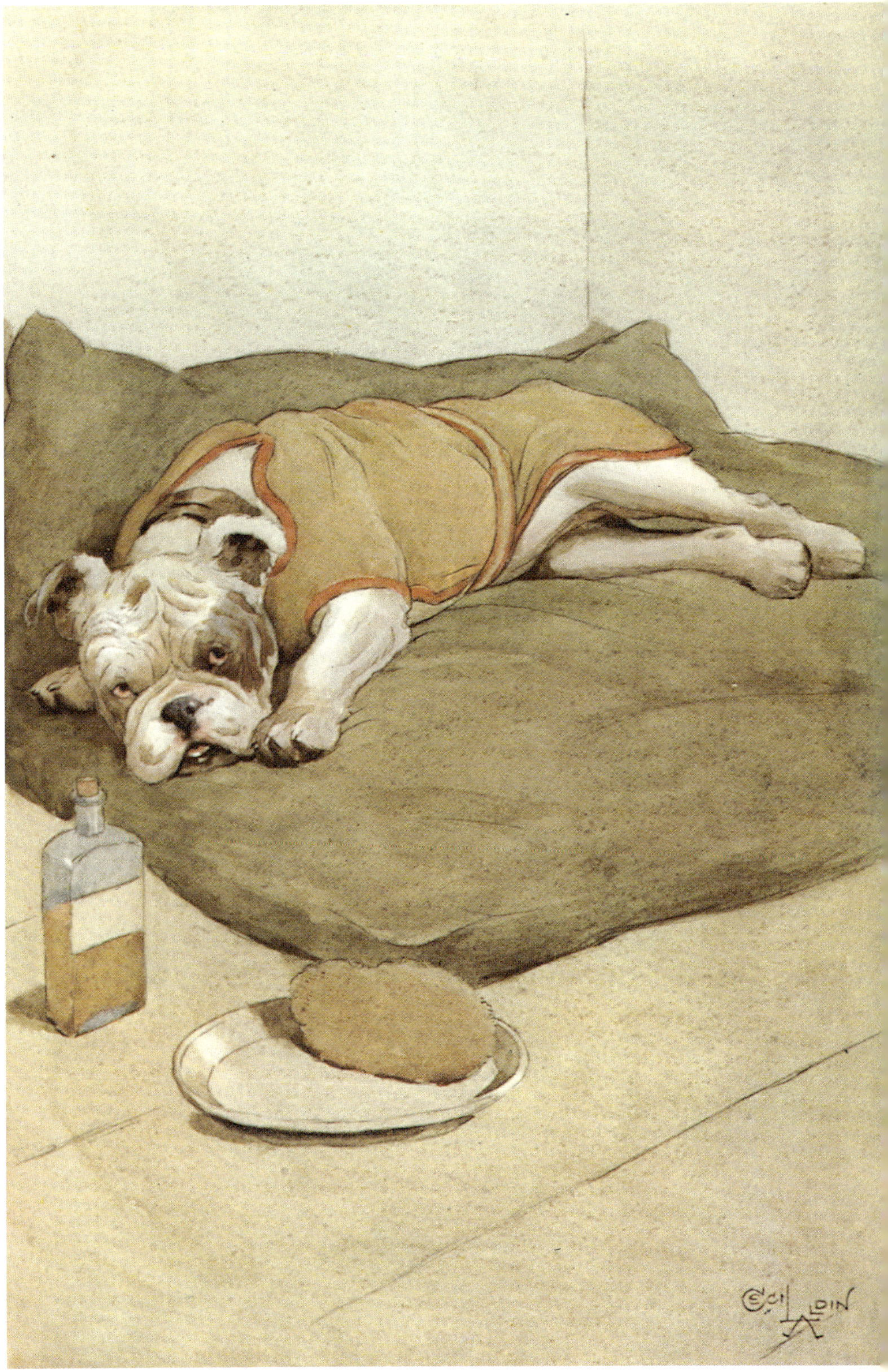

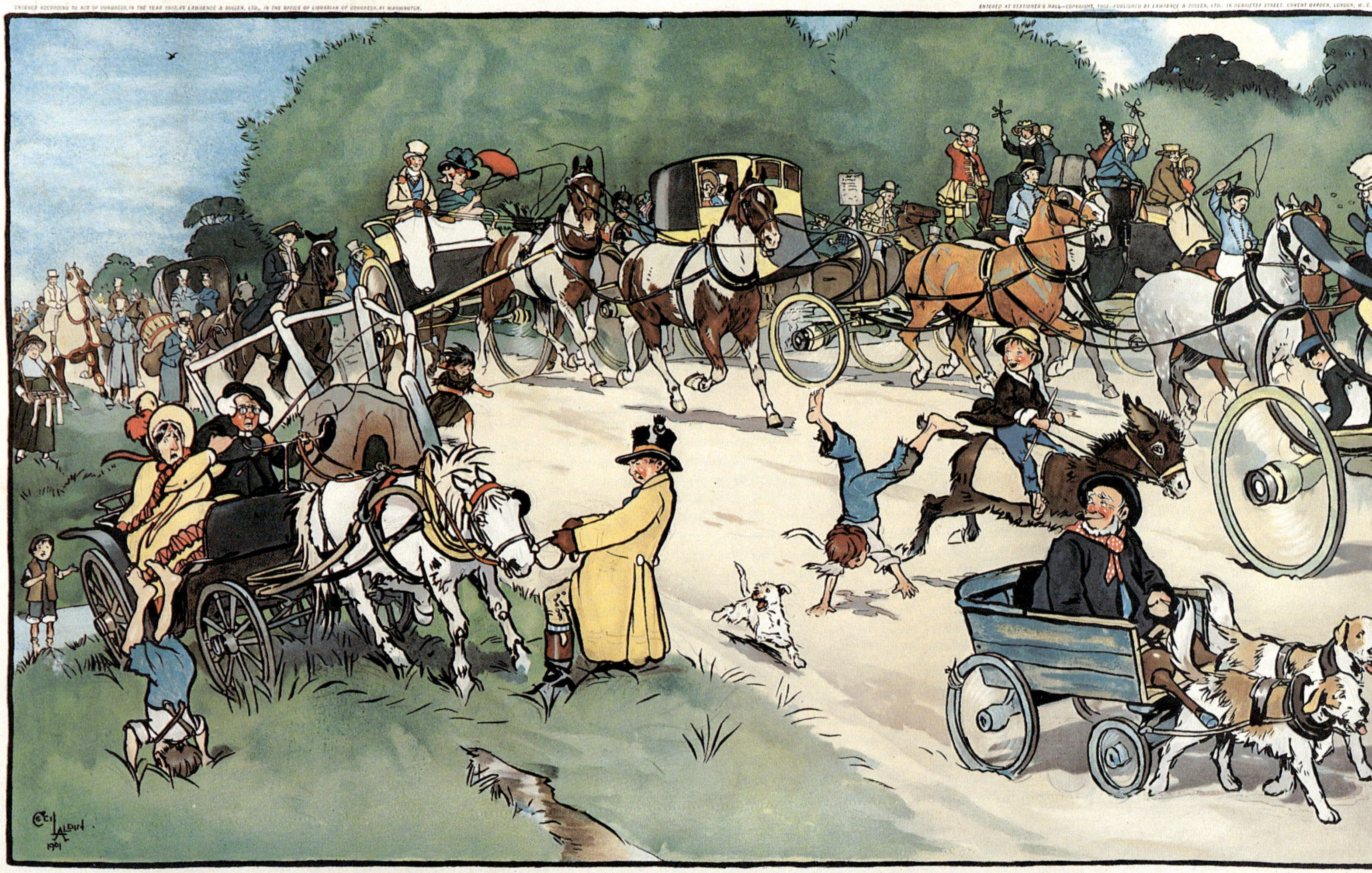

THE BLUEMARKET RACES.

On the Road.

These two prints are from 'The Bluemarket Races' series of racing prints.
Aldin is driving the tandem in the print above, drawn by two piebald horses, with his wife carrying a red parasol.
These piebald horses were often used as models around this time.
Once again, as in so many of his prints, it is the canine embellishments which make them so wonderful.

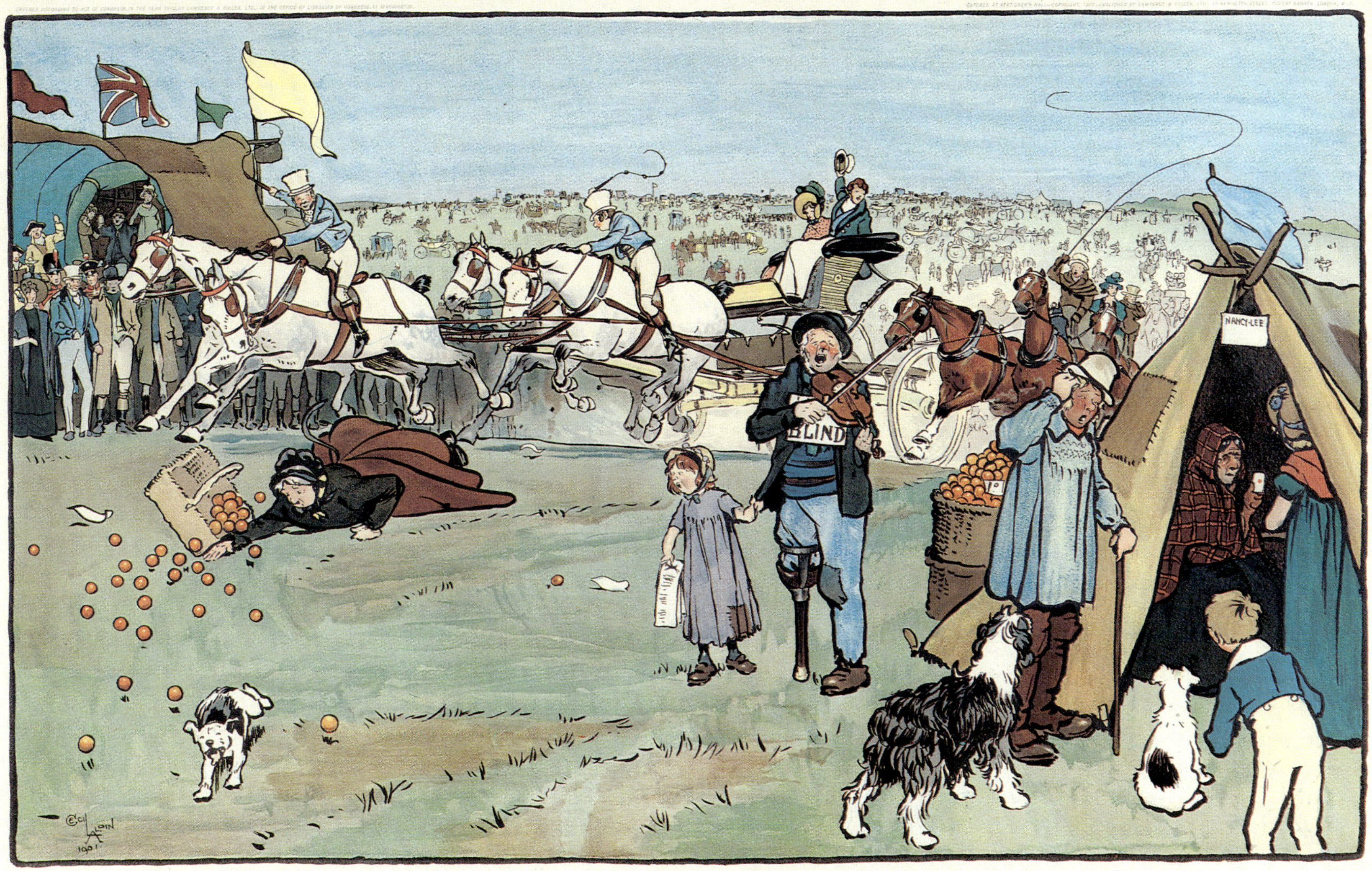

THE BLUEMARKET RACES.

The Arrival on the Course.

Aldin had recently been to Flanders and was quite fascinated by the use of dogs as draught animals and was to draw them as such many times around 1905.

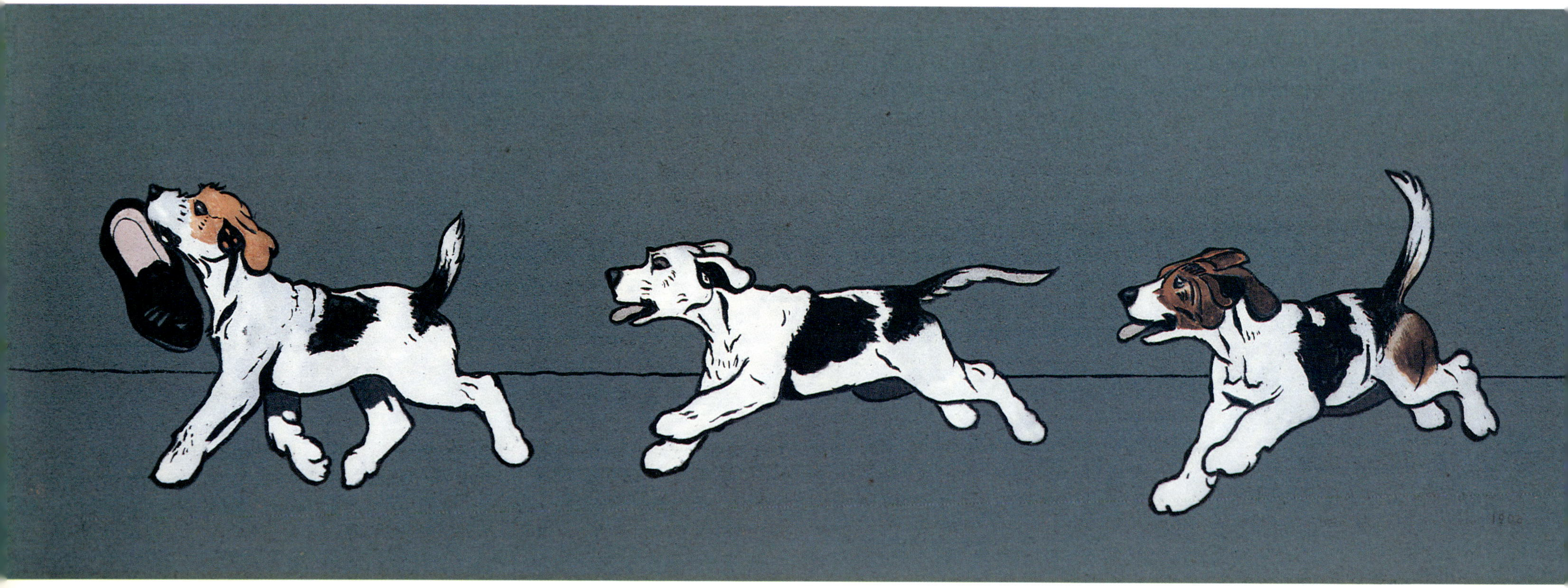

'Hunt the Slipper'. The above painting executed towards the end of the 1890's was later turned into a print. It shows the influence of the bold, highly coloured Japanese prints which were so fashionable in London's artistic circles in the 1890's. Aldin painted it on dark green board using strong poster paints.

This type of work is very reminiscent of Aldin's style, so widely acclaimed in his large posters for Bovril, Cadbury's and other major firms.

Chapter Two
The Golden Years (1901 to 1914)

By 1901 Cecil Aldin's workload and output was prodigous. He was a regular contributor to most of the sporting and social periodicals of the day, illustrated more and more books annually, had prints coming out on a regular basis and even found time to start producing large posters for such prestigious firms as Bovril and Cadbury's. Aldin's bold designs and strong colouring were greatly admired and we can trace the origins of his poster style to the Japanese prints which were then fashionable in the artistic circles in which he moved.

By 1902 or 1903 Aldin was very much accepted as one of London's leading illustrators and artists. Such highbrow magazines as *The Poster* were giving his work and, for that matter, Aldin himself, remarkably good reports. There was no sign at this stage of his career of him becoming such a great dog artist as he was to prove later. Admittedly he could paint dogs well, but he could also paint horses and coaching scenes well. In short he was a leading all-round artist.

Aldin must have been 'a bundle of energy' as not only did he produce a vast and varied amount of work, year in year out, he hunted at least two days a week from November until March and was a great one for a party. Aldin was very much the leader of his *coterie* of artists when it came to organising social events in the various Bohemian clubs where he was a member. Artistically the most important of these was The London Sketch Club where he was considered to be a leading light, not only on the artistic side, but very much on the social side.

If 1900 was the year in which Cecil Aldin made his breakthrough into the big time as far as prints were concerned, 1902 was to be his great year for books. The illustrations for *A Sporting Garland* are undoubtedly some of his best, although I believe they had been executed, or at least roughed out, in 1897 or 1898 and are a natural link between his earlier, less fanciful, work of 1895/1896 and his highly stylised and colourful work first shown to the public in 'The Fallowfield Hunt' series.

I appreciate that the drawings are clearly dated 1902, but it must be remembered that signatures are regularly 'dropped in' to artist's originals by printers. Just because a print is dated 1902 or 1910 does not mean that it wasn't executed by the artist a number of years earlier, and his signature and a convenient date added by the printer.

Aldin regularly submitted a series of unsigned drawings to publishers with one signature which was 'dropped' onto all of the illustrations for uniformity. This habit can cause considerable problems when dating his work, as one will sometimes find an illustration in one magazine dated, say 1898, and exactly the same illustration will appear in a book dated 1923 - the same work but with different signatures and dates.

The other great book Aldin was associated with in 1902 was *A Dog Day, or The Angel in the House* on which he co-operated with Walter Emanuel for the first time. It must have been one of the best-selling dog books ever, as over 100,000 copies were sold between 1902 and the outbreak of World War I.

In 1904, Aldin moved his family, dogs and horses to Henley-on-Thames and took up residence in a large house and garden right in the centre of the town, where the Post Office now stands. It must have been a severe culture shock to leave his fellow Bohemians and move down to Henley, as he was the most sociable of men, but I have found no hint of complaint about his new environment. The main problem seemed to be with one of his dogs which took to killing chickens in a major way and had quickly to be found a home back in London. Of course, living in the proper country, hunting became easier and better.

Throughout the early years of the century Aldin's work became more and more popular, not only in the British Isles, but particularly in France and the U.S., and he travelled to both countries staging successful exhibitions. He certainly loved France and the French and spent a few weeks in 1908 there, staying near Chantilly, hunting with various French packs, but mainly with the 'Foret d'Halatte'. On his return to Britain, Aldin re-formed a pack of harriers, based near Reading, and going by the name of the Peppard Harriers. He did much of the work and hunted hounds himself.

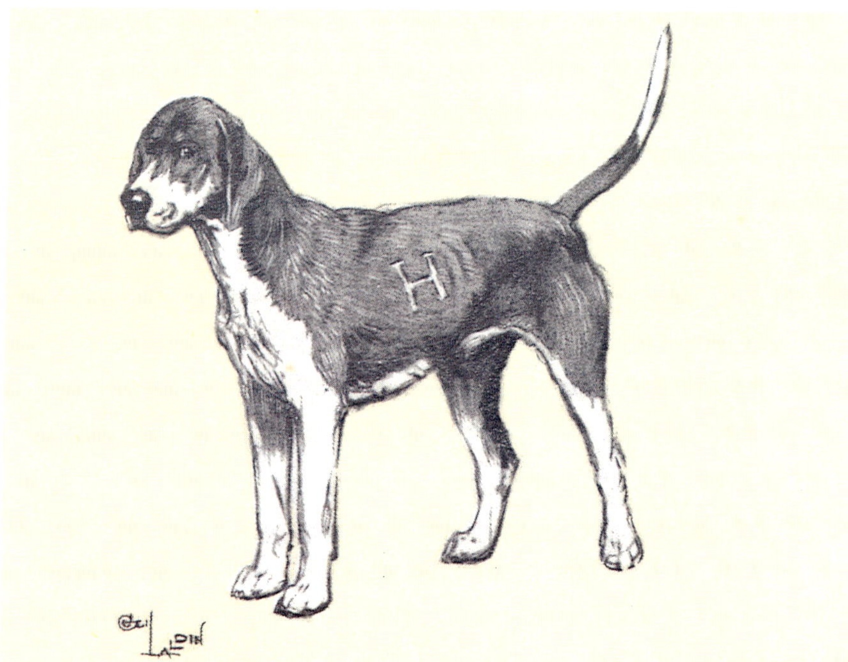

The next great landmark in Cecil Aldin's career came rather by chance in 1909 with the publication of his first large format childrens' book entitled *Pickles, A Puppy Dog's Tale*. Aldin wrote and illustrated this initially for his daughter Gwen, but these childrens' books soon became a major commercial proposition. *Pickles* was followed by other similar books such as *Rough and Tumble* also in 1909, *The Twins* in 1910 and *Merry and Bright* in 1911. These books are approximately 12" by 10", printed on semi-stiff paper and are nowadays worth well over £250.00 in fine condition.

Aldin's workload during the last five years of peace before the outbreak of World War I must have been comparable only to John Leech's in the previous century and he regularly worked twelve to fourteen hours a day. Firstly there was an enormous amount of illustrations for books (nearly fifty), many of which he wrote as well as illustrated, and which were mainly for children. Some were smaller editions of the semi-deluxe books such as *Pickles* and *Rough and Tumble* and included such lovely books as *The White Puppy Book* , *The Black Puppy Book* and *Farmyard Puppies*. Two famous books he illustrated in these years were *Black Beauty* by Anna Sewell and *Handley Cross* by R.S. Surtees.

In 1912 Lawrence & Jellicoe started issuing the famous hunting prints 'Twelve Hunting Countries' which were to be the forerunners to the even better-known series executed in the twenties and thirties by Lionel Edwards. These took Aldin an immense amount of time as they necessitated him visiting hunts and not only doing watercolours of famous coverts, but making notes of individual riding styles. Aldin always claimed that this series did little more than pay his out-of-pocket expenses, but he certainly must have enjoyed them as, not unnaturally, the hunts chosen for this were some of the best and most fashionable such as The Quorn, Pytchley, V.W.H. (Cricklade), and the Duke of Beaufort's to name but a few.

By now Aldin had taken to going down to Exmoor each year for at least one month in August/September with his wife and two children, a large number of dogs, nearly as many horses and ponies and assorted servants for a combined hunting holiday and work.

'A Dog Day or An Angel in the House'.

A chance meeting in 1902 with Walter Emanuel led to Cecil Aldin illustrating his book *A Dog Day.*

The book was an instant success as Emanuel's brilliant text worked superbly with Aldin's illustrations and edition after edition in various formats were rushed from the presses. I sold a copy of the book to my sister, a great dog person, who told me she laughed so much the first time she read it that she was sick and every time she re-reads it laughs so much she normally cries.

Aldin and Emanuel were to co-operate on a number of other highly successful books in the next few years including *The Snob* in 1904, *A Gay Dog* in 1905 and *Dogs of War* in 1906.

THE STORY SO FAR ...

'A Dog Day' is the story of a mongrel puppy who becomes a hero for a day after disturbing a burglar. Unfortunately, on his way out with the family silver, the burglar treads on the pup, making him yelp with pain. The ensuing noise wakes up the household and the silver is saved.

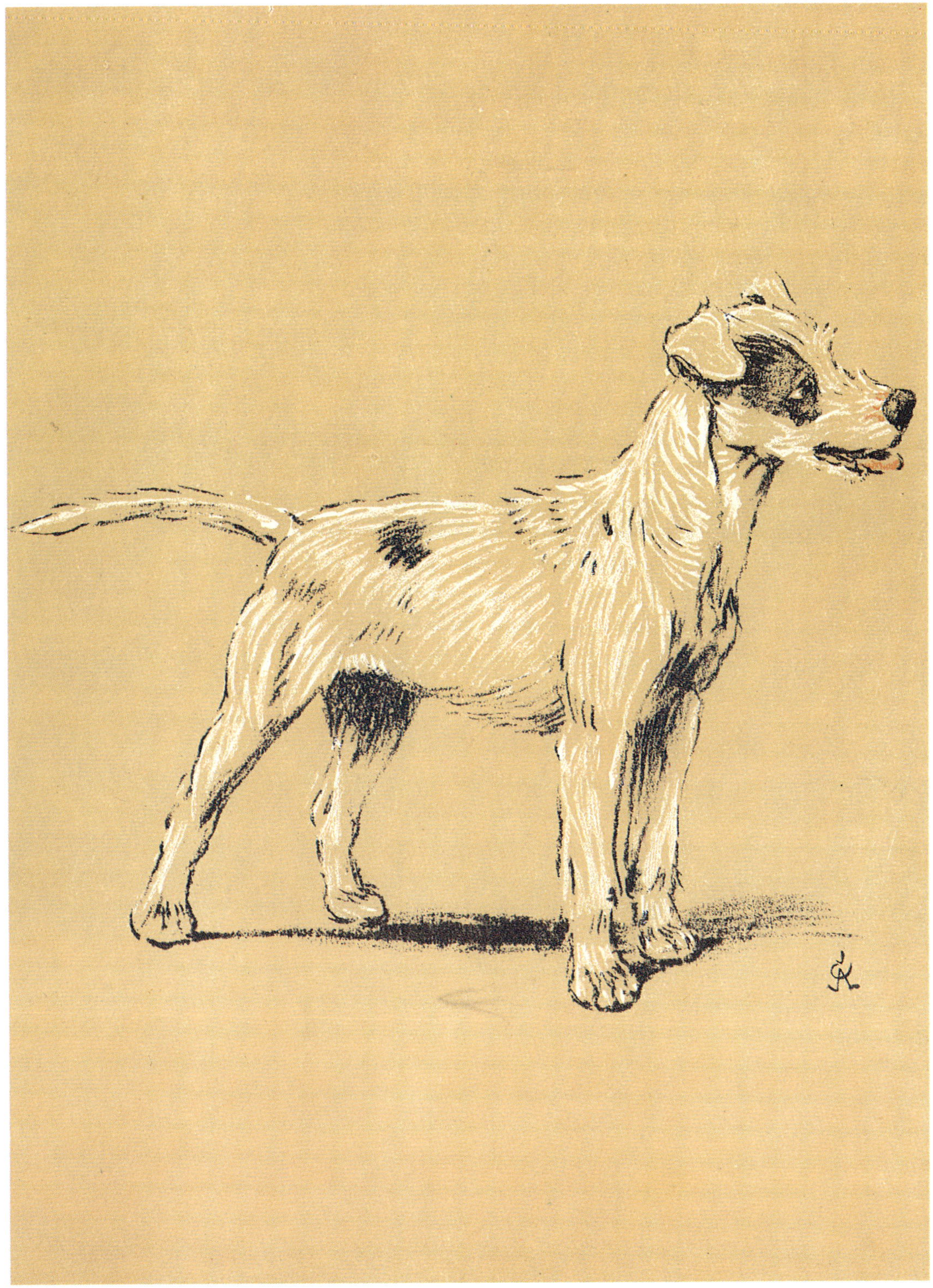

10 to 10.15 Wagged tail.

1.25 Upstairs into dining-room. Family not finished lunch yet. Young Mr. Brown throws a bread pellet at me, hitting me on the nozzle. An insult. I swallow the insult. Then I go up to Miss Brown and look at her with my great pleading eyes. I guessed it: they are irresistible. She gives me a piece of pudding. Aunt Brown tells her she shouldn't. At which, with great pluck, Miss Brown tells her to mind her own business. I admire that girl more and more.

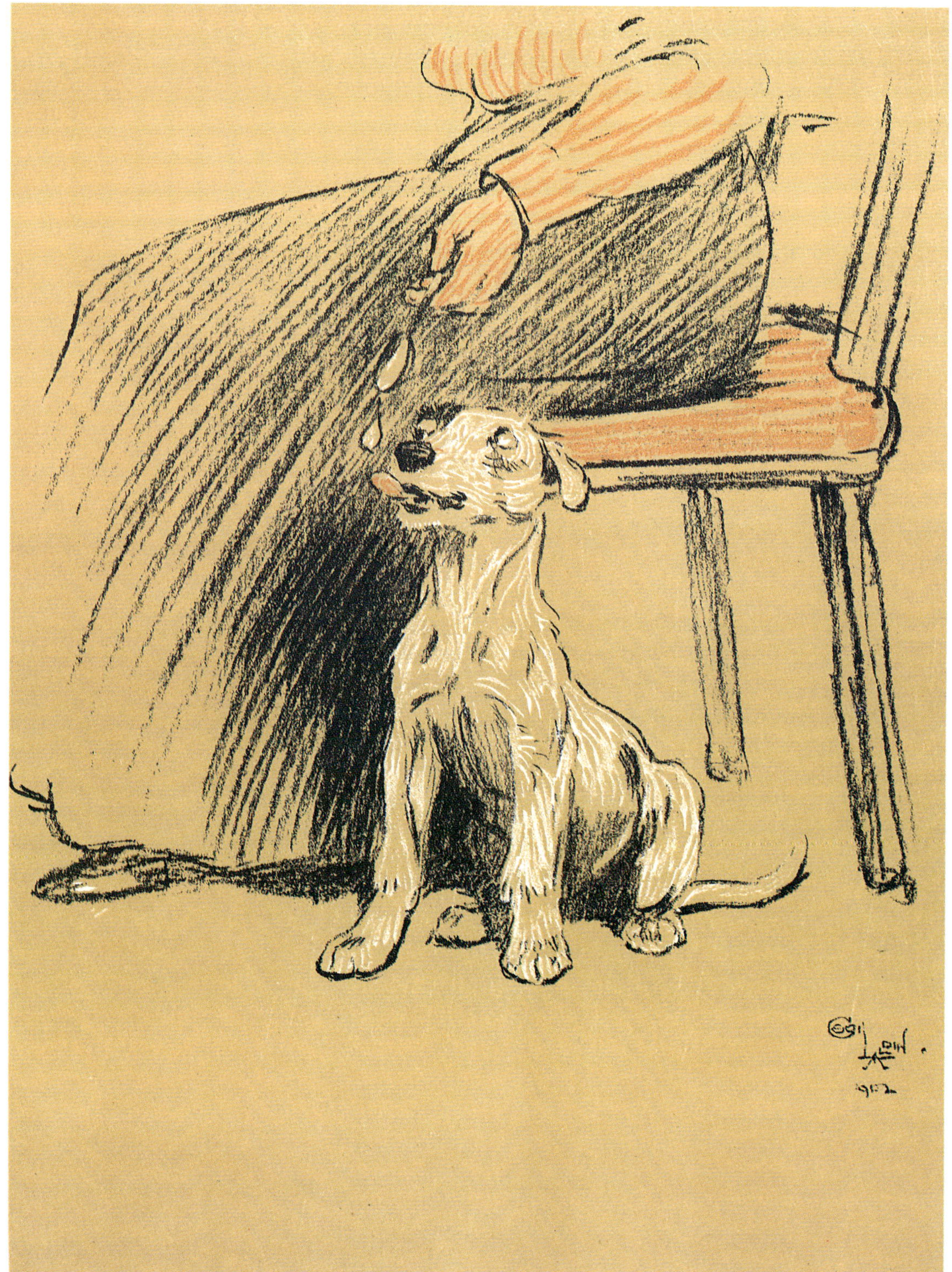

1.30 A windfall. A whole dish of mayonnaise fish on the slab in the hall. Before you can say Jack Robinson I have bolted it.

1.32 Curious pains in my underneath.

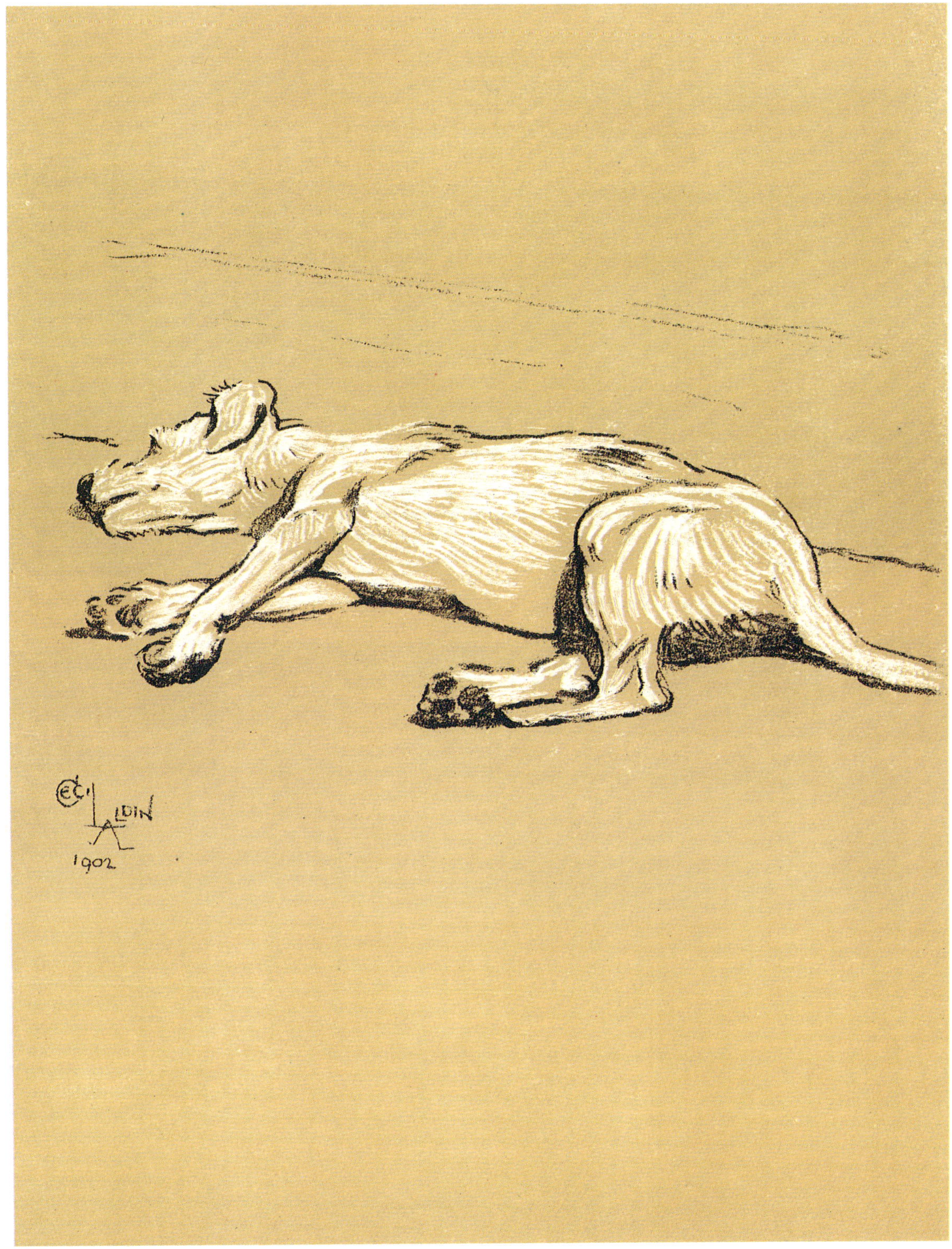

l.33 Pains in my underneath get worse.

l.34 Horrid feeling of sickness.

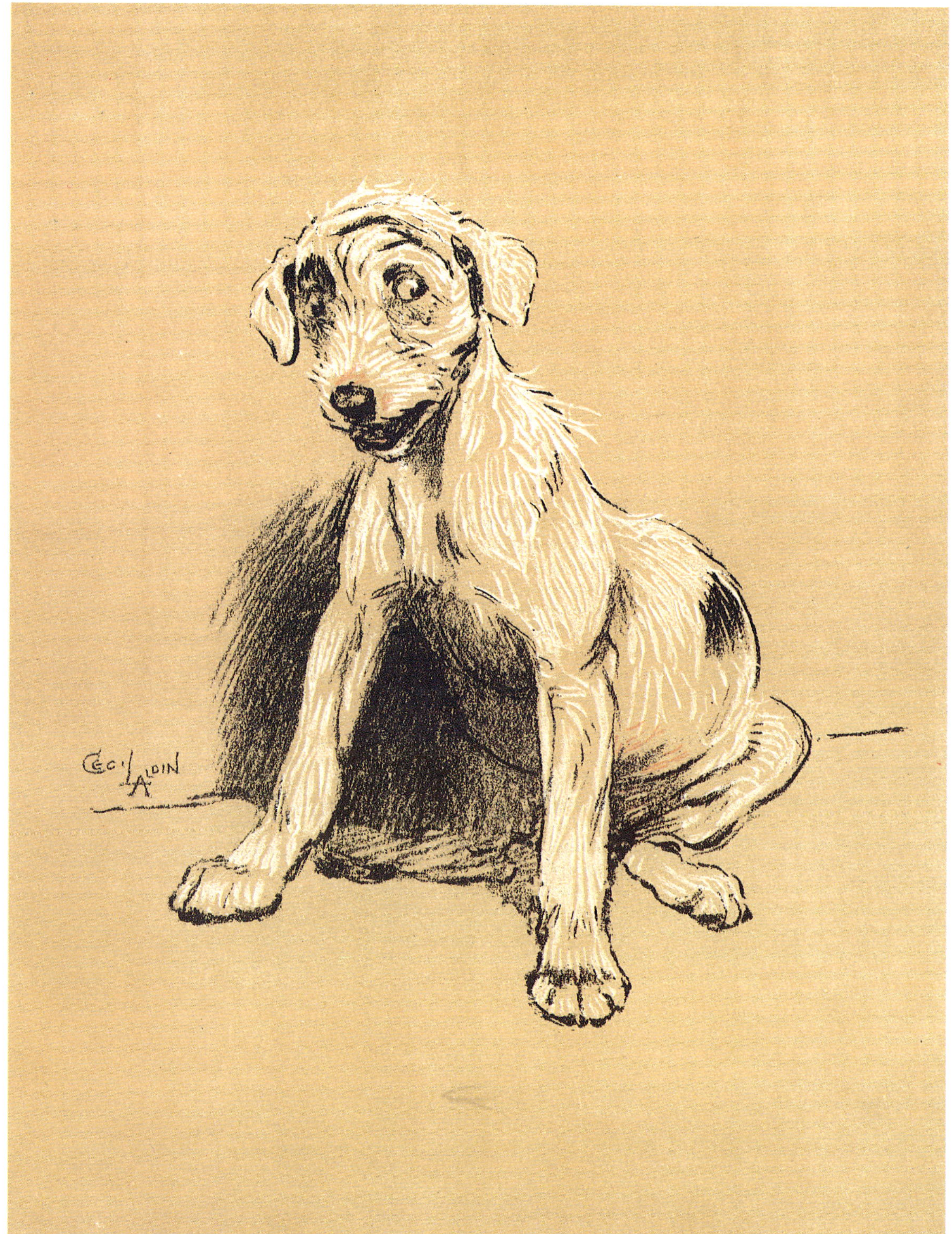

1.35 Rush up into Aunt Brown's room, and am sick there.

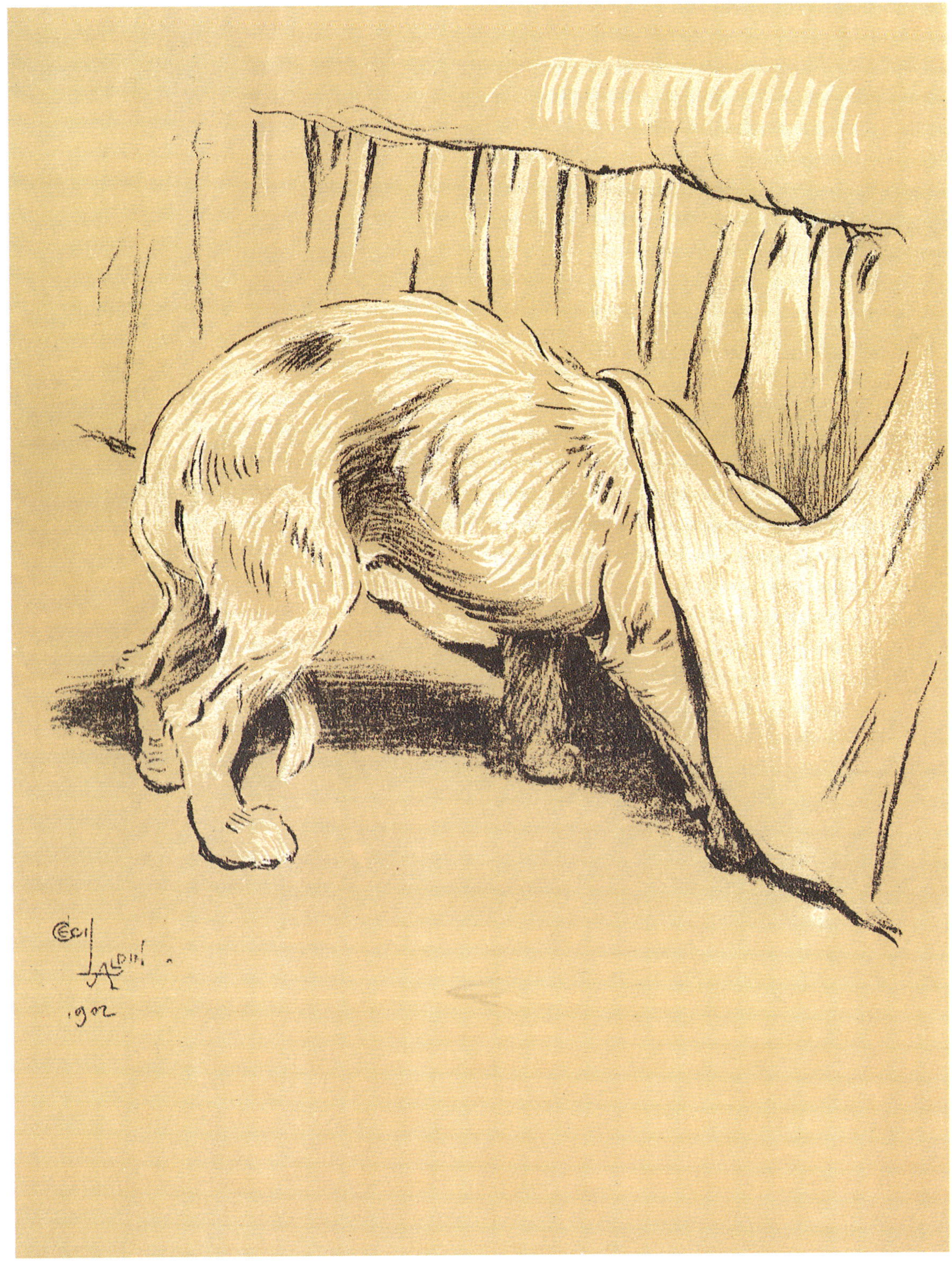

1.37 Better. Think I shall pull through if I am careful.

1.40 Almost well again.

1.41 Quite well again. Thank Heavens! It was a narrow shave that time. People ought not to leave such stuff about.

1.42 Up into dining-room. And, to show how well I am, I galumph round and round the room, at full pelt, about twenty times, steering myself by my tail. Then, as a grand finale, I jump twice on to the waistcoat-part of old Mr. Brown, who is sleeping peacefully in the arm-chair. He wakes up very angry indeed, and uses words I have never heard before. Even Miss Brown, to my no little surprise, says it is very naughty of me. Old Mr. Brown insists on my being punished, and orders Miss Brown to beat me. Miss Brown runs the burglar for all he is worth. But no good. Old Mr. Brown is dead to all decent feeling!

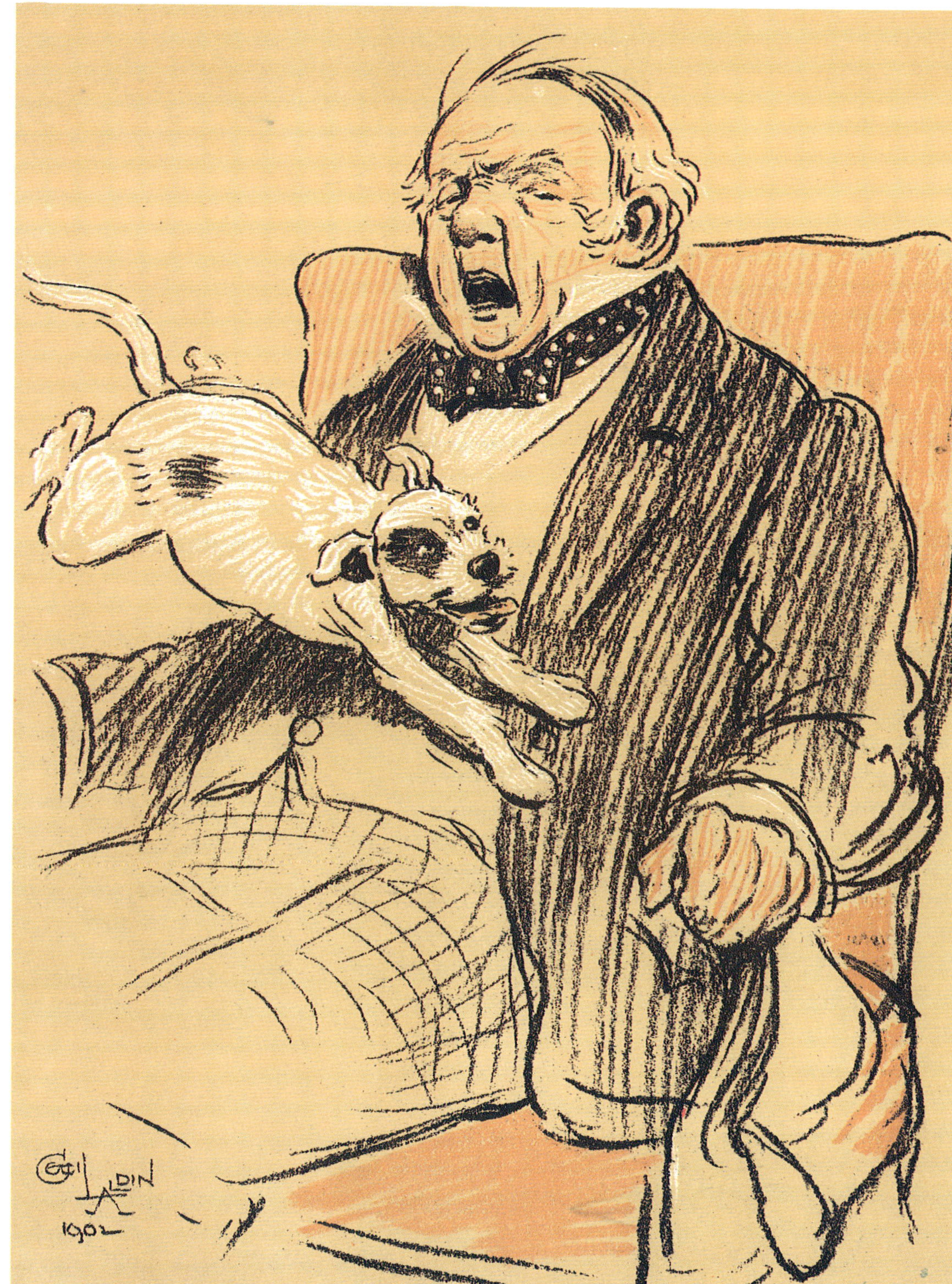

So Miss Brown beats me. Very nice. Thoroughly enjoyable. Just like being patted. But, of course, I yelp, and pretend it hurts frightfully, and do the sad-eye business, and she soon leaves off and takes me into the next room and gives me six pieces of sugar! Good business. Must remember always to do this. Before leaving she kisses me and explains that I should not have jumped on poor Pa, as he is the man who goes to the City to earn bones for me. Something in that, perhaps. Nice girl.

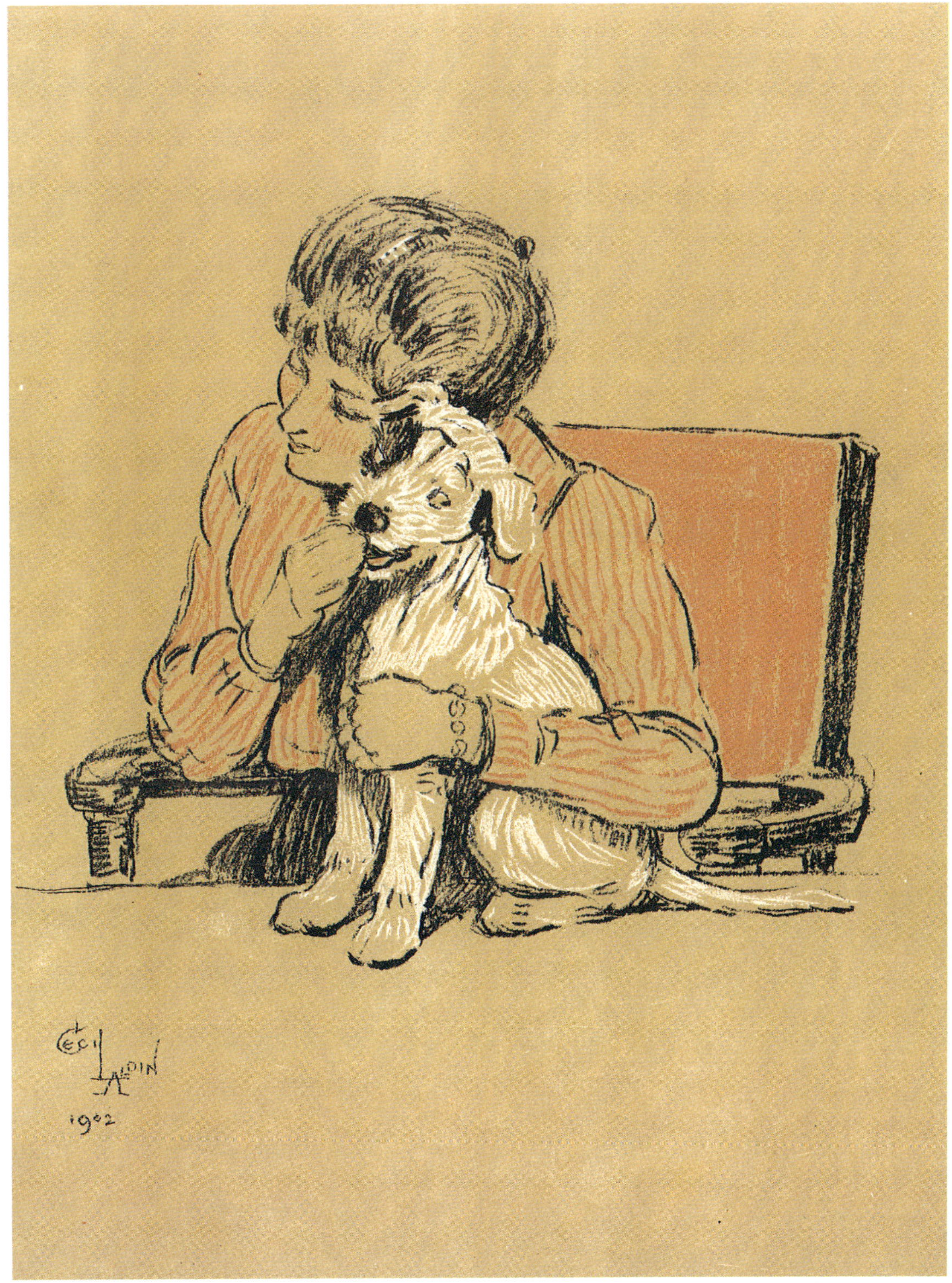

A Black and White Exhibition

Now he's been and gone and done it!

We visited the scullery, just out of curiosity. Most interesting things there,—potatoes, blacking-bottles, bones in saucepans,—but, owing to a sudden alarm that sounded like Cook, we moved too fast. Immediately all the bottles and pails became tippy and wobbly. The silly blacking-bottle has upset itself all over me; and Tumble—ha! ha!—has fallen into the whitewash!

Result, two piebald puppies. It doesn't so much matter for Tumble: a little white upon his sooty skin is rather an improvement on the whole. But me—with nasty wet black boot-stuff all over my beautiful snow-white coat! . . . .

Tumble, it was a bad day for me when you were invented. Oh, yes, laugh! Laugh, if you like. I mean to have nothing more to do with you, Tumble. Nothing more whatever.

Rough and Tumble.
Rough, the white puppy, is the narrator.
Tumble, the black puppy,
comes to visit.

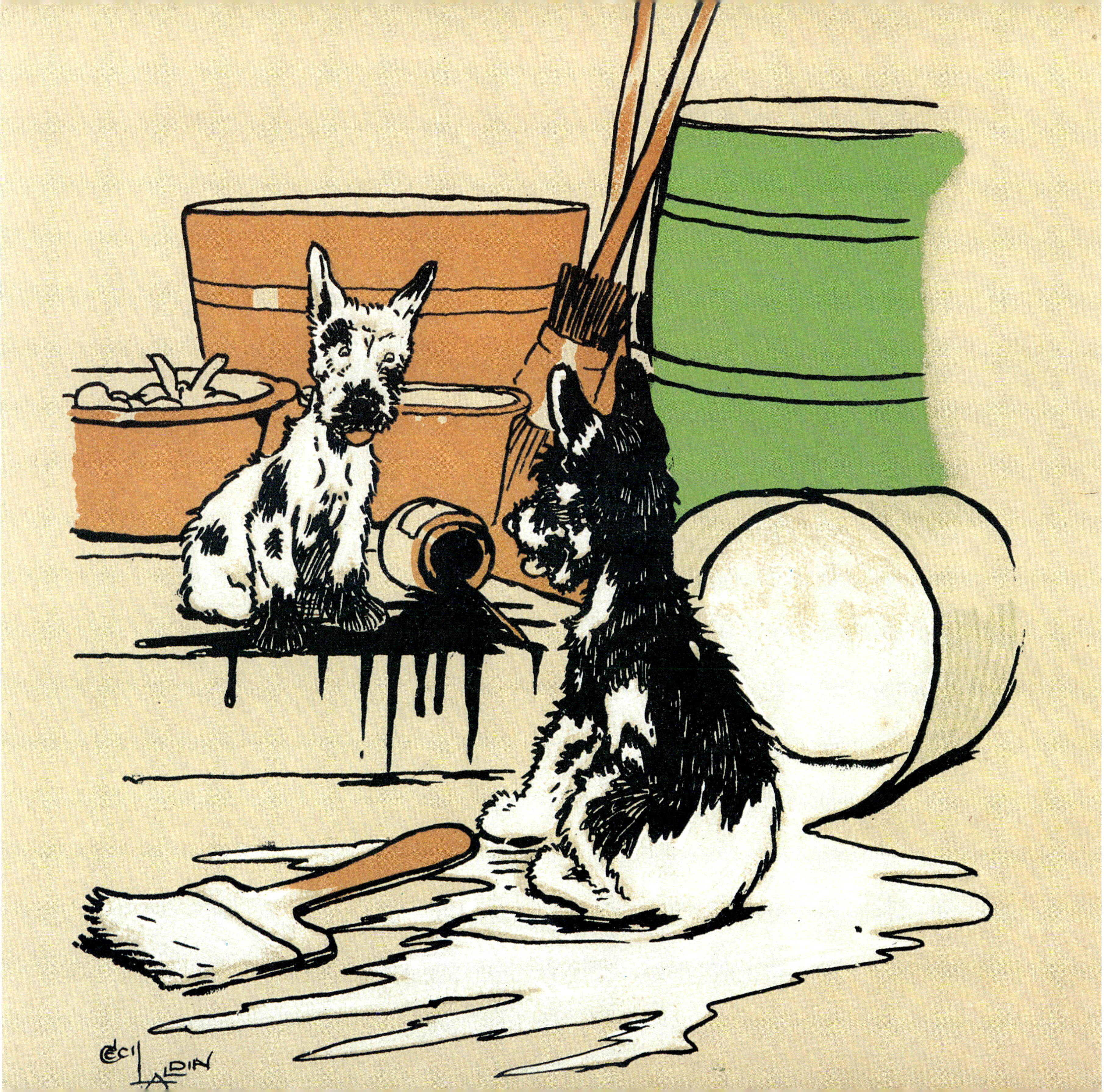
Cecil Aldin

A Good Ducking

What's that you say? The only thing for it is to go down to the pond. Very well, then, go. But I shan't put myself into the same pond with you, Tumble; I don't care for mixed bathing. I always wash in a sensible, gentlemanly, good old English tub at home.

There, you see! Obliged to annoy <u>some</u>-body! You leave those ducks alone, and they'll leave you alone. I daresay, once upon a time, you were a respectable puppy, and were properly trained and had a good education. Now you go about the country teasing ducks.

Tumble, you are no fit companion for me, that's plain—nearly as plain as you are. And, anyway, you might have headed those ducks over in my direction. I can scare ducks just as well as you can—every bit of it.

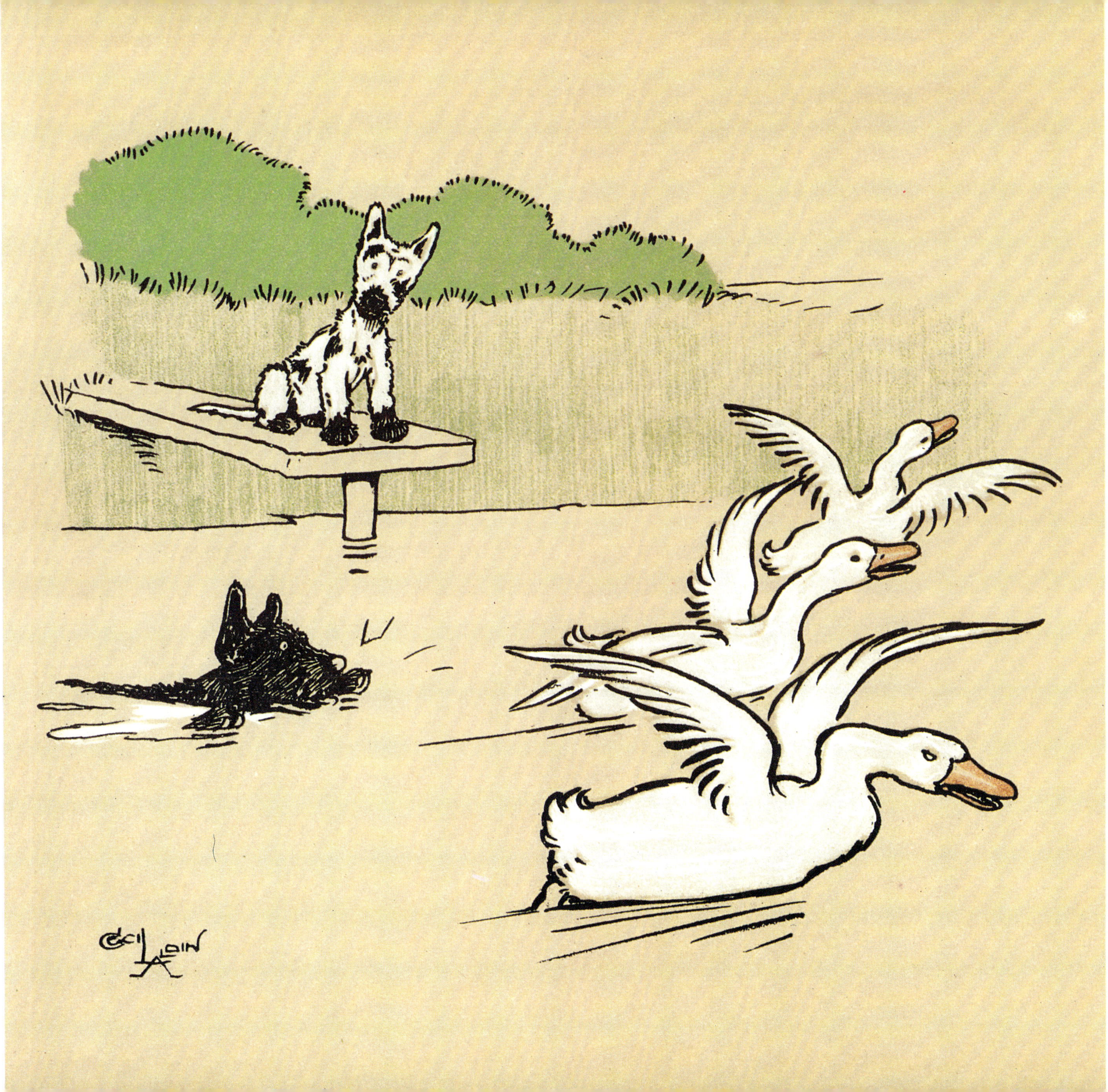
Cecil Aldin

The Wanderer's Return

I went home to avoid that Tumble—I wouldn't be seen within a mile of him. But, now I've come to the back kitchen door, he has turned up at precisely the same moment.

Cook doesn't know him. She thinks he's a strange dog. So he is, a very strange dog indeed. But she knows me, far, far too well, in spite of my sadly changed appearance.

Cook has a very thoughtless way of expressing herself. She just lets go. She doesn't know when to stop. And the worst of it is, she rubs in her remarks with the rolling-pin.

That Tumble is trying to make up to Cook, waggling and wriggling all round her feet,—purring, one might almost say. I do despise a dog that purrs. But that Tumble is mean enough for anything!

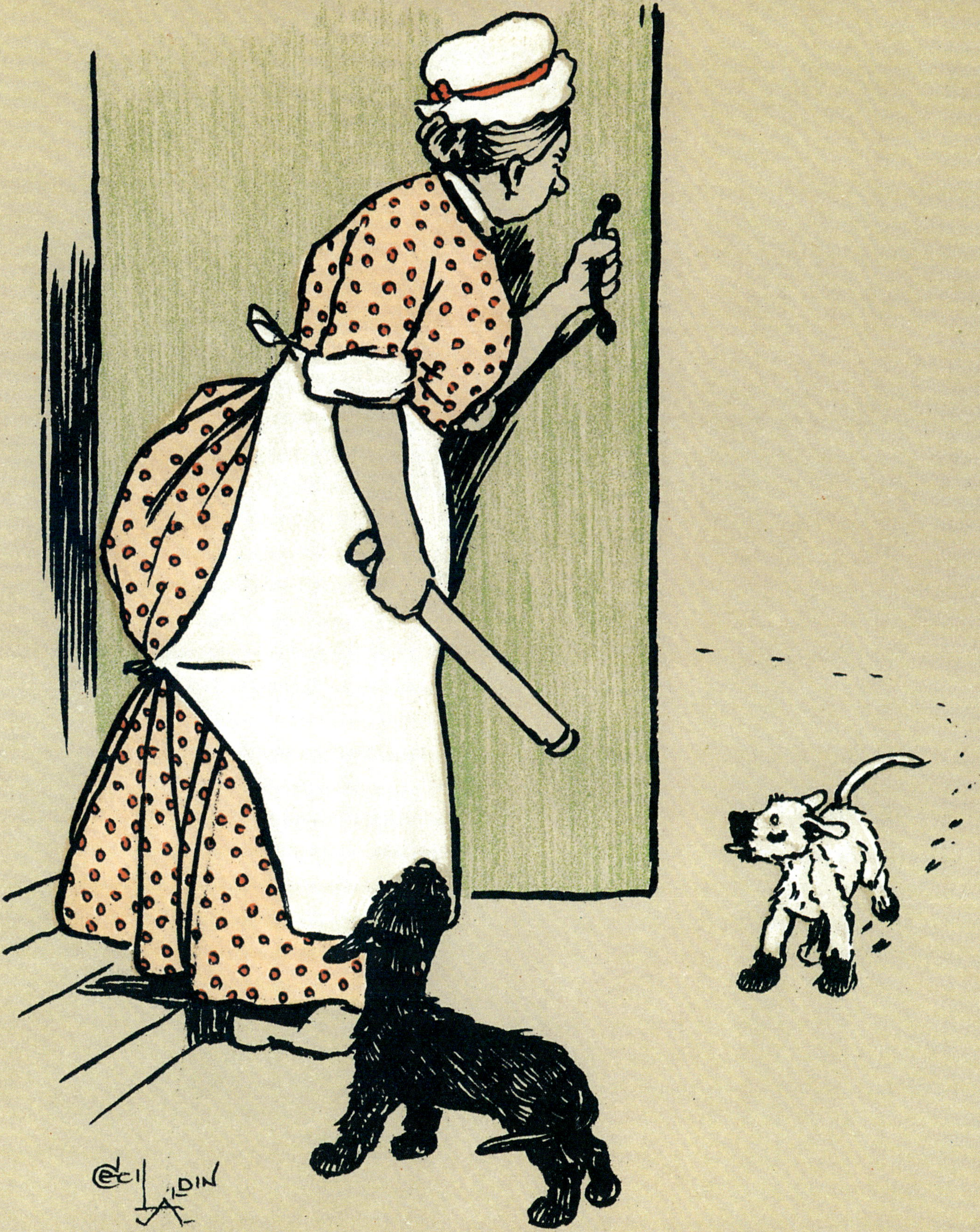
Cecil Aldin

A Brush with Cook

This is what I've been brought to!

This is what comes of keeping bad company.

Tubbed TWICE in one day. Not only tubbed, but scrubbed. Monkey Brand and a stiff scrubbing-brush applied to my nice soft elegant person!

Oh! what a thing it is to have a hard-hearted Cook, who encourages strange dogs, and lathers her own little Roughie!

I don't like Cook. Nor Susan. Nor anybody. The world is dark, and dismal, and disagreeable, and hatefully damp. All the fault of that Tumble.

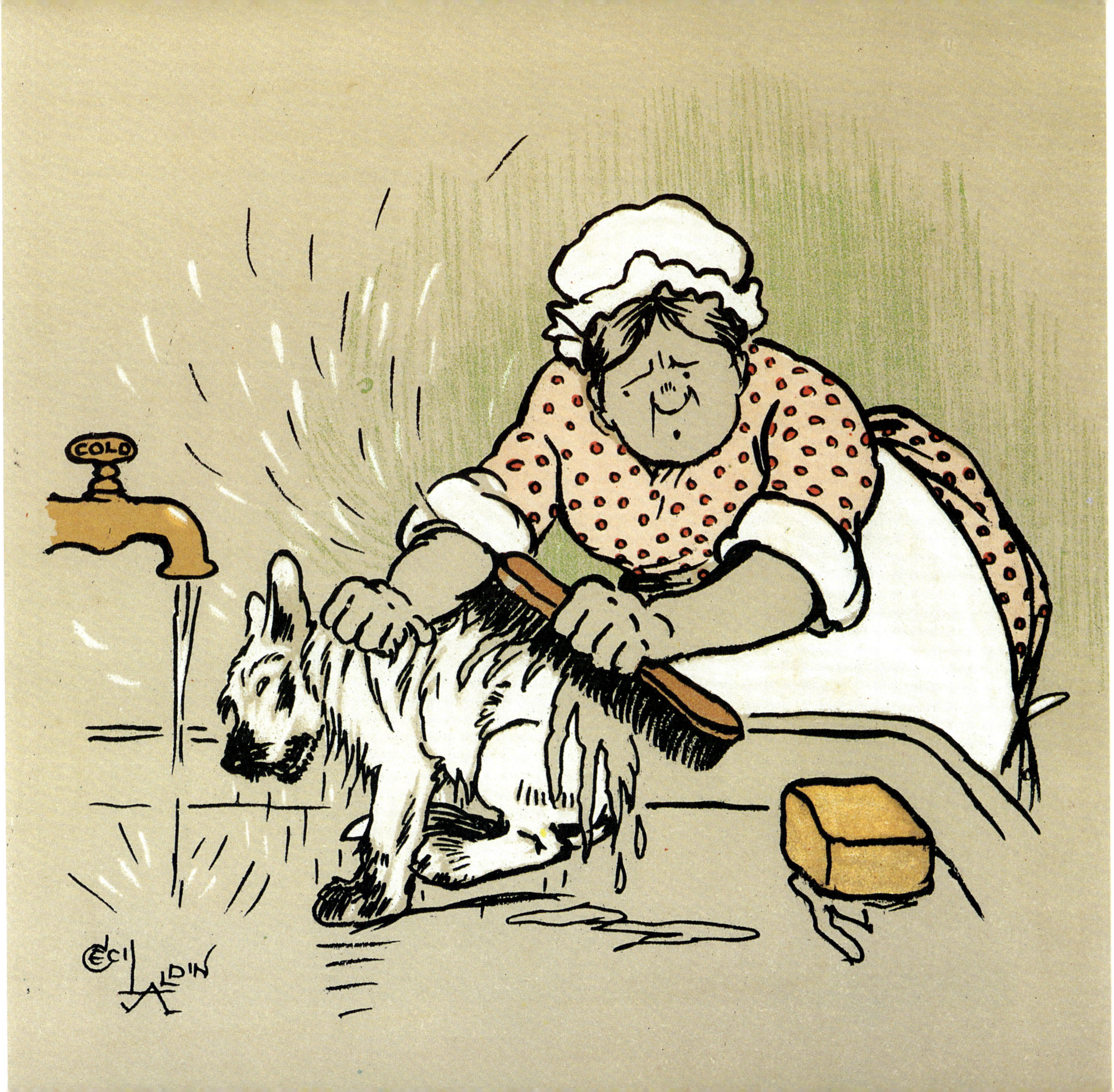
COLD
CECIL ALDIN

More Injustice

Meanwhile that Tumble is not being rubbed and scrubbed and scolded and unjustly treated. Oh, dear no! Far from it. He has arranged himself very comfortably in the cot where the old baby sleeps,—I mean the last baby but one. He is rolling and kicking to his heart's content.

Is there no justice anywhere? No common-sense? Nobody to roll out and kick out that Tumble?

If not, why not?

But it doesn't seem like it, so far.

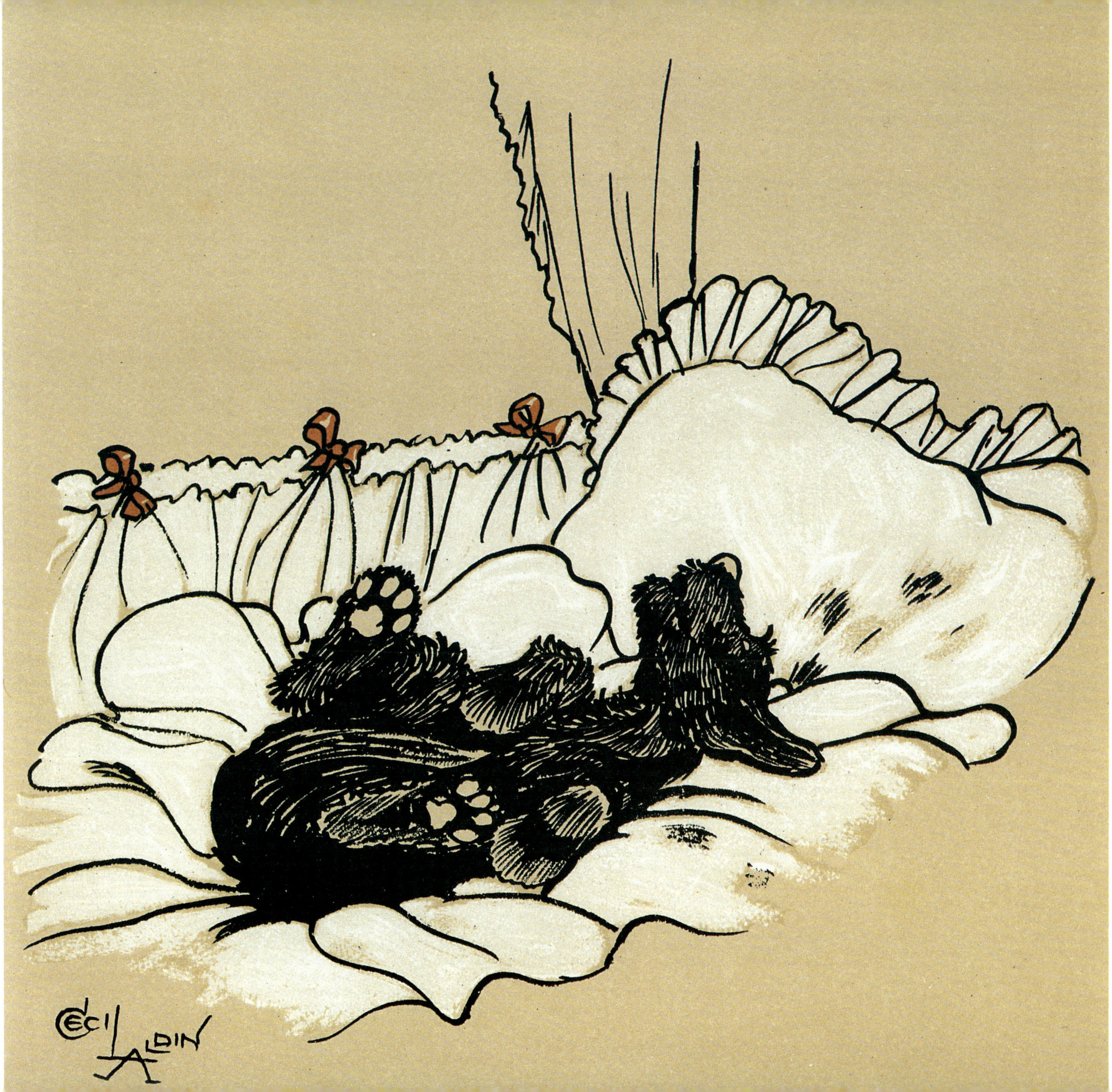
CECIL ALDIN

Handley Cross & Hunting Countries

In 1912 the first of Aldin's great hunting prints, commonly known as 'Hunting Countries' were published. These are long, narrow prints and came out in two sizes. The first editions were approximately 15″ high by 24″ long and the smaller, latter reprints, 8″ high by about 12″ long.

1912 was also to see a two volume edition of *Handley Cross* by R.S. Surtees, illustrated by Aldin and published by Edward Arnold. These two volumes included 24 colour plates by Aldin and 97 black and white drawings. Quite frankly, this book has never been a great success with the public, although this was probably Aldin's favourite book, as it must be said that the public have always favoured editions illustrated by John Leech. Aldin's illustrations, like those of G. D. Armour, are heavily influenced by the Leech original illustrations.

The criticism, in many ways fair, levied at Aldin for his paintings of hounds during the four year period 1910/1914 is that they are in many ways 'sausages on sticks'. I wouldn't disagree with this rather unkind description; however, in Aldin's defence it must be said that the hounds were not meant to be studies of individuals, but merely part-players in the overall scene. In *Handley Cross* his black and white illustrations, when it came to hounds, were very much more effective than his colour.

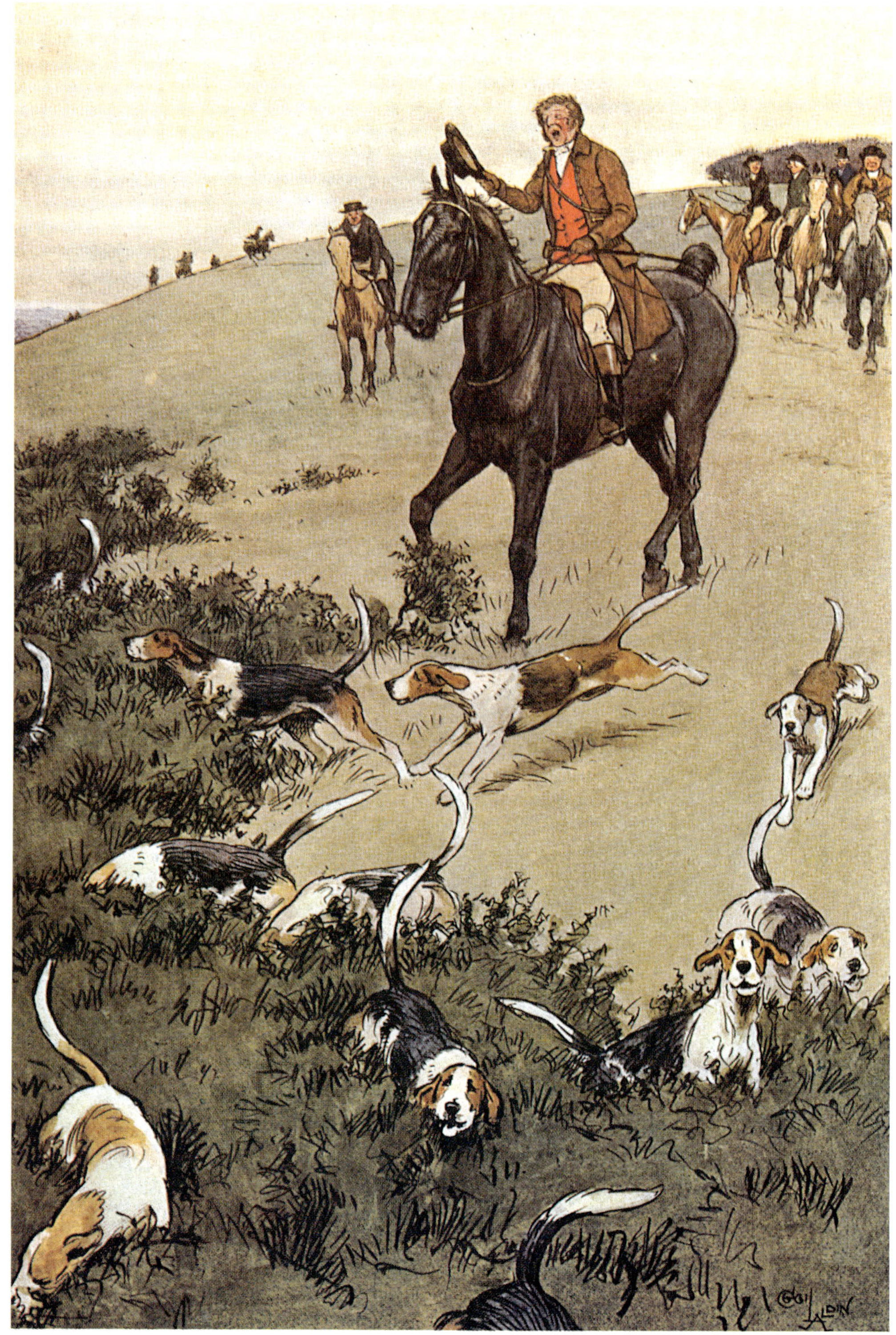

Michael cheered them to the echo.

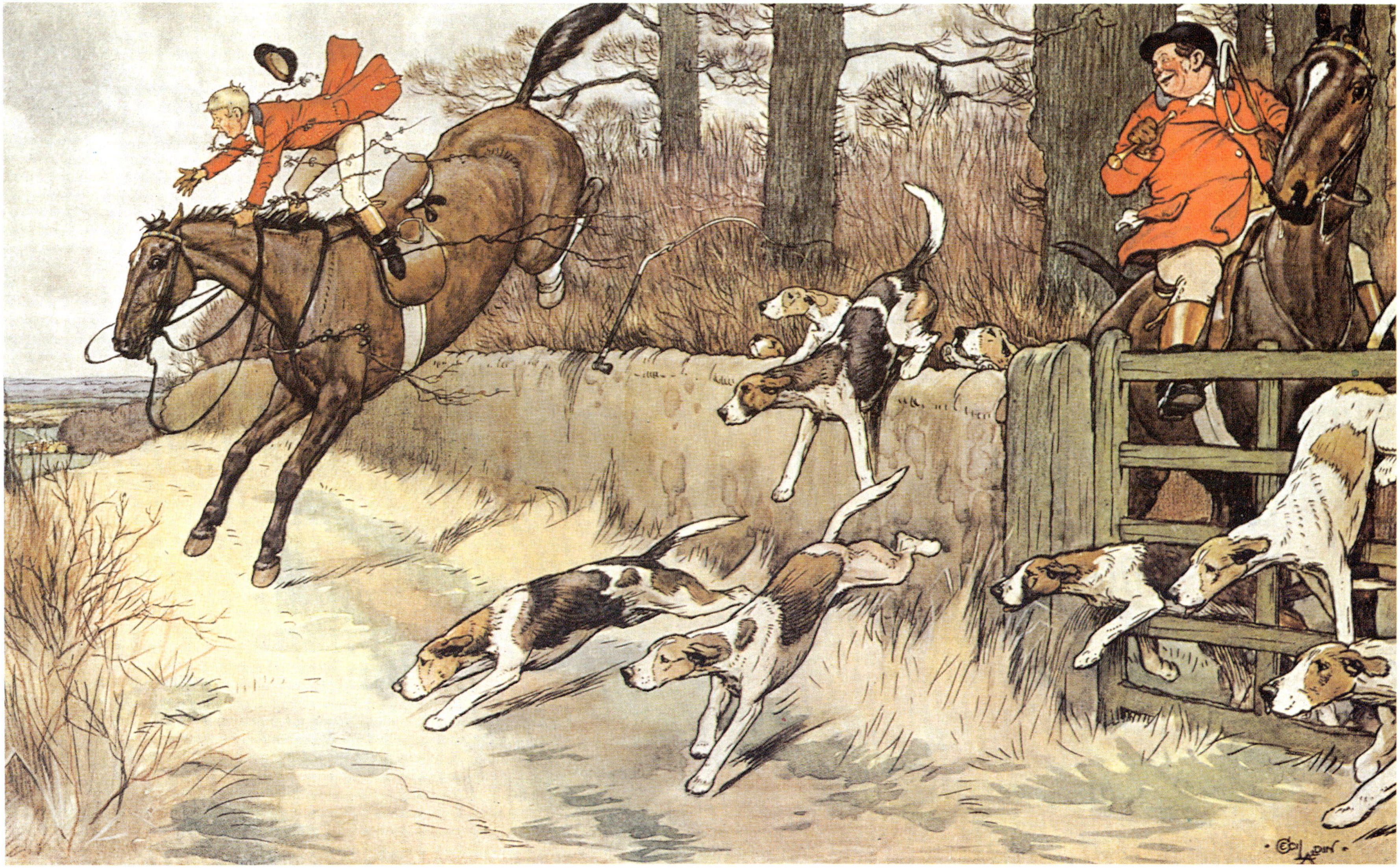

"Hoff, for a fi'pun note!"

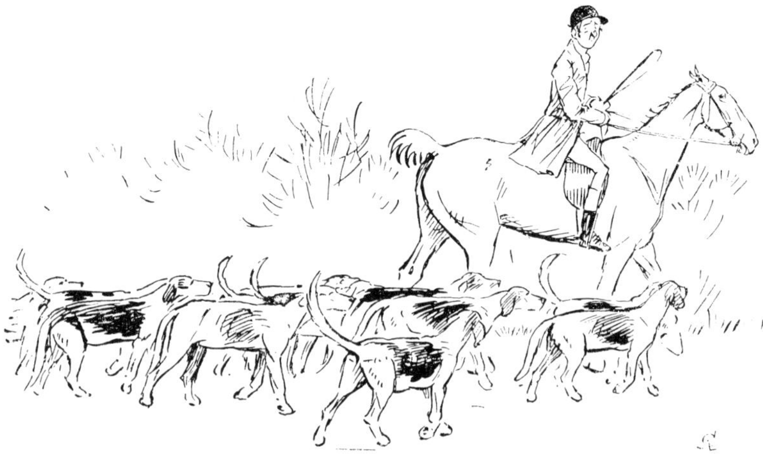

" The hounds proceeded sluggishly to cover."

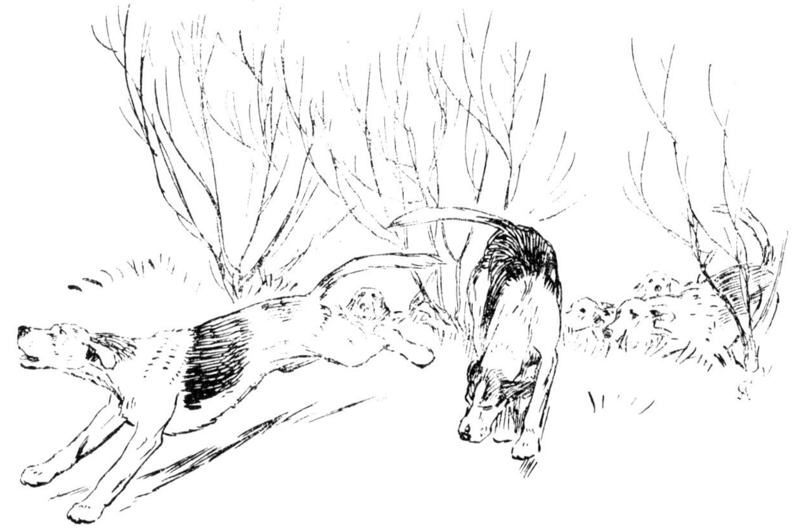

" 'A fox for a pund!' "

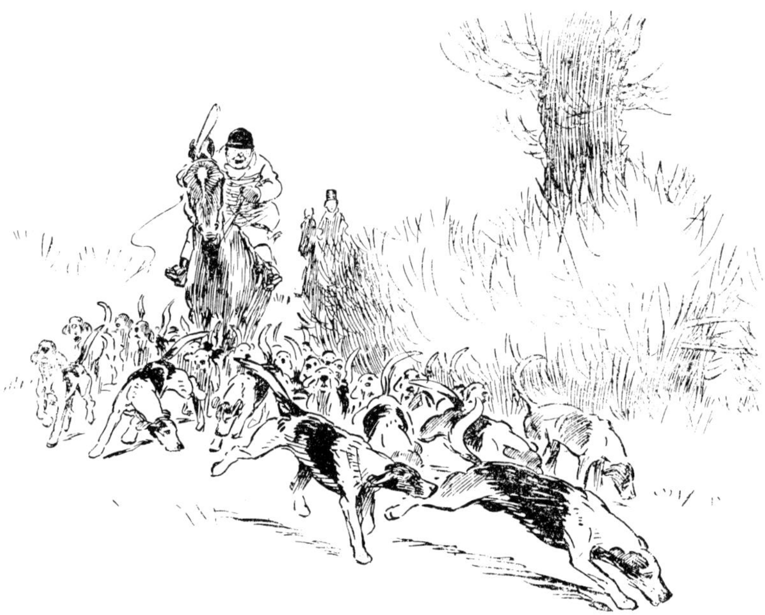

" 'A fox ! for a million !' roared he."

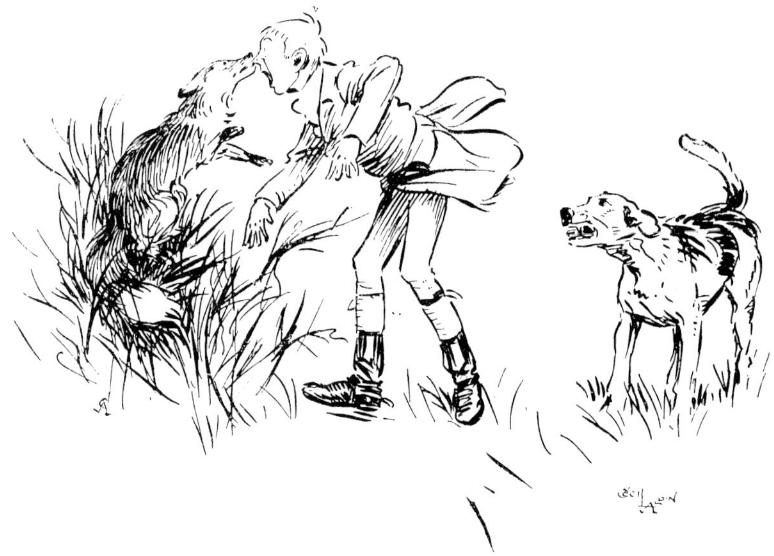

" Seized Ben by the nose."

DECEMBER 21, 1904.] PUNCH, OR THE LONDON CHARIVARI. 433

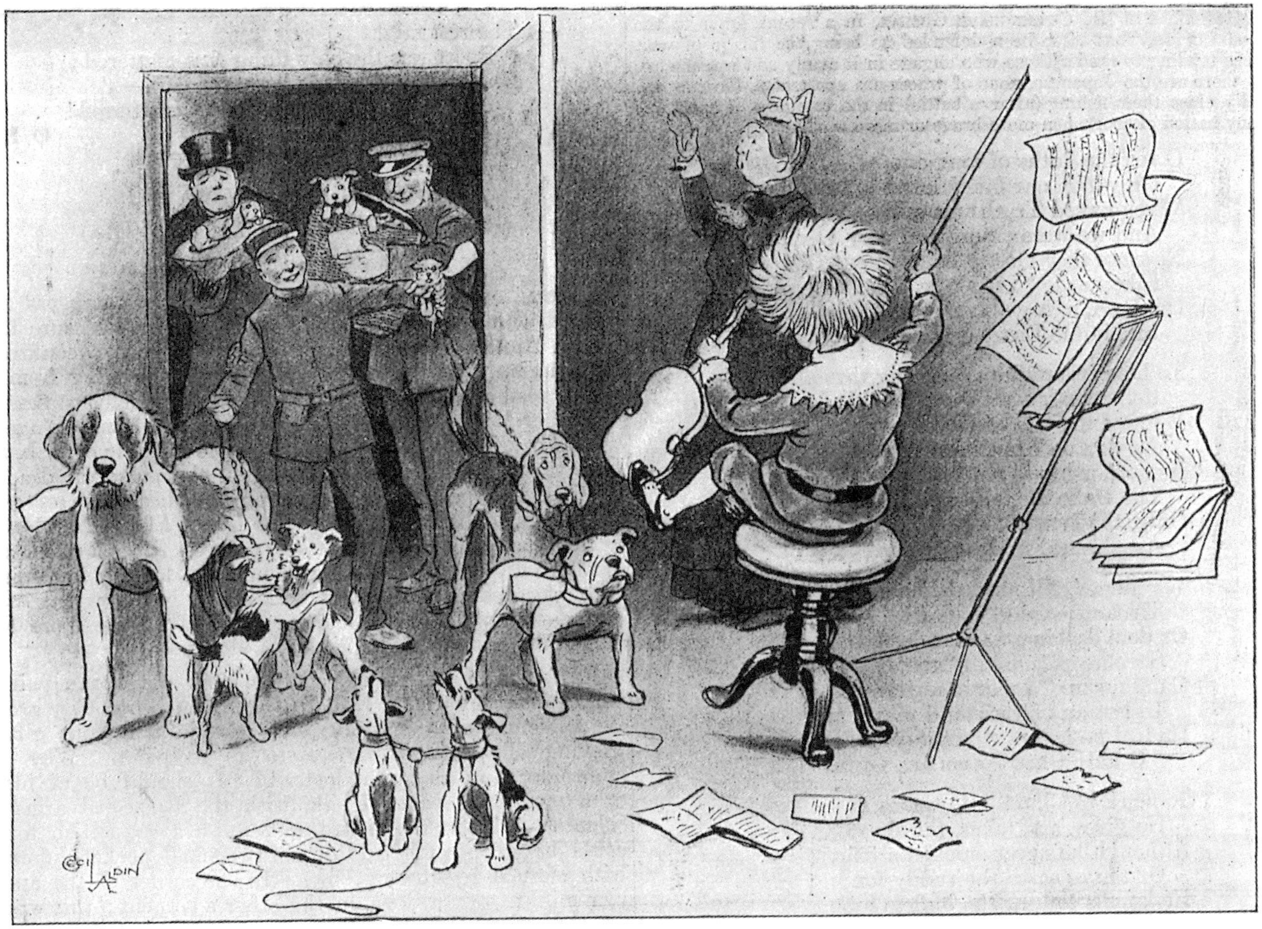

THE PERILS OF POPULARITY.

"I WISH SOMEONE WOULD GIVE ME A DOG."—*Infant Prodigy to an Interviewer.*

OUR ARTIST DEPICTS THE SCENE NEXT DAY.

From 1904 onwards Aldin was a regular contributor to *Punch,* as well as many other illustrated magazines. It cannot be said that his illustrations in *Punch* were a success, either by his standards or by *Punch's* standards.

Aldin's style, using a large amount of black ink wash did not suit the paper's style and, equally important, did not reproduce well on the rather course, soft paper Punch was then using. G. D. Armour, whose work was much stronger when it came to pen and ink drawing, was very much more successful as a purveyor of sporting and animal drawings to the magazine.

Farmyard Puppies & Other Childrens' Books

Farmyard Puppies was written and illustrated by Cecil Aldin and was first published in 1911 by Frowde & Hodder. Frowde & Hodder also published *Rough and Tumble* in 1909, extracts from which have already been shown in this book. *Jock and Some Others* was published by Gale & Polden down in Aldershot initially and then in French by Hachette et Cie of Paris.

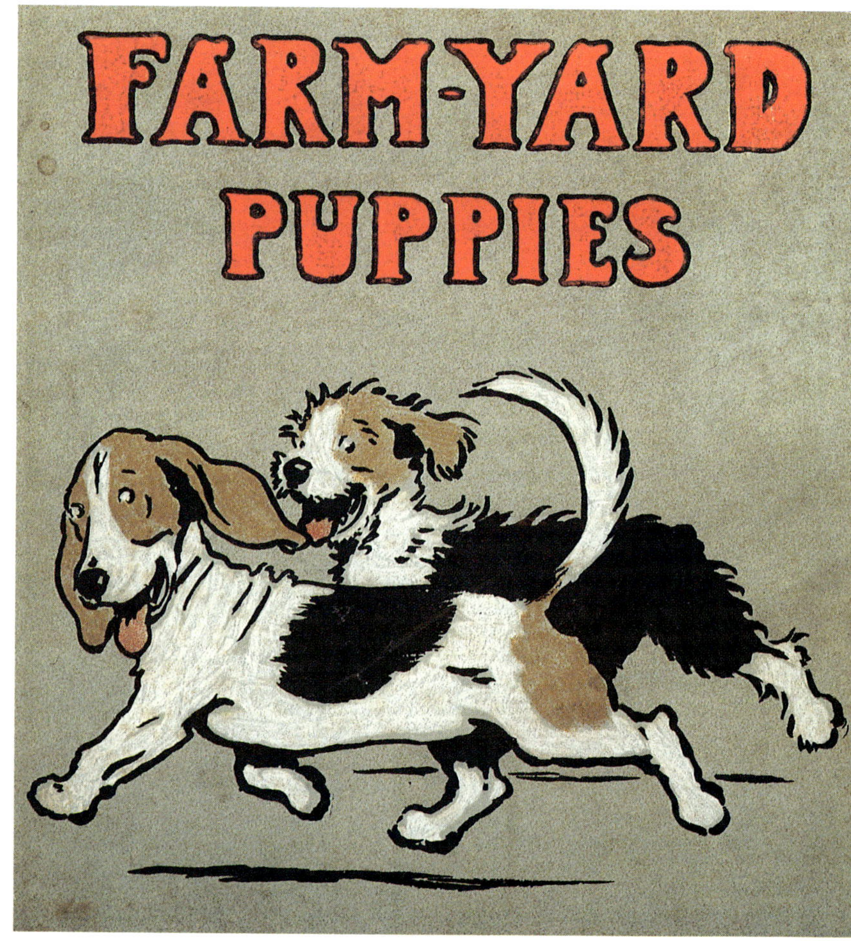

Farmyard Puppies was in the same style as many of the other 'childrens' books' written and published by Aldin in the five years leading up to World War I such as *The White Puppy Book, The Black Puppy Book* and *The Bobtail Puppy Book* and consisted of twelve colour plates with text opposite. Even in those days their appeal was universal and they were purchased by adults, not only for children, but for their own enjoyment.

As well as writing and illustrating his own books for children, Aldin also built up a successful relationship with May Byron and did equally wonderful illustrations to accompany her text. Undoubtedly the most successful of their co-operations was Cecil Aldin's *Happy Family* which consisted of six childrens' books - *Hungry Peter, the Pig; Rufus, the Cat; Forager, the Puppy; Rags, the Dog; Humpty and Dumpty, the Rabbits* and *Master Quack, the Duckling.* Noel Coward starred in a musical based on these books and Cecil Aldin helped with the design work for it.

An Attack in the Flank . . .

Chips remarked (what a fearful shame!)
That he found the Farmyard distinctly tame.
What did he expect, I'd like to know—
An elephant-hunt, and a tiger or so?
There's no big game in our yard at present.
Still, pig-stalking is decidedly pleasant.
Old fat Porko (from whom I take
A very short cut when he's wide awake),
Was snoring away like a buffalo there.
"Chips," I whispered, "let's give him a scare!"
We jumped the moment that I commanded.
With a piercing war-cry, down we landed. . . .
Porko is ever so large and fat,—
But still he has teeth. I'd forgotten that.

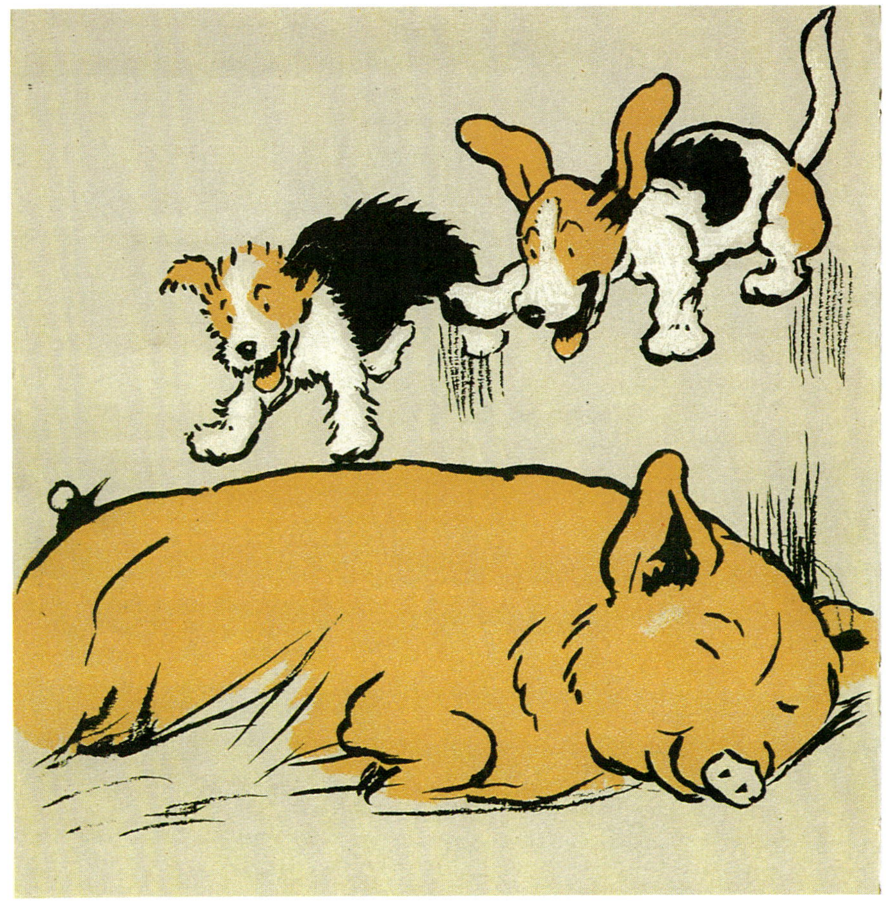

A City of Refuge . . .

Out of the pig-stye, extra quick,
We made our way to the nearest rick.
Chips was white to the very lips.
He's a shocking poor hand at adventures,
Chips.
I've often known him go perfectly pale,
And trembly, too, to the tip of his tail.
It isn't the sort of a tail you'd call
A traveller's tale,—by no means at all.
He was meant to sit by the kitchen fender,
And grumble because his chop isn't
tender.
But with bold bad brigands, or pirate
ships,
Or even Red Indians—no good, is Chips.
In fact, I found him an absolute stick
At simply climbing a farmyard rick.

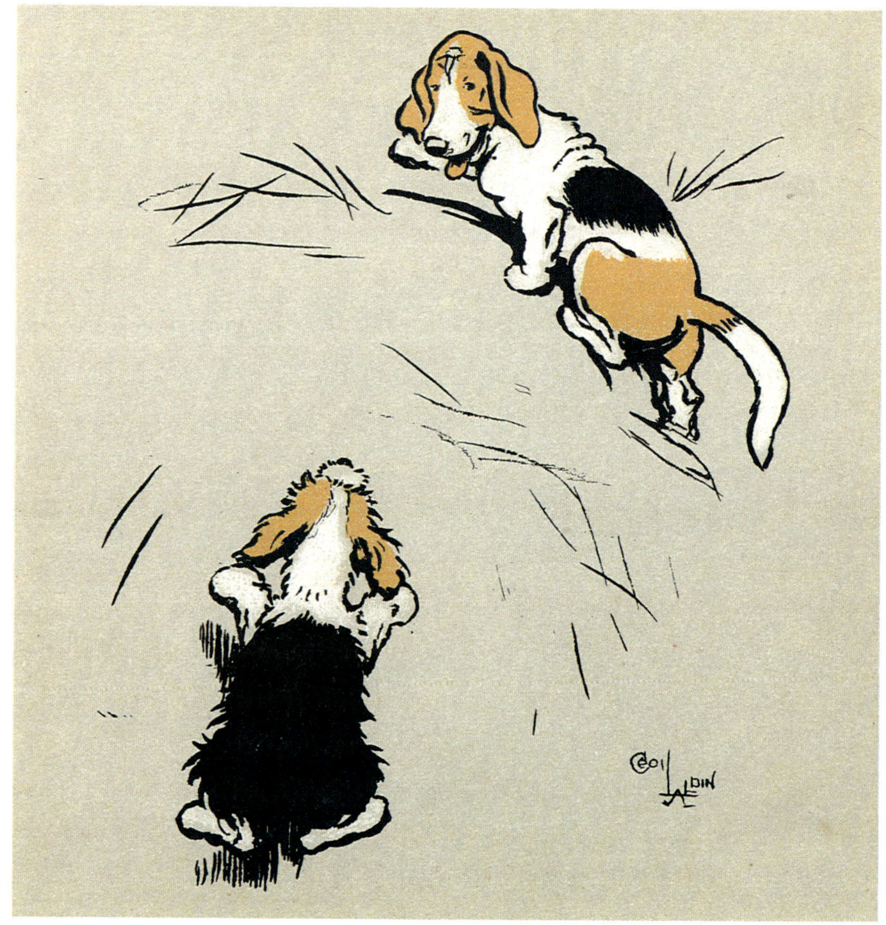

A Hair-raising Adventure . . .

I seized him fast by the ear and the scruff,—
My gracious, I hope it was hard enough!—
And grabbed him dreadfully tight, as if
He were hanging over a straight-down
cliff,—
The sort of breathless scene, you know,
One sees in a picture-palace show.
I dragged him up by sheer brute force,—
And bellowed "Saved!" till I grew quite
hoarse.
And he said, "Thanks awfully!" Think
of that!
The kind of thing he'd say to a cat
If she left him some milk she didn't care
for.
No: Chips is a regular slacker; therefore,
I mean to teach him a bit what's what:
And Chips, my boy, you will find it hot!

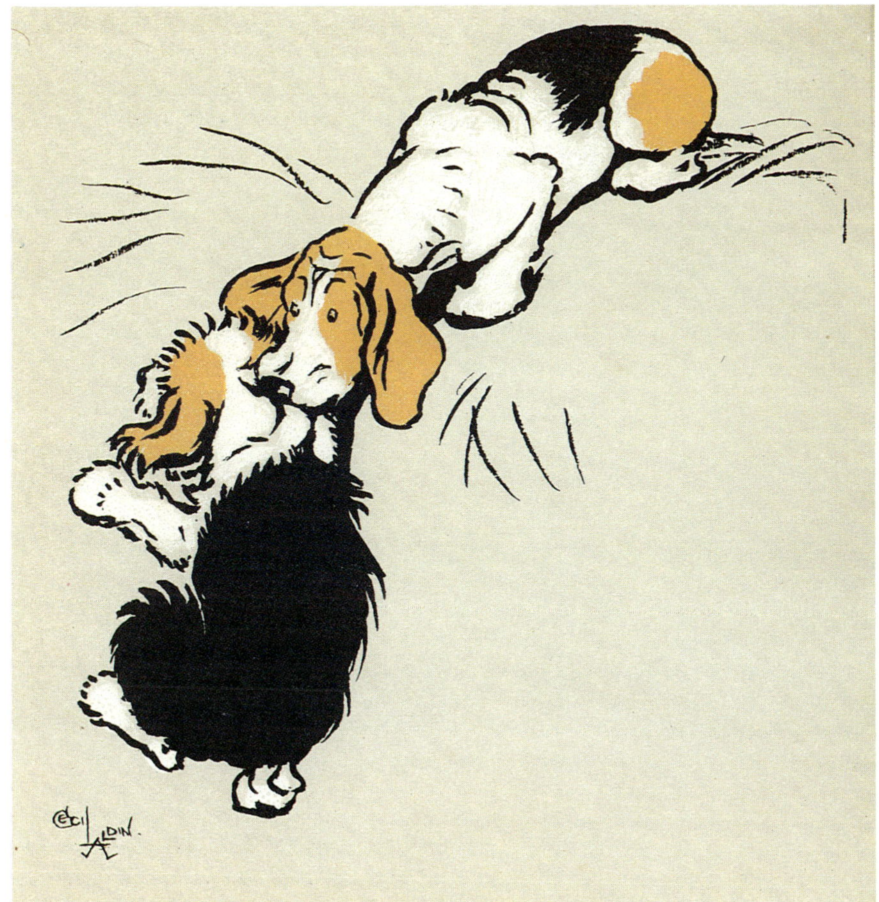

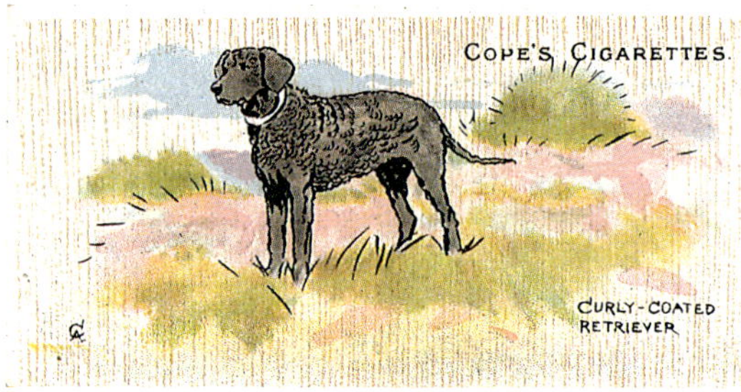

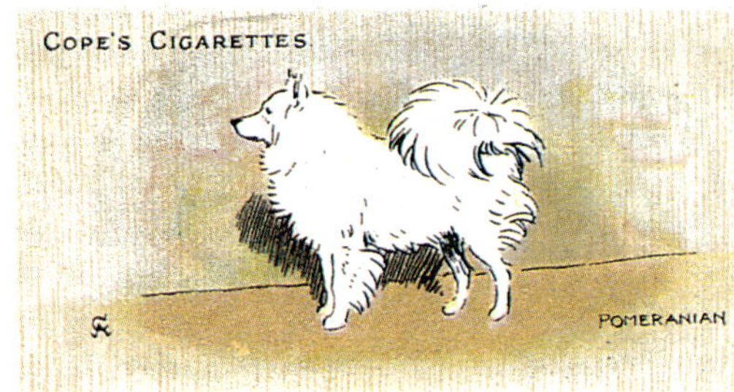

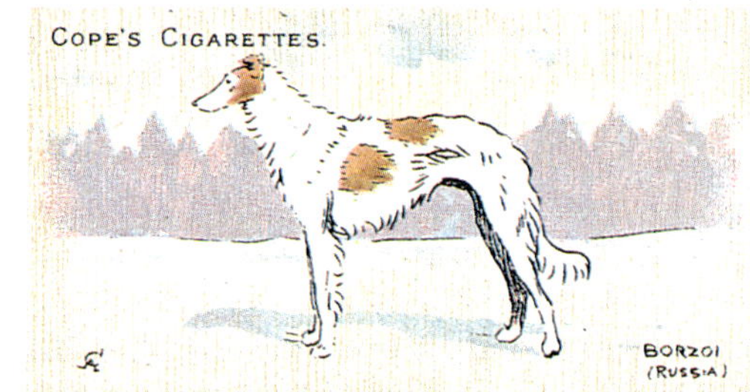

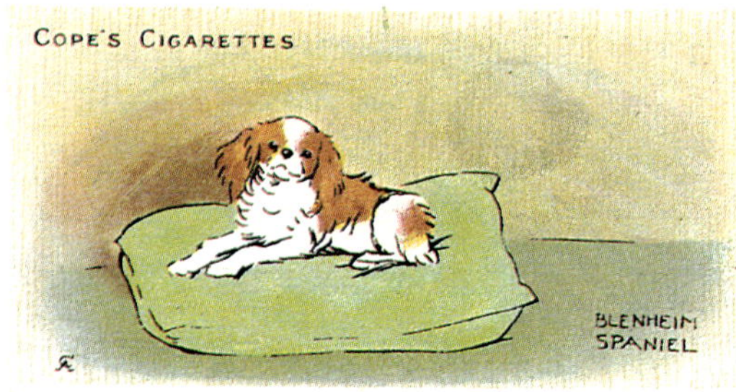

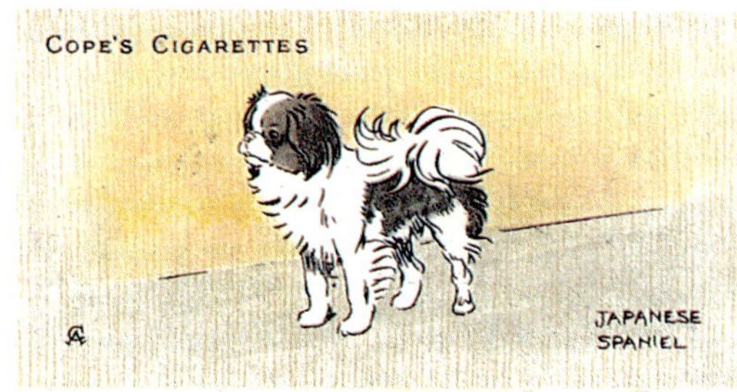

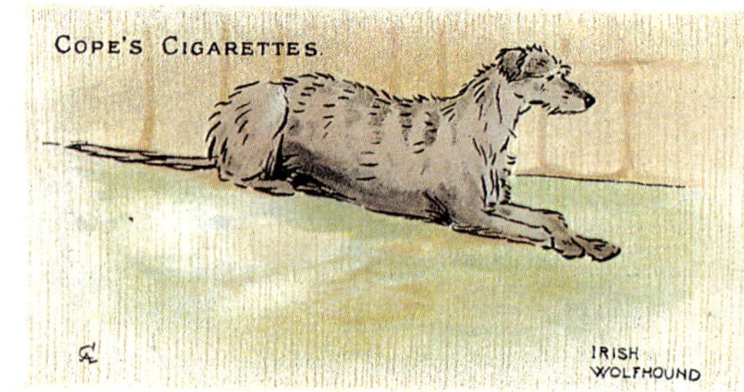

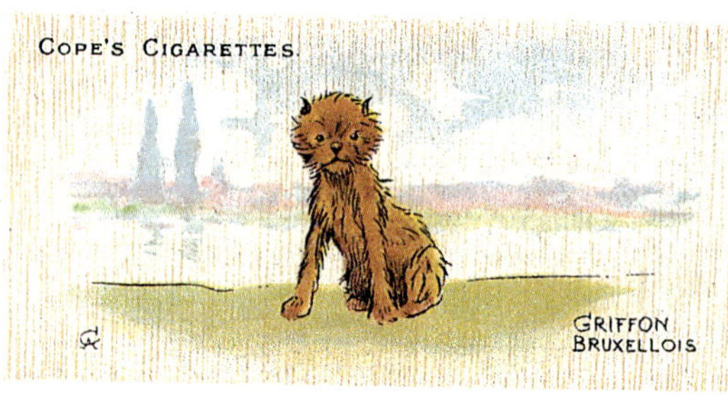

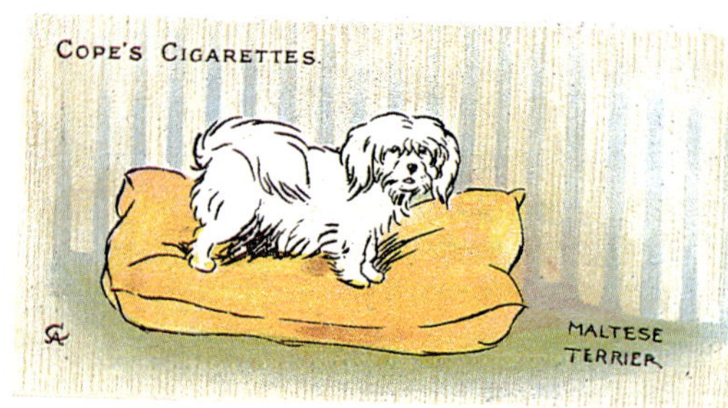

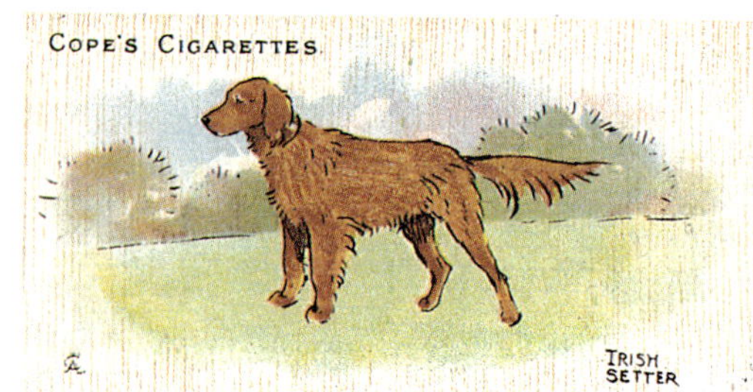

In 1911 Cope's issued a set of fifty 'Dogs of the World' cigarette cards by Aldin.
On the reverso they said "A series of 50 pictures from Drawings by Cecil Aldin, R.B.A., the most celebrated modern painter of Horses and Dogs."
At this time Aldin was the most successful and famous sporting artist in the British Isles, having overtaken in popularity such artists as Finch Mason and Cuthbert Bradley of the older generation and being very much more popular than the giants of the 1920's and 1930's such as Lionel Edwards, Alfred Munnings (later President of the Royal Academy) and Snaffles.

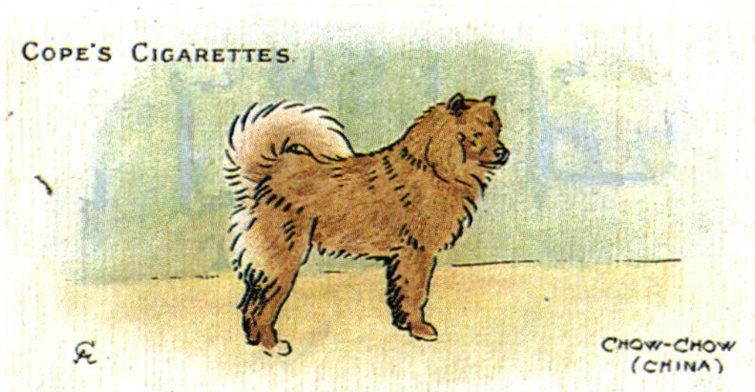

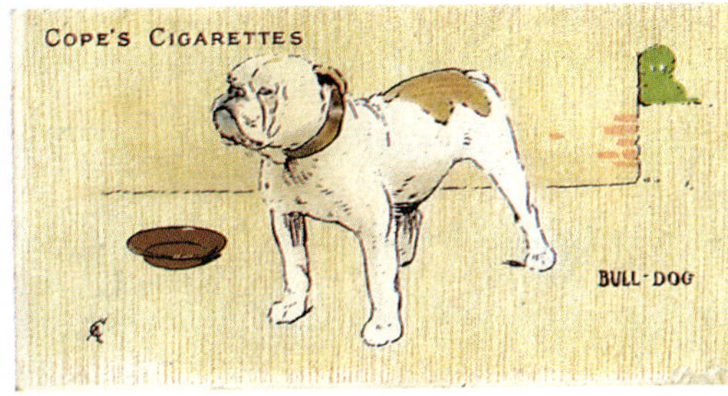

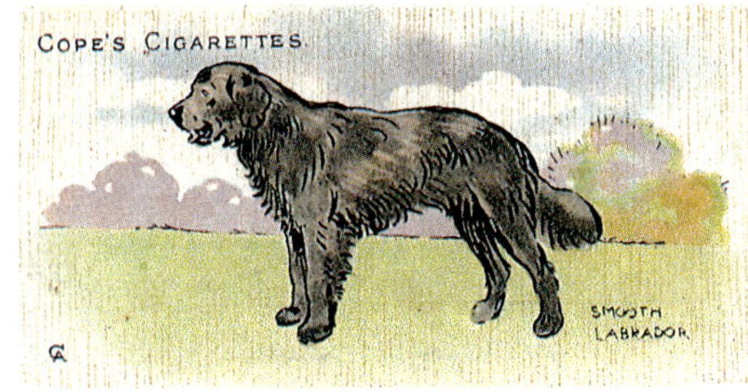

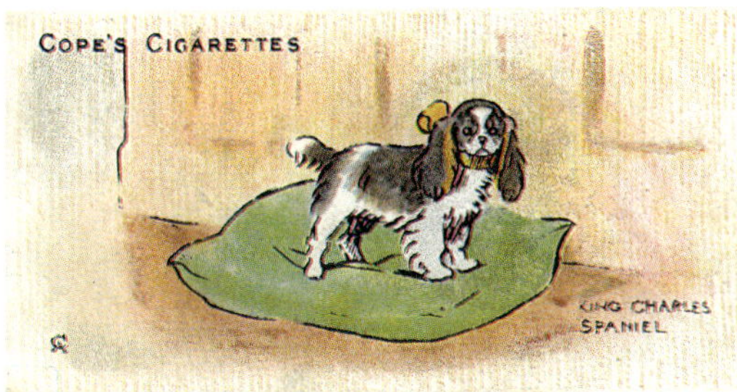

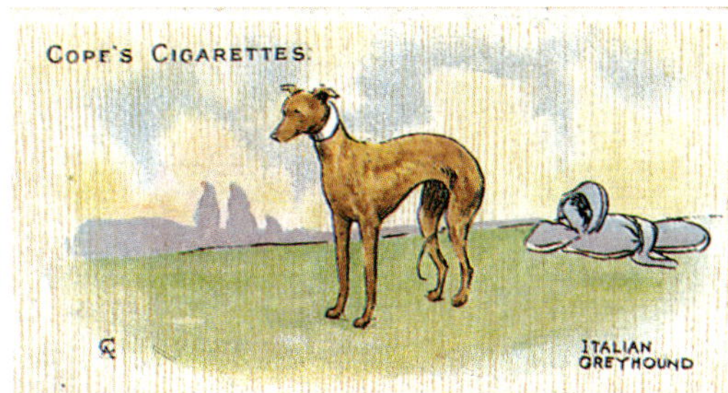

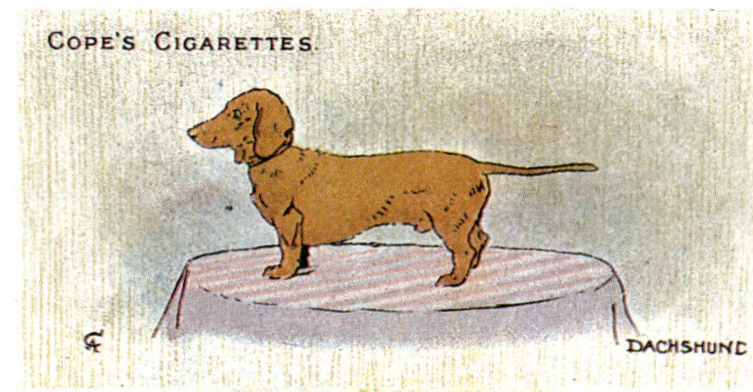

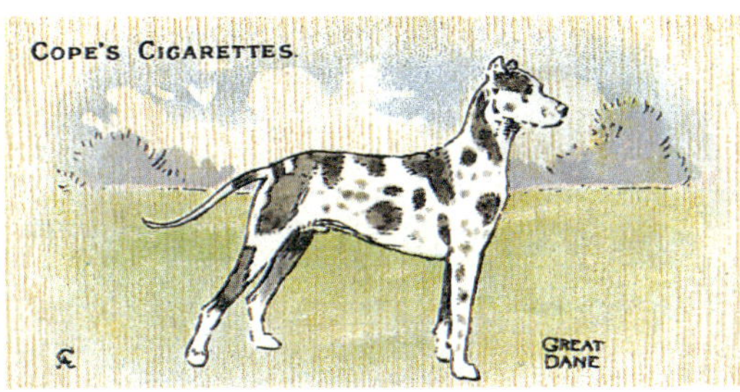

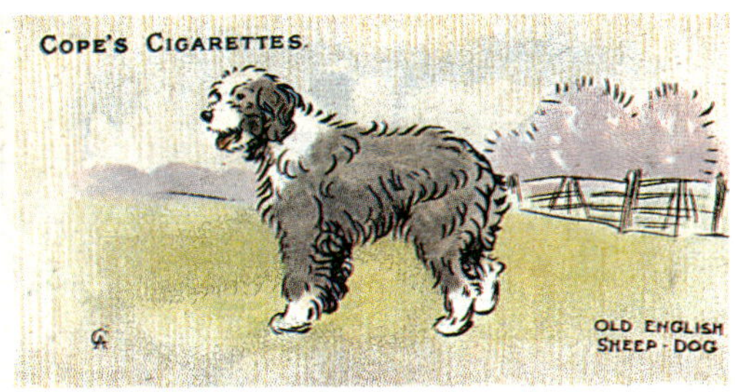

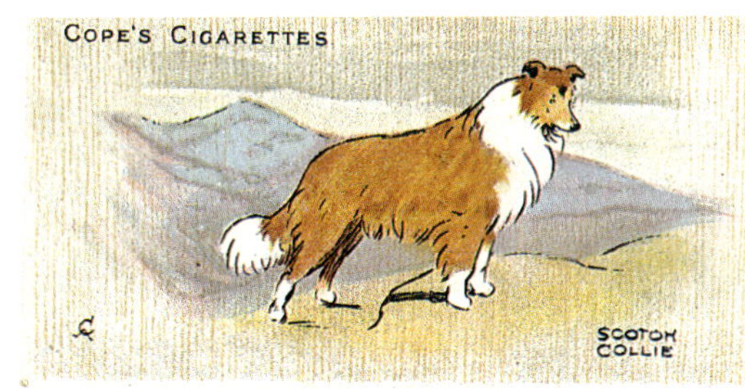

Cope's were quite a small cigarette company and as a result full sets of cards are now rare and worth many hundreds of pounds.

Clearly at this stage of his career, Aldin was still very much better at depicting large dogs such as old English sheepdogs or great danes than small dogs such as griffon bruxellois or blenheim spaniels.
In the 1920's and 1930's, when dog paintings represented the large majority of his output, he could paint all types and sizes of dogs with unsurpassed skill and feeling.

'Jock and Some Others'

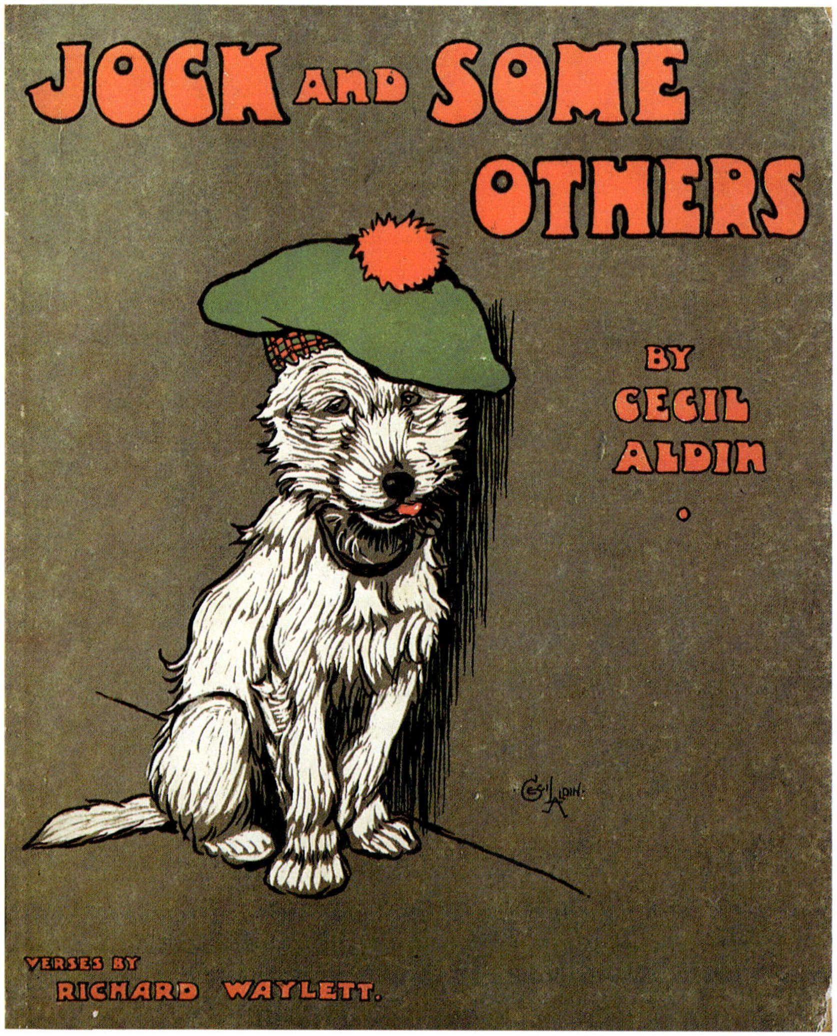

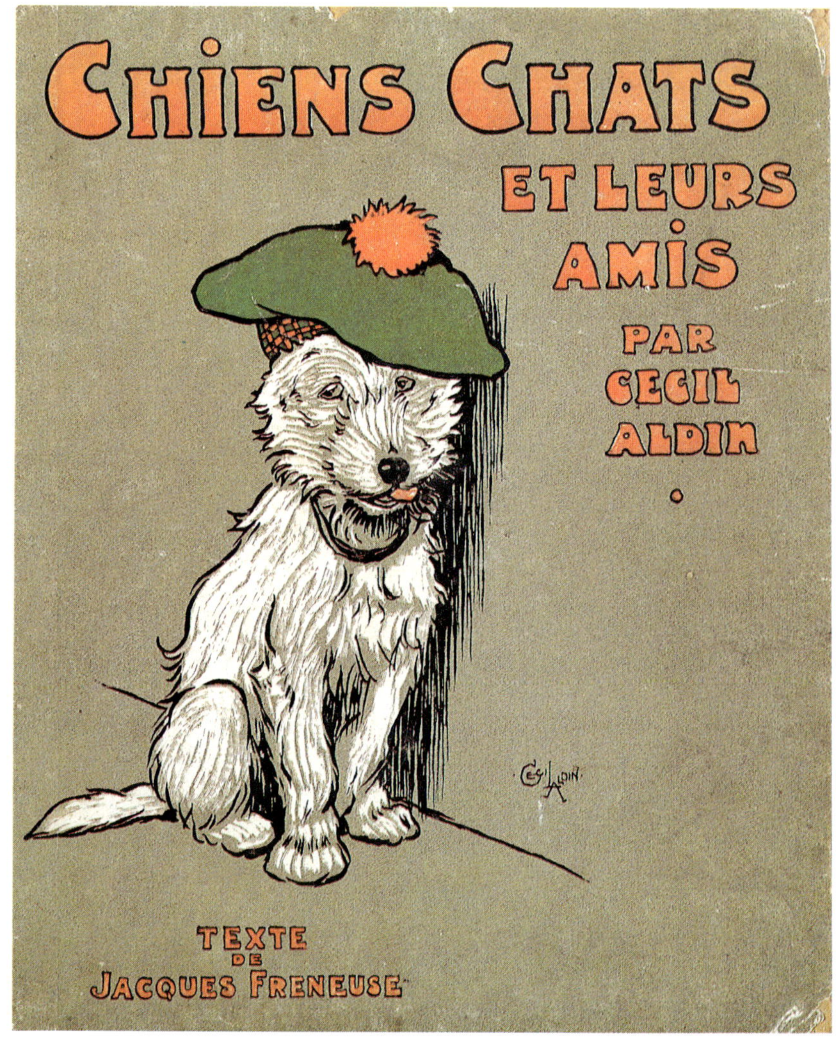

was just one of the many books published
in France.

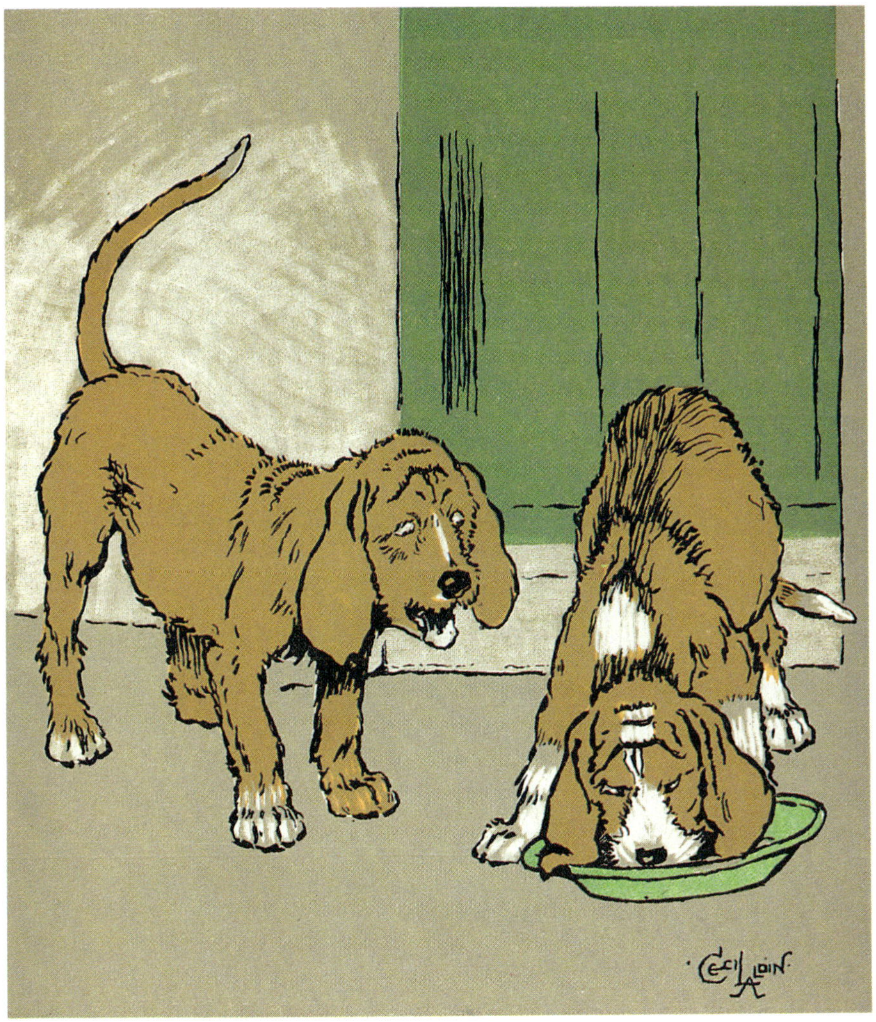

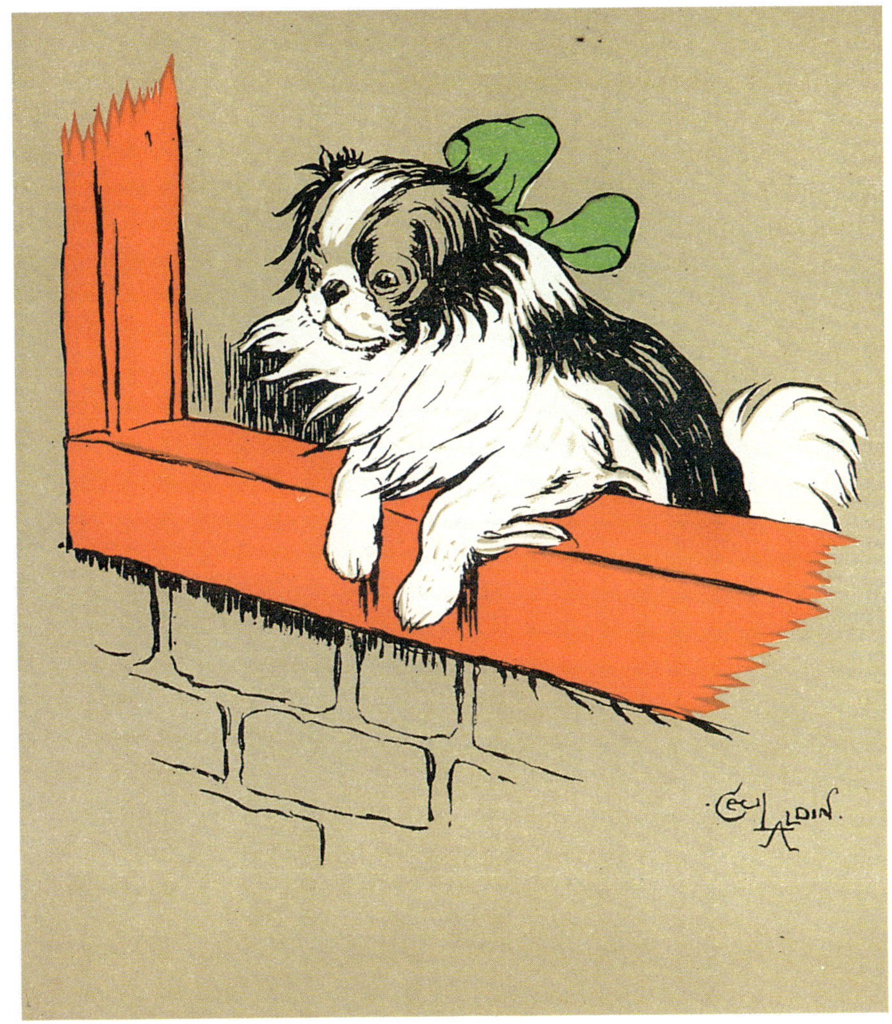

Pictures had and still have universal appeal.

Chapter Three
The First World War (1914 to 1918)

The First World War broke out in August 1914, soon after Aldin had been elected with his great friend, Eric Palmer, as joint Master of the South Berks.

Aldin, by then aged forty-four, was too old to serve with the Colours but immediately rallied to the country's aid by becoming a Remount Officer. At that time the horse was still the main method of transportation in the Army and with the outbreak of war tens of thousands of horses of all types were needed. Not only were horses needed for the Cavalry and Mounted Infantry, but heavy horses were also required for The Royal Artillery and draught purposes.

As far as I am aware, Aldin hardly picked up a pencil or brush during the whole of the hostilities and what little spare time he had was spent in keeping his beloved South Berks Foxhounds going.

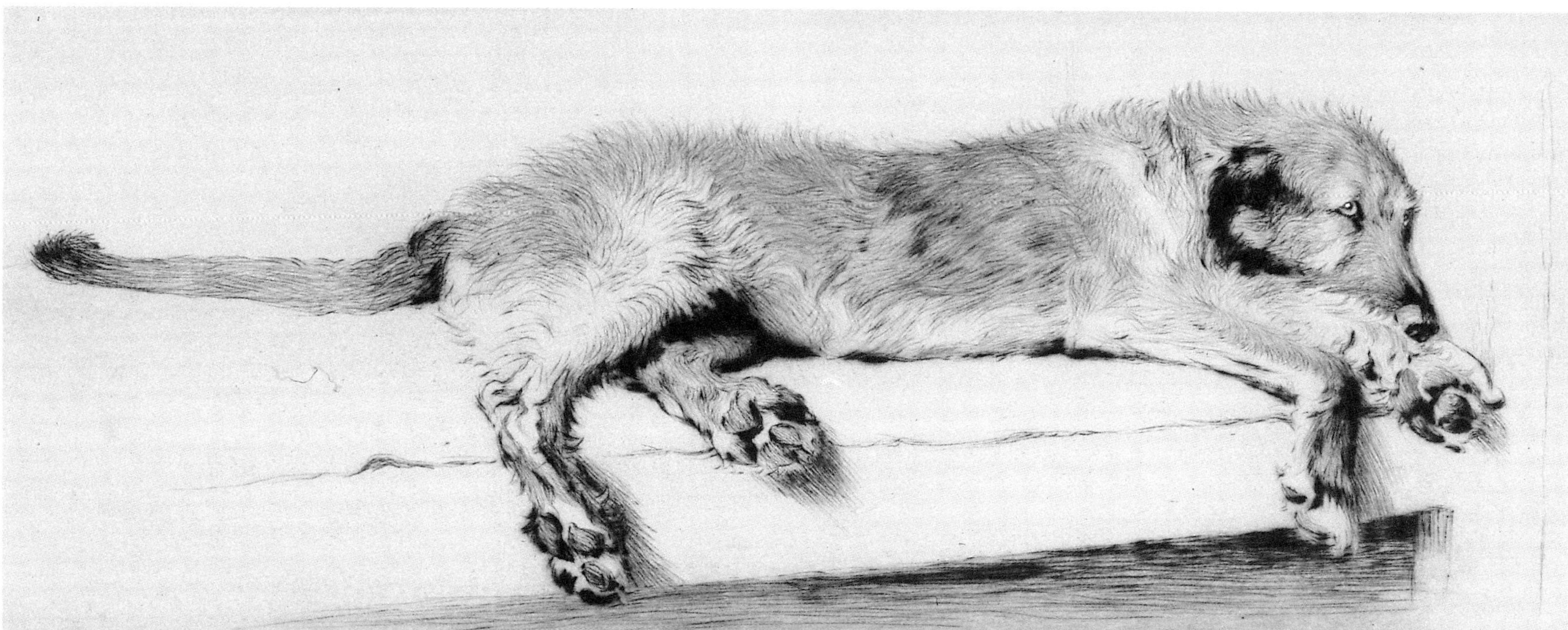

The Aldin Family, like so many others, paid a most awful price in terms of human tragedy as Aldin's only son, Dudley, was killed at Vimy Ridge in 1916. He was just nineteen and had graduated as an Officer in the Royal Engineers a few days before. Throughout the rest of his life Cecil Aldin could not bear to discuss the tragedy nor, for that matter, could he even write of it fully in his memoirs.

Certainly by the end of the war Aldin was a very different man to the wonderfully carefree person of August 1914. His work after World War I was completely different from that before. There were to be no more amusing childrens' books like *The Farmyard Puppy Book* or *Rough and Tumble*. However, the seventeen or so years he was to live after World War I were his greatest years as a dog artist.

Soon after the war ended, Aldin acquired two puppies: Micky, the Irish wolfhound and Cracker, the bull-terrier. By 1927 these were the two most famous dogs in the British Isles and, as far as I am aware, with the possible exception of Lassie, if she ever existed, remain so.

← Micky, the Irish wolfhound

Cracker, the bull-terrier →

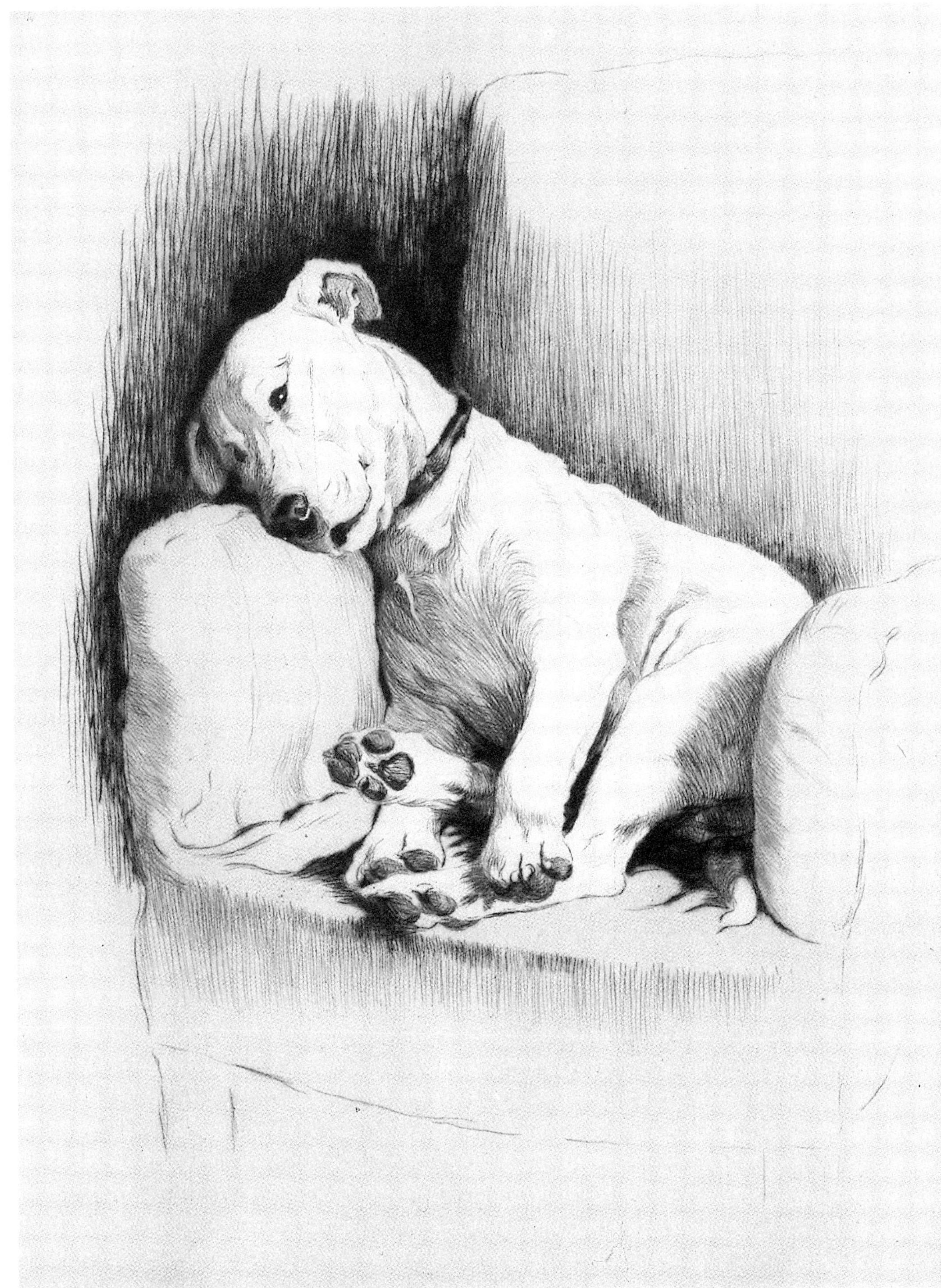

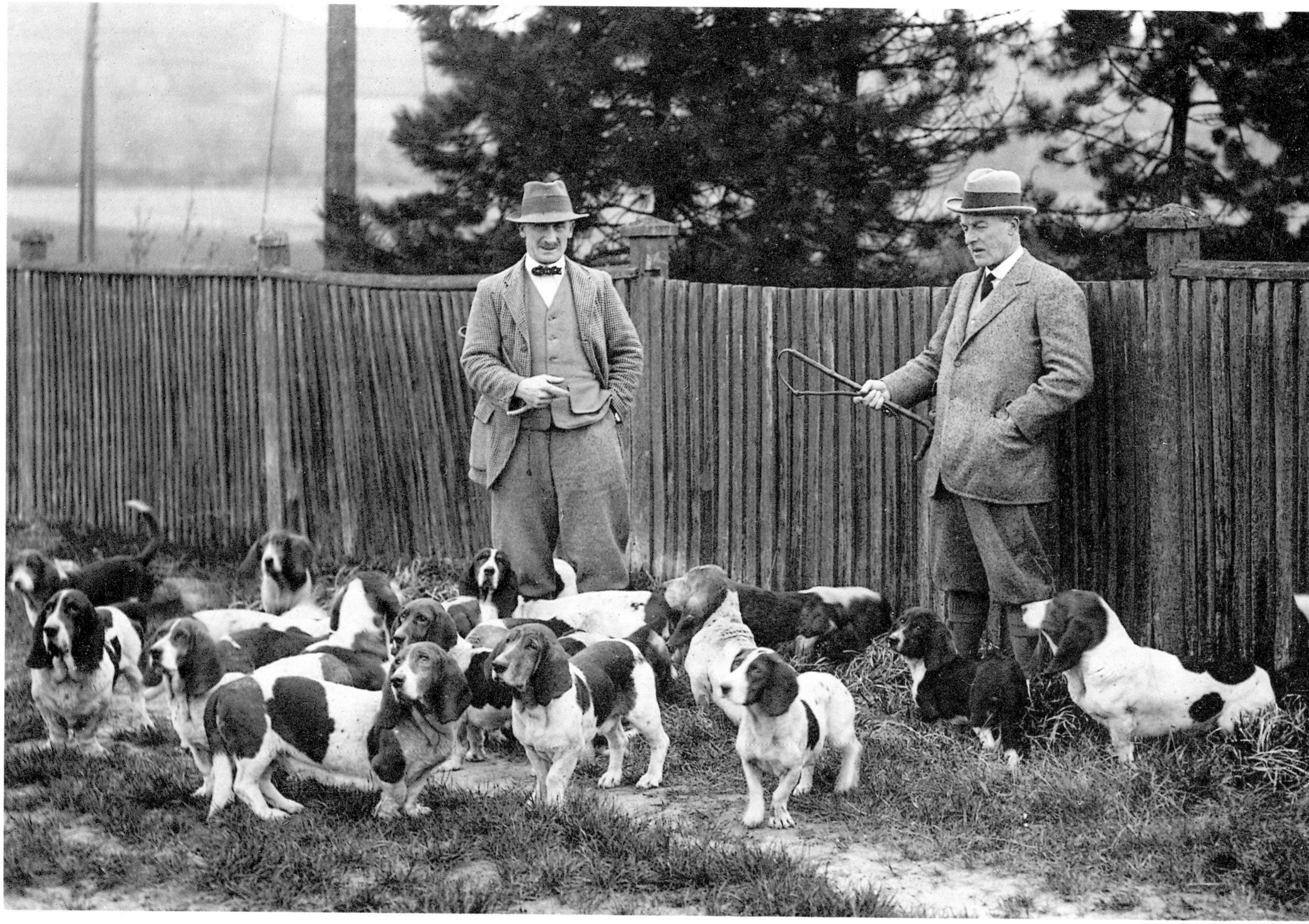

Cecil Aldin, facing camera, wearing bow-tie, and his bassets.
Merryman is the hound facing the camera to the left of the pack. Aldin had a way with all animals, especially dogs and hounds, and although he didn't start to hunt his harriers until he was nearly forty, he found controlling packs of hounds no problem.

Chapter Four
Great Paintings and Great Books (1918 to 1935)

Personal tragedy or not, as soon as hostilities came to an end Aldin's output went back to its enormous pre-War level. His work after a break of nearly five years was very different in style and character to that produced before the War.

Firstly, Aldin took up drawing architecture in pastel and spent much of the two years directly after the War away from home drawing old inns. He would go off in his car with one of his terriers for days at a time and found that by working in pastel he could work within the car; this saved him the embarrassment of having to work in public which he considered only suitable for amateur lady artists. The result of this was a trilogy of much admired books where the colour illustrations were of course from pastel drawings, *Old Inns* published in 1921, *Old Manor Houses* published in 1923 and *Cathedrals and Abbey Churches* published in 1924. Many of the plates from these were turned into limited edition prints and, as one would expect, dogs enlivened the scenes in some of them.

Aldin handed over the Mastership of the South Berks, which he had retained single-handed throughout the War (his joint Master had retired when he left for the Front in 1915), but continued to hunt two days a week with them and still helped in the kennels. He had long been fascinated by bassets and had kept a stray one, Potamus, as a pet when his children were fairly young.

One of Aldin's hunting friends, Godfrey Heseltine, had a lovely pack of bassets, many of whom were winners in the show ring, but at the end of the War Godfrey wished to stay out in India and continue to hunt the Ootacamund Hounds (the "Snooty Ooty" as Aldin's friend Snaffles used to call them). Consequently, the pack was sent down from Rosyth in Scotland, where it had spent the War with the R.N., and Aldin became Master with Mr. C. Carter. Now nearing fifty, he used to hunt them on foot once or twice a week during the season. The most famous hound in the pack was Champion Merryman, of whom Aldin painted a life-size portrait which he was later to swap with Godfrey for a stagecoach. The painting and the stagecoach were probably each worth in the region of £100 back in the mid 1920's, although nowadays the painting would certainly be worth in excess of £10,000 which, even taking inflation into account, shows the value now put on Aldin's work by collectors.

The trilogy of books – *Old Inns, Old Manor Houses* and *Cathedrals and Abbey Churches of England,* was a great success, *Old Inns* being reprinted a number of times in the twenties. For the rest of Aldin's life book-writing and production were to be an important part of his work. His daughter, Gwen, has put forward the theory that as arthritis in his hands made long hours at the easel or drawing block more and more difficult, he took to writing as a substitute. However, I cannot see that holding a pen would be any easier than holding a paintbrush. I believe that he genuinely liked writing books; he certainly greatly enjoyed the production of the childrens' books before the War, which is why he spent so much time and care on them.

In 1926 Aldin wrote and illustrated a semi-autobiographical instructional book on hunting entitled *Ratcatcher to Scarlet* and, in 1933, a companion volume was published, entitled *Scarlet to MFH*.

Leaving aside the purely visual side of Aldin's books, undoubtedly the most historically important work for which he was to be responsible was *Romance of the Road* first published in 1928. This was a luxuriously illustrated and magnificently produced history of coaching. Aldin had always been interested in coaching and coaching inns and, of course, this all tied in with his own make-believe Camelot world first shown in his great large print series 'The Fallowfield Hunt' and 'The Bluemarket Races'. After the First World War he started seriously researching coaching in all its aspects and *Romance of the Road* is a highly respected book amongst 'historians of the road'. Although Aldin had been a failure academically and had left school aged sixteen, books such as *Romance of the Road* prove that he was intelligent, able to carry out painstaking research, not only in libraries but in the field, and was also highly articulate.

Good as *Old Inns, Old Manor Houses* and *Romance of the Road* were, it was his 'dog' books of this era which really captured the public imagination and made him and his dogs so famous.

The first of these magical books was *Dogs of Character* first published in August 1927. It was to be published in many different forms over the next ten years and although not perhaps such a success as *A Dog Day*, proved to be one of the best-selling dog books of all time. It very much followed the format of *Ratcatcher to Scarlet* although it was more autobiographical and frequently featured Micky and Cracker. *Dogs of Character* gave serious and good advice on buying, training and keeping dogs and also included a light-hearted section on showing, which couldn't have found much favour with the Kennel Club authorities.

Dogs of Character was followed by *Sleeping Partners* in 1929 devoted solely to Cracker and Micky. Cracker was, in all probability, Aldin's favourite dog, due to his sense of humour. He was not the first bull-terrier Aldin had owned, as prior to the war he had another by the name of Sturdee. Micky was a wolfhound and once again Aldin had owned another before the war, so he was familiar with both breeds when he acquired these two dogs who were born within days of each other soon after World War I.

Micky, by the time *Sleeping Partners* was published, was credited with being the third largest dog in the British Isles at that time. Anyway, by 1929, Micky and Cracker were undoubtedly the two best-known dogs in the British Isles.

Two other great dog books were to follow: *An Artist's Models* in 1930 and *Just Among Friends* in 1934. Like the first editions of *Dogs of Character* and *Sleeping Partners* these were beautifully and expensively produced and the four books remain some of the most collected books on canine subjects ever produced in the British Isles.

Successful and popular as these two series of books, Old Inns and Coaching and Dogs were, Aldin was still conquering other new artistic fields. In around 1924 he started to produce limited edition engravings and not unnaturally the first subjects were dogs. For me, to suddenly start working in such a specialised and difficult medium as copper engraving when aged well over fifty is yet another demonstration of Cecil Aldin's unlimited ability and talent as an artist.

Many people believe these dog etchings are the greatest ever produced anywhere in the world. Although some of them are extremely appealing, they show none of the 'sickly sweetness' which so often spoils similar work.

It also says much for Aldin's strength of character that in his mid-fifties he should embark on such a tricky and entirely unknown venture as producing etchings; we know that his early efforts were fairly unsuccessful and works were not sold commercially until he had completely mastered his new skill. It hardly needs to be said that the public demand for these etchings, normally limited to 150, was tremendous and the editions quickly sold out. Also in the twenties Aldin took to working on ivorine which I will deal with in more detail elsewhere.

Continued on page 78

"Potamus"

Cecil Aldin writing in *Dogs of Character,* first published in August 1927, tells of the game he and his children used to play around 1905/1910, as follows:-

"A game we used to have was with a bloodhound and an old basset-hound, Hectopotamus, of whom I shall tell you more later.

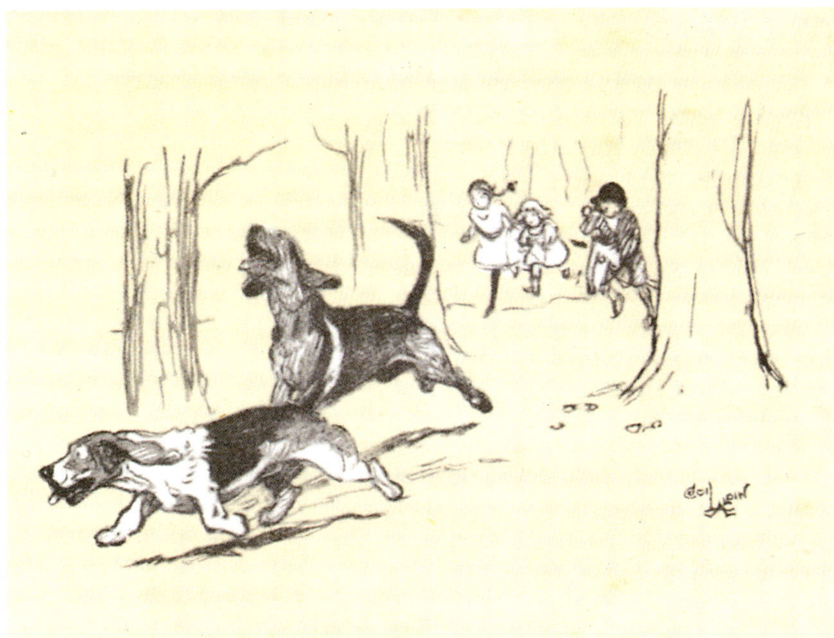

This game was known as "Hunting the Criminal" – "Bunny," that is myself, always taking the part of the quarry.

A party of children would be invited, and I need hardly tell you that everybody eagerly accepted, for the opportunity of participating in a real "man-hunt" was much too thrilling to be neglected. I enjoyed it as much as the children and, incidentally, the exercise kept me in good condition. The criminal, having perpetrated some imaginary, dastardly deed, was allowed to escape from his prison into the pinewoods surrounding my house.

After a quarter of an hour Hectopotamus and Buster Brown, the basset and bloodhound, were laid on the line and the hunt commenced.

Now, Potamus (his abbreviated name) had a habit of giving tongue from the moment he was laid on the line until he finally got the criminal "treed" and stood baying beneath him.

This, I am afraid, he did whether he was on the line or not, and was probably the reason that, being a good-looking basset-hound but a stray dog when I found him, no one could ever be found to claim him.

Notwithstanding this, his music helped matters with the children's hunt, the bloodhound always doing the serious work, notifying to the field in deep bays when he was on the line of his quarry.

To the villagers I was always expected to be torn to pieces when caught, but to the field of children a man-hunt was great fun, especially when Hectopotamus played a continuous orchestra until I was "eaten".

At last he had found an audience who appreciated his music. But I must tell you how "Potamus" came to me, and of his appetite when he arrived.

A thin, stray basset-hound once came to the Hunt kennels, and as no owner could be found for him, he was given to me, as M.F.H.s do not always admire the beautiful leg curves of the common or garden basset-hound.

He was first christened "Hector" by my children, but later, as he rapidly increased in avoirdupois, "Hippopotamus" was added to it.

"HECTORHIPPOPOTAMUS,"

however, was rather a mouthful to say quickly, so we gave him a kennel name, combining the two of

"HECTOPOTAMUS,"

and at a subsequent date abbreviated it to plain

"POTAMUS."

Hectorhippopotamus (it takes such a long time to write that we will call him "Potamus" in future) had a most abnormal appetite, possibly on account of the lean days of his straydom period, for he certainly never meant to have an empty tummy again, and of this appetite and how it saved his life I will tell you.

Now, the woman who has agreed to share for life all my doggy and other troubles would take a collection of the dogs with her when walking to the village, including the hefty Potamus.

These morning trips were the joy of the once thin basset.

Slowly he would plop, plop, plop, plop behind her, gradually "filling" up from every cottage rubbish heap, and from the outsides of the butchers', fishmongers', and bakers' shops, his

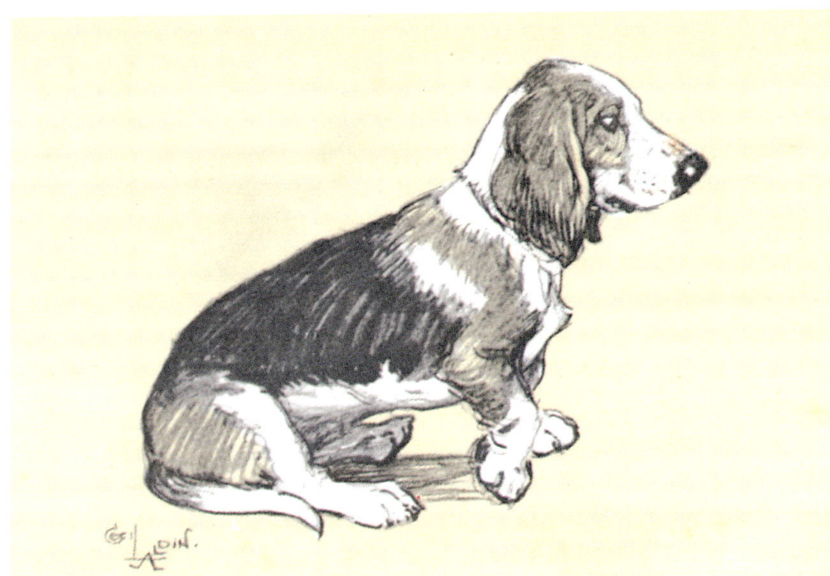

"The lean days"

keen nose never missing the minutest crumb in the way of food.

At the end of an hour's "shopping" Potamus's larder would be well filled and he would be ready to start to waddle home again.

One hot day, when he had been more than lucky in flotsam and jetsam and, in consequence, was feeling rather sluggish, a car came slowly chugging its way up the hill behind him.

My wife called to him to get out of the way, and the chauffeur, seeing the dog, slowed his car down to walking pace.

Meanwhile, Potamus went on, still keeping in the centre of the road, day-dreaming, no doubt, of the supper to come to him in the evening.

Hoot-hoot-hoot-hoot-hoot went the motor-horn, and our friend took a slow step to the side, but not quite quick enough to miss the near front wheel. Then came a shriek from my wife as the basset collapsed under the wheel itself.

The car had just enough "way," or enough horse-power, to rise partly the big mound of the tightly-packed middle of Potamus, climb to the top, then, "konking out" slowly trickled back again on to the road.

Rushing to the spot, my wife expected to pick up the corpse of the once bonny basset hound, but no more serious damage was done than a bent back rib.

My family ever afterwards put this down to the tightness of the packing in his tummy - which tightness had obviously stopped him from being killed and the car from completely surmounting so steep an incline. It was always afterwards an excuse for the children to give him some more to eat in case he was run over by another car."

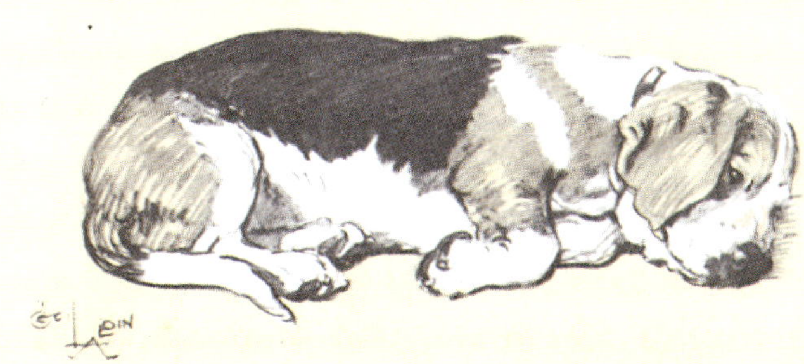

"Rapidly increased in avoirdupois"

It would be fair to say in fact that although by 1925 he was aged fifty-five, the next five years leading up to his sixtieth birthday were as productive and fruitful as any other five year period of his life - there was no slowing down, either on the work front, when it came to enjoying himself hunting, or organising childrens' pony shows or mongrel dog shows. For Aldin art was work. It did not have a capital A and like any other strong-willed person Aldin was meticulous about spending long hours working. In most weeks he certainly put in fifty hours in his studio; he established a daily routine which suited his family, his kennel of dogs and his artistic output.

After the First World War Aldin continued to go to his beloved Exmoor every August and September and as his fame increased through the 1920's, was called on more frequently to participate in local events such as judging horse shows.

I have already mentioned how Aldin took a fairly jaundiced view of proper dog shows and, one can assume, of proper horse shows; however, he adored children, loved fun and light-heartedness, and started to arrange, single handed, childrens' pony shows at Dunster Castle and mongrel dog shows. The latter were widely reported in the press and I think some of his most amusing work was based on them and reproduced in *The Cecil Aldin Book* published in 1932, extracts of which can be found later in this chapter.

Alas, by 1930, age, arthritis and, more seriously, Aldin's weak heart had all taken their toll and his doctors advised him to move to a warmer climate. His lifestyle had not of course helped his general health. He continued to hunt two days a week, and sometimes more, until the spring of 1930, in all weather and, incredibly bravely or perhaps, incredibly foolishly, continued to ride in point-to-points, although nearly sixty. It was a fall in 1929 or 1930 which gave his poor heart a shaking which it could well have done without and made a move abroad imperative.

His horses were given away and in his sixty-first year he moved lock, stock and barrel to Majorca. Most people would have been devastated at having to give up their way of life and move to an island where they knew no one at such an age, but not so Aldin. He looked upon this as yet another of life's adventures.

His daughter Gwen, who by now was married herself with two children, took his kennel of dogs out to Majorca by ship. Cecil Aldin and his wife Rita normally travelled across France and Spain by train rather than taking the longer sea journey. Cracker emulated his previous bull-terrier, Sturdee, and ate his way out of his kennel on board every night, giving Gwen a terrible fright every morning until she found him as she was always afraid he may have fallen overboard in the night looking for his master.

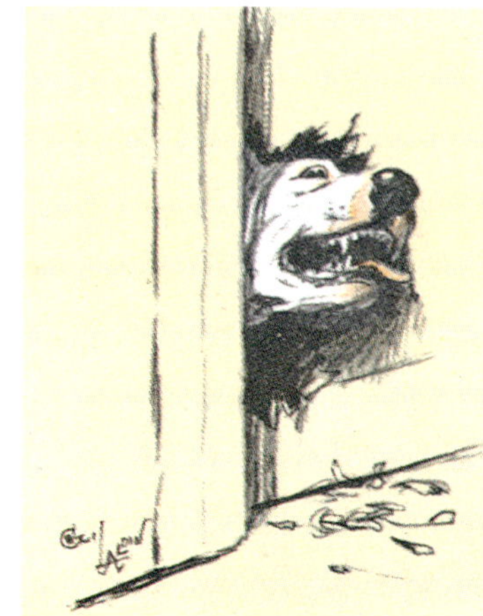

Sturdee

Aldin was soon happily ensconced in a house and studio on the island and working his eight or ten hours a day, six days a week. By now arthritis had greatly slowed his output but the quality was not to suffer. He did illustrations when in Majorca for the last of his four great dog books, *Just Among Friends*, and these are as good as any dog paintings executed by anyone.

In the autumn of 1934 he suffered a heart-attack, returned to England by ship and in early 1935 died in the arms of his old hunting pal, Henry Tiarks, in the London Clinic.

On his death obituaries appeared in all the leading newspapers in England, as well as in many foreign countries and the Royal Veterinary College was to benefit from a Memorial Fund launched by Lord Rosebery and supported by one of Cecil Aldin's greatest admirers, Lord Lonsdale, 'The Yellow Earl', which still provides money for student prizes.

Micky had died in 1932 in Majorca but Cracker was to survive his beloved master until the end of July 1938. On Cracker's death Rita returned to England and survived Cecil by twenty years, dying in 1955.

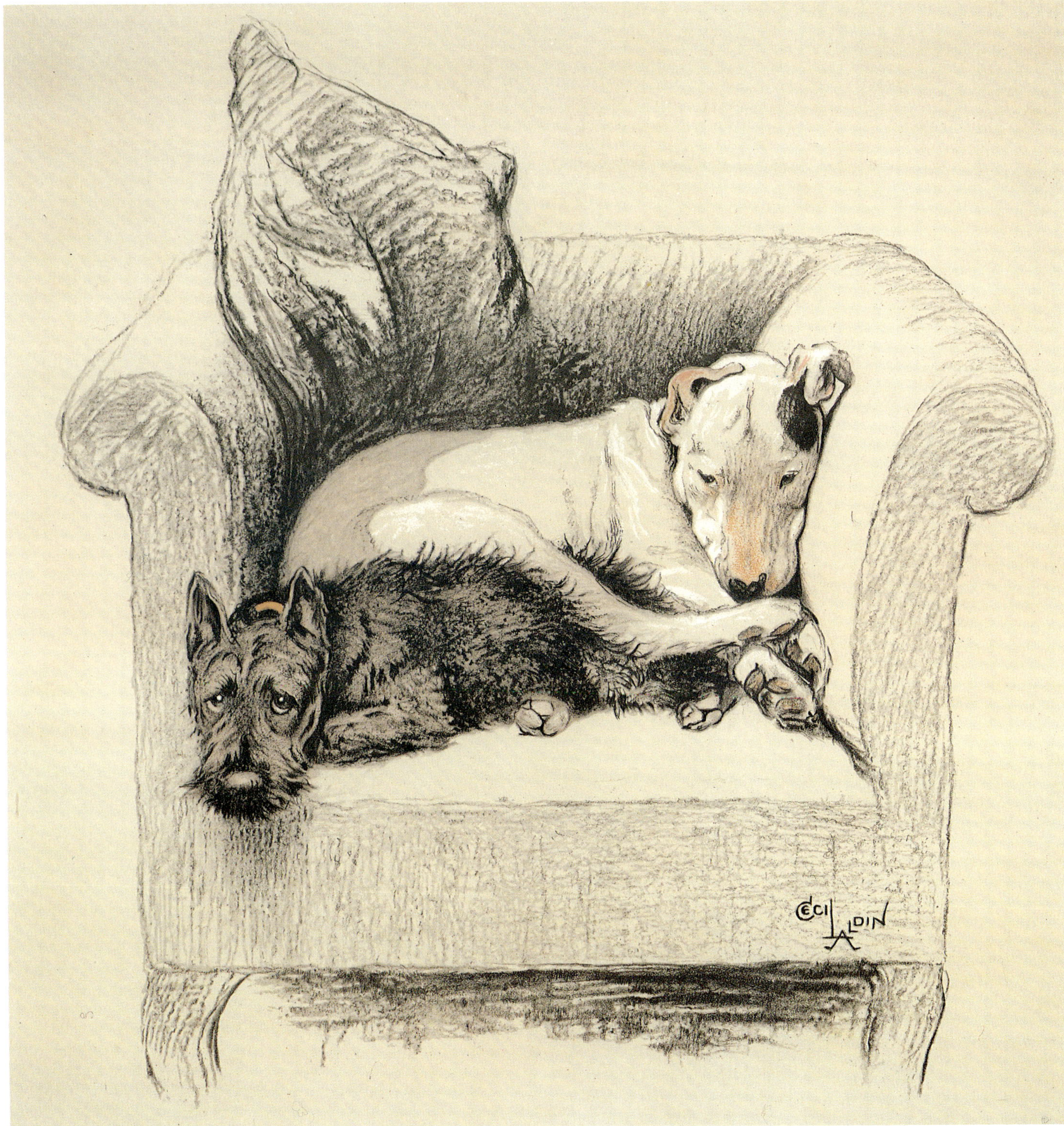

"Weight Will Tell"

Ivorines

In the mid 1920's Aldin started working in ivorine – thin sheets of white plastic. This new material suited Aldin's painstaking and accurate style perfectly and for many people his ivorines represent the very best of his canine work.

The two ivorines shown on this spread are two of my favourites.

The drawing on this page of 'A Meynell Hunt Terrier' is very atypical as it was clearly done quickly and with little or no scratching out.

The drawing opposite – 'A Resident and two Guests' can be dated accurately to 1926. The alsation depicted, whose name we do not know, only stayed for three days. Aldin clearly sat down and executed the drawing then and there and it has none of the 'stiffness' which can be found in certain of his works on ivorine.

Certainly these ivorines now present considerable problems with regard to cataloguing and identification. These stem from the fact that during Aldin's lifetime he reproduced the same image many times. It can be clearly seen from the less good ones that he used some type of 'printed base' for the outline and for some of the base colouring. This was clearly done by some mechanical means. I personally think he used a stencil and then over-painted and finished the image, while other people are under the impression that some photographic process was used for the outline and base colouring.

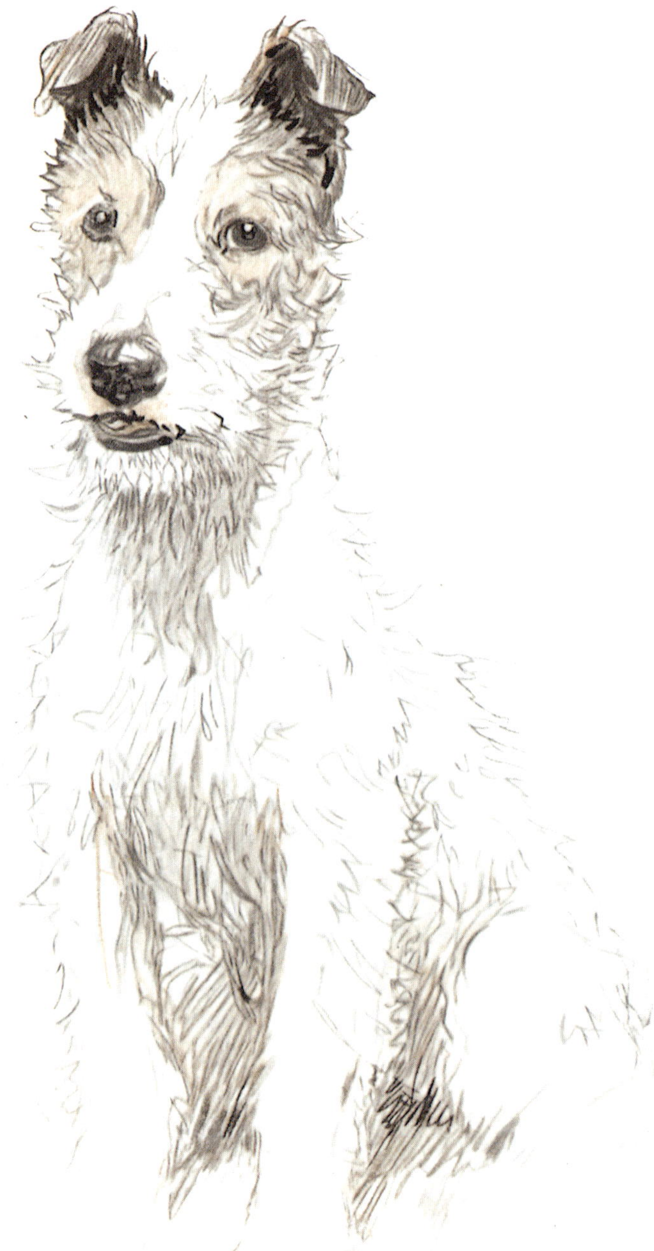

The two drawings shown on this page have no mechanical reproduction on them at all, while the four on the next page all had a mechanically produced base which Aldin hand-finished. The ones with no mechanical base are normally far more spontaneous and lively than those with a mechanically produced base which tend to show uncharacteristic stiffness.

In the last ten years forgers have been photocopying black and white Aldin drawings onto ivorine, crudely hand-colouring them with crayon and putting them into auctions. These are of course forgeries and as such valueless. The image selected for this trickery is often taken from a large book entitled *The Berkshire Vale* and the image reduced by about 80%. Therefore Aldin's signature virtually disappears and another, larger one is added by the forgers, so one way to identify these is to check if there are two signatures, something which is always wrong.

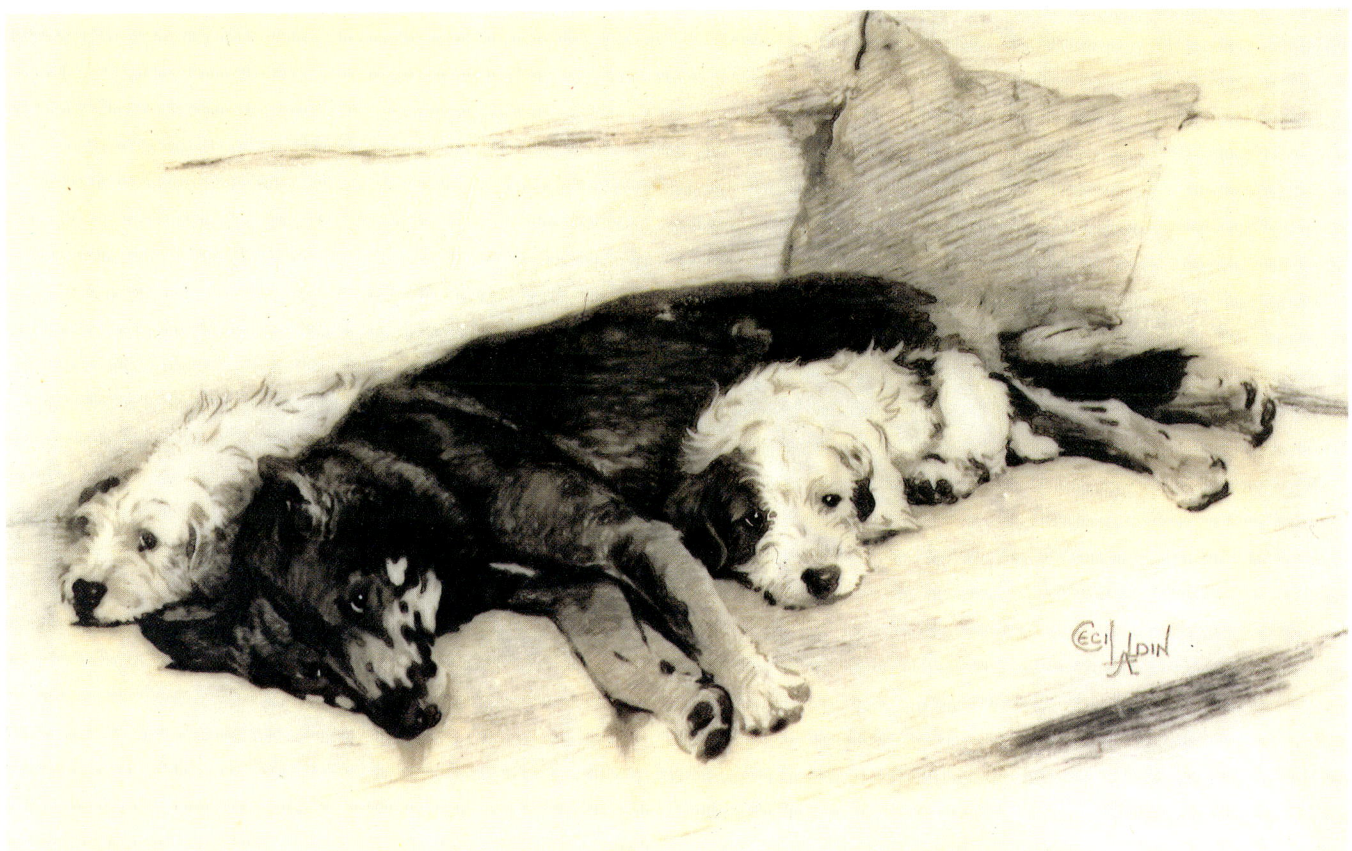

← 'A Meynell Hunt Terrier'.

'A Resident and Two Guests'. →

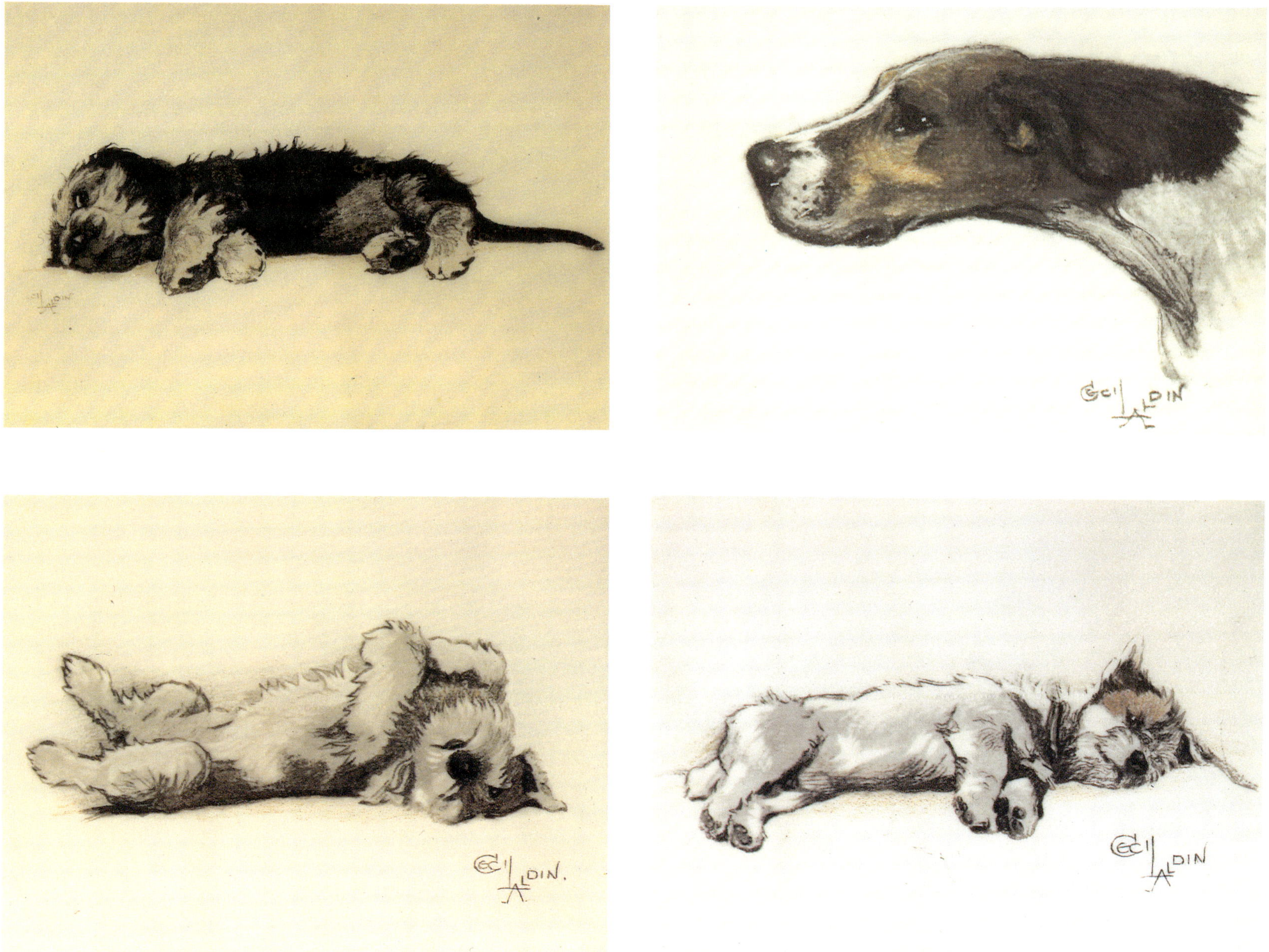

Four small ivorines.

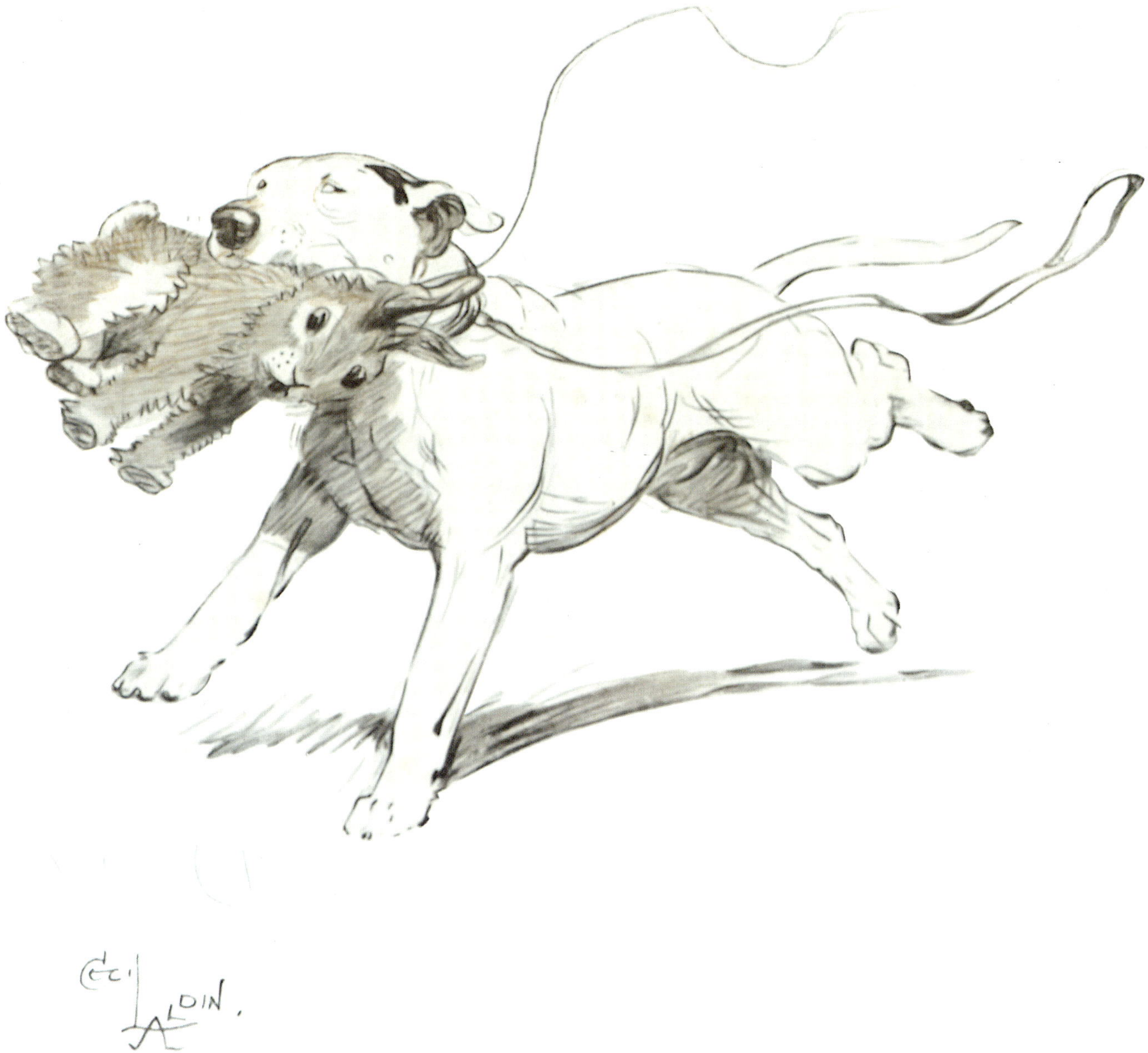

'Cracker.'

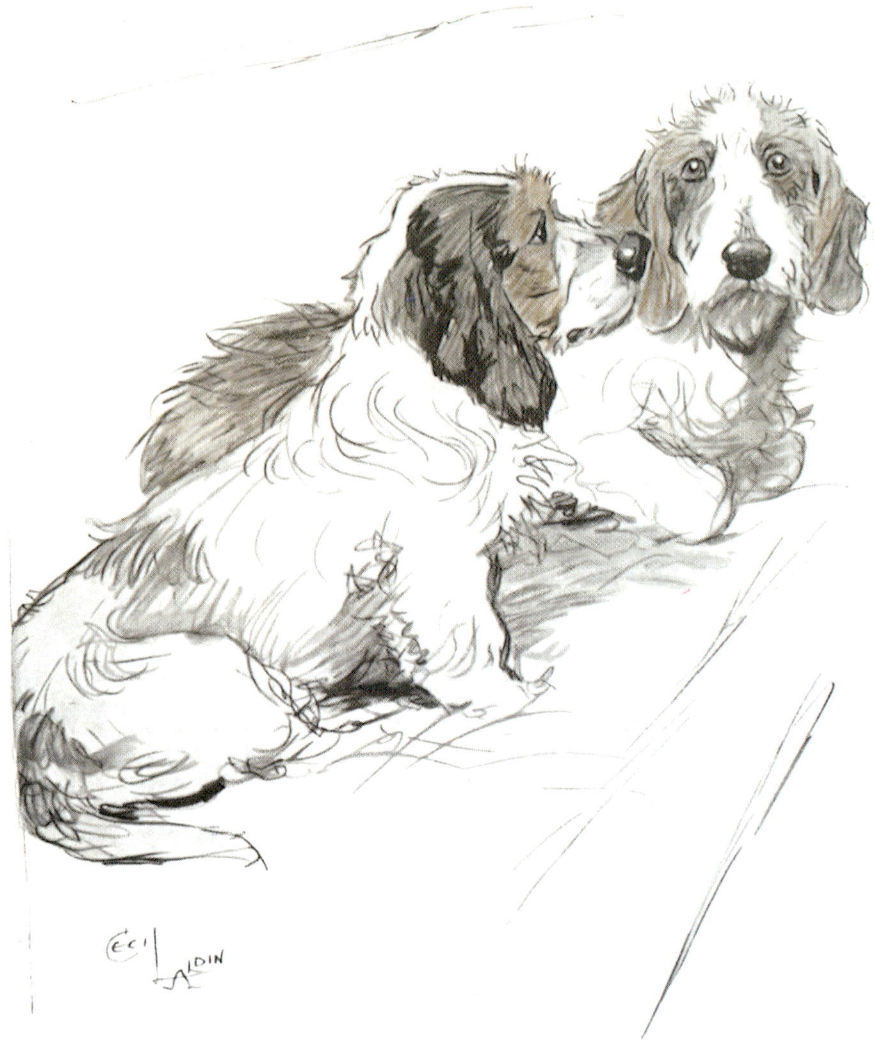

These bassets, belonging to H.R.H. The Prince of Wales (later H.M. King Edward VII)
were originally drawn in the 1890's, but reworked on ivorine,
as above, in the late 1920's.

South Berks and Ratcatcher to Scarlet

After World War I Aldin continued to have his famous long, narrow 'Hunting Countries' prints published. The majority were published by Lawrence & Jellicoe but in the twenties Alfred Bell produced three which were rather more sophisticated than his previous prints and included 'The South Berks', 'The Garth' and 'The Devon and Somerset Staghounds'.

The two illustrations over the page are of Aldin's own South Berks. I think the hounds here are better than those which are illustrated from *Handley Cross*, but he was still using plenty of artistic licence to thin the hounds down, making them look 'herring-gutted', to increase the impression of speed.

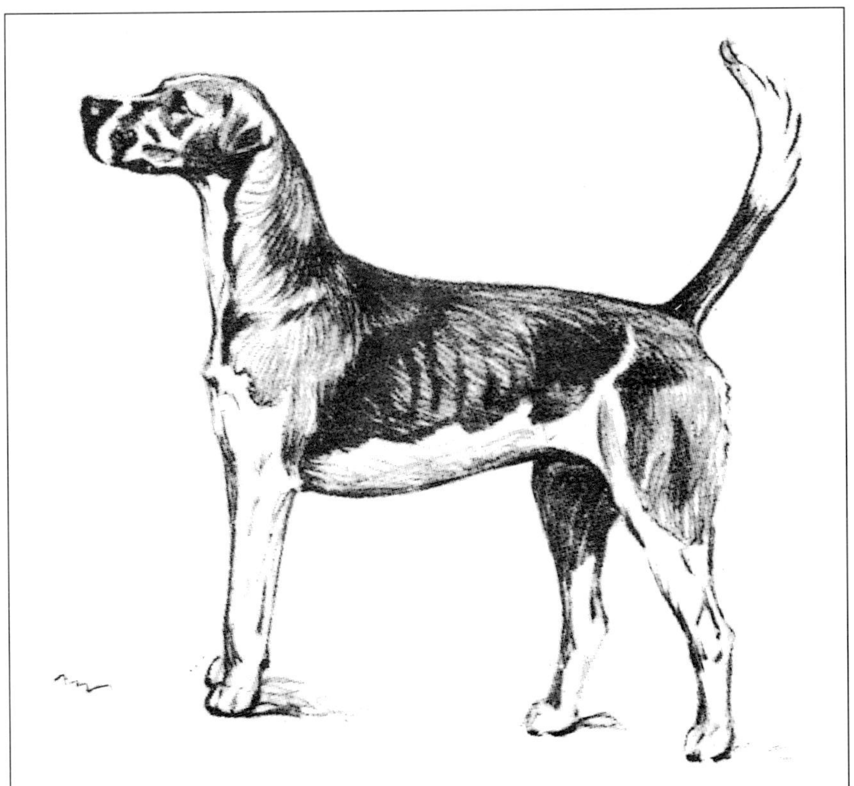

Certainly by the time Aldin was coming to work on *Ratcatcher to Scarlet* the hounds were no longer 'sausages on sticks', and he had certainly overcome the technical difficulties hounds had seemed to present to him in the first fifteen years of the twentieth century. It must of course be remembered that the majority of illustrations for *Ratcatcher to Scarlet* and, later on, *Scarlet to MFH,* were drawn on ivorine, on which he did much of his best work. Furthermore, many of the hound illustrations for these two books were done purely as studies of hounds and not as mere supporting players in a larger, overall scene as was the case in 'Hunting Countries'.

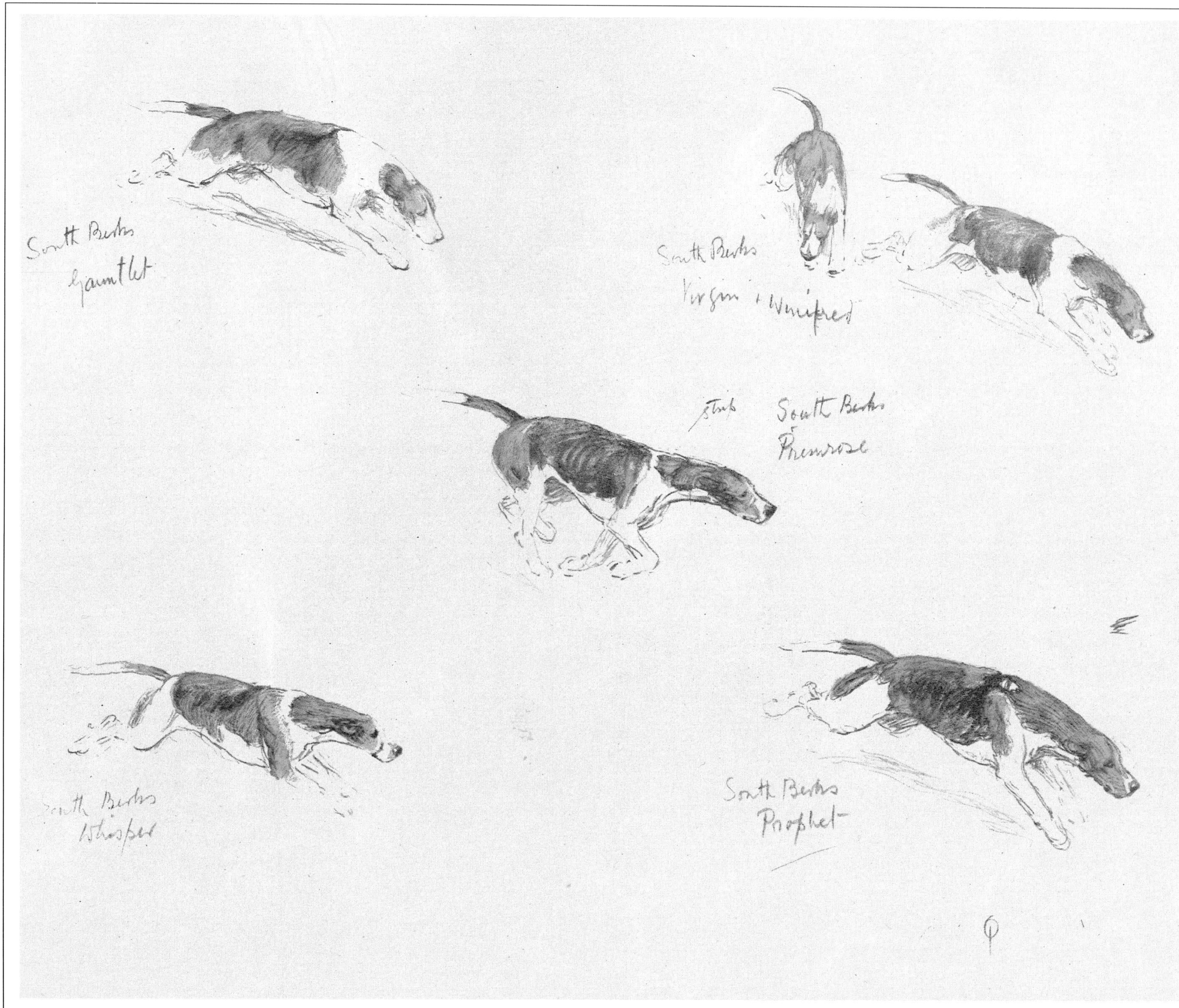
South Berks
Gauntlet
South Berks
Virgin + Winifred
South Berks
Primrose
South Berks
Whisper
South Berks
Prophet

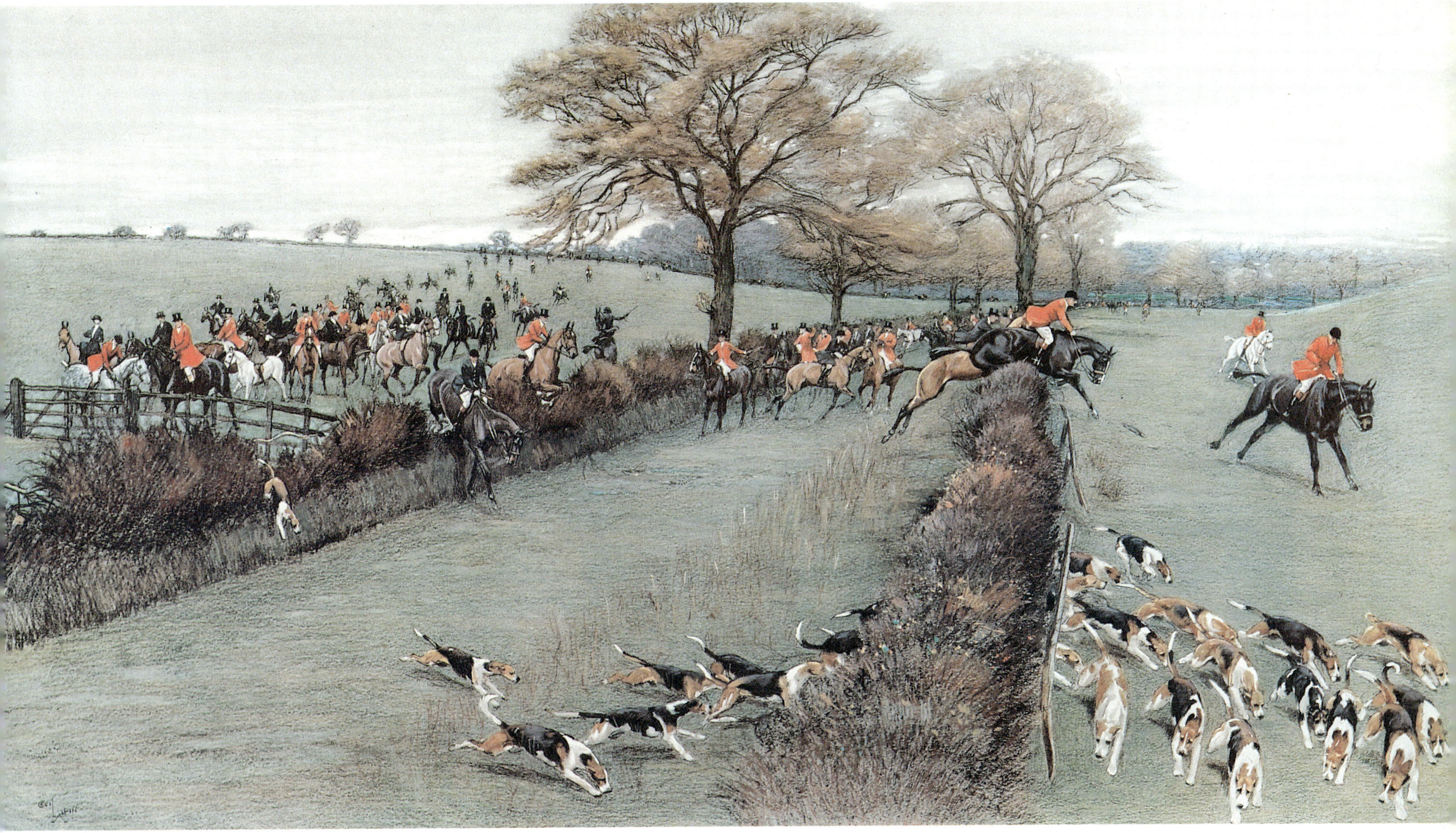

Cecil Aldin, in the black coat and huntsman's cap, is jumping down in the green lane.

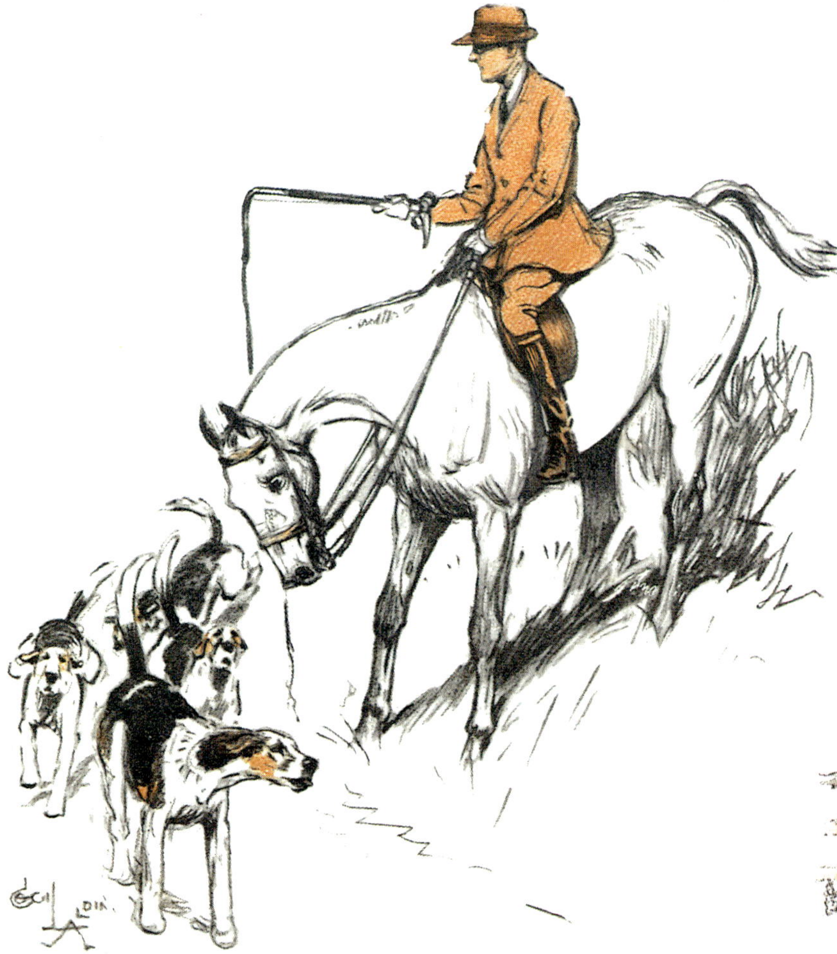

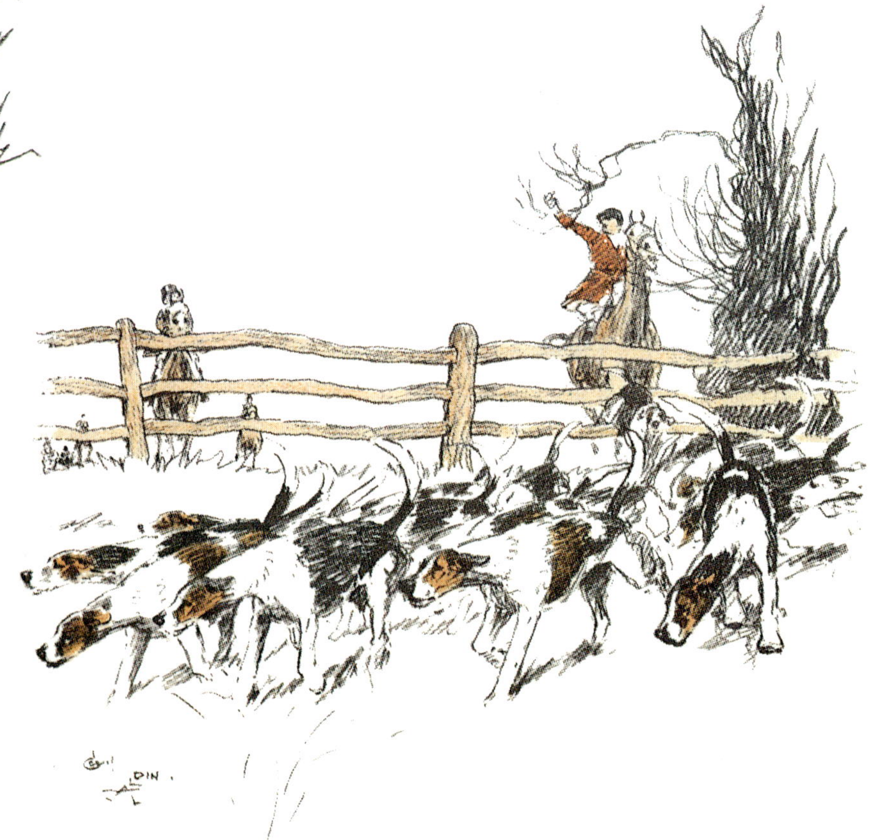

These drawings, for *Ratcatcher to Scarlet,* were drawn on ivorine.

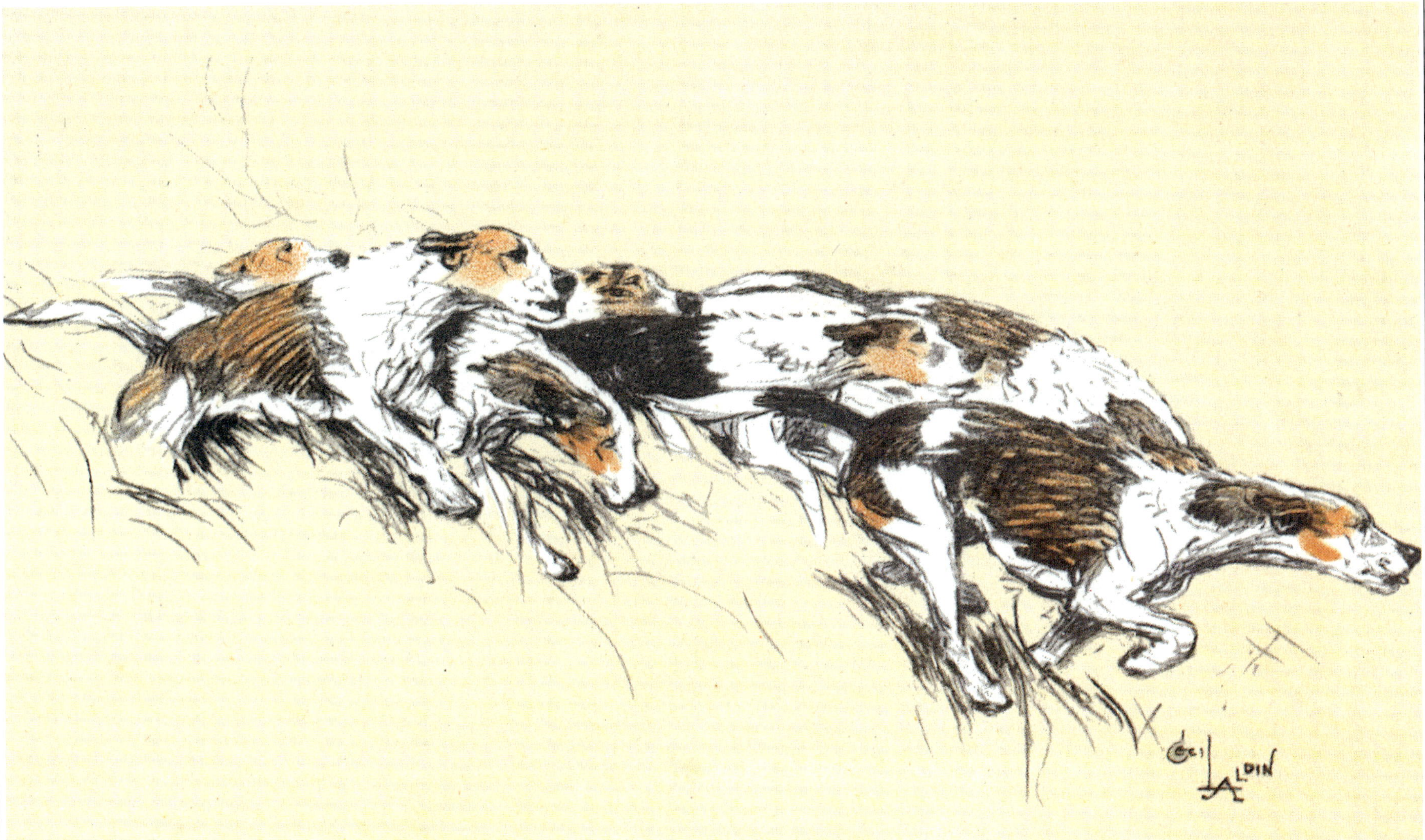

Once again from *Ratcatcher to Scarlet*,
this drawing was also executed on ivorine, and one can immediately see how by the mid-1920's Aldin's depiction of hounds is very much better than his pre-War work on the subject.

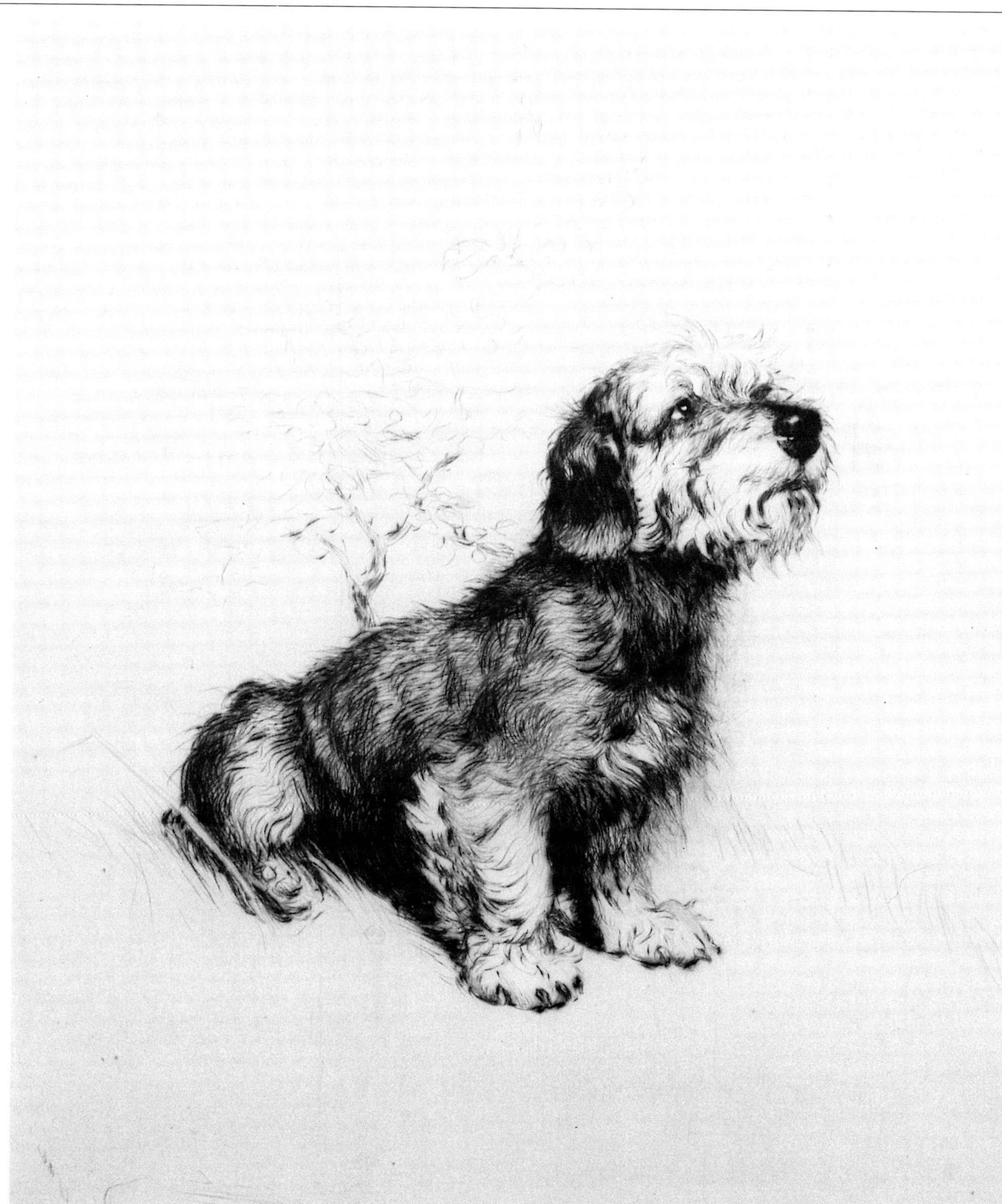

'Mutt Dog'.

This lovely etching is not, as one would immediately think, of 'Turps', who had not yet arrived on the scene. 'Mutt Dog' was a mongrel which obviously had a lot of rough-haired dachshund or dandy dinmont in him.

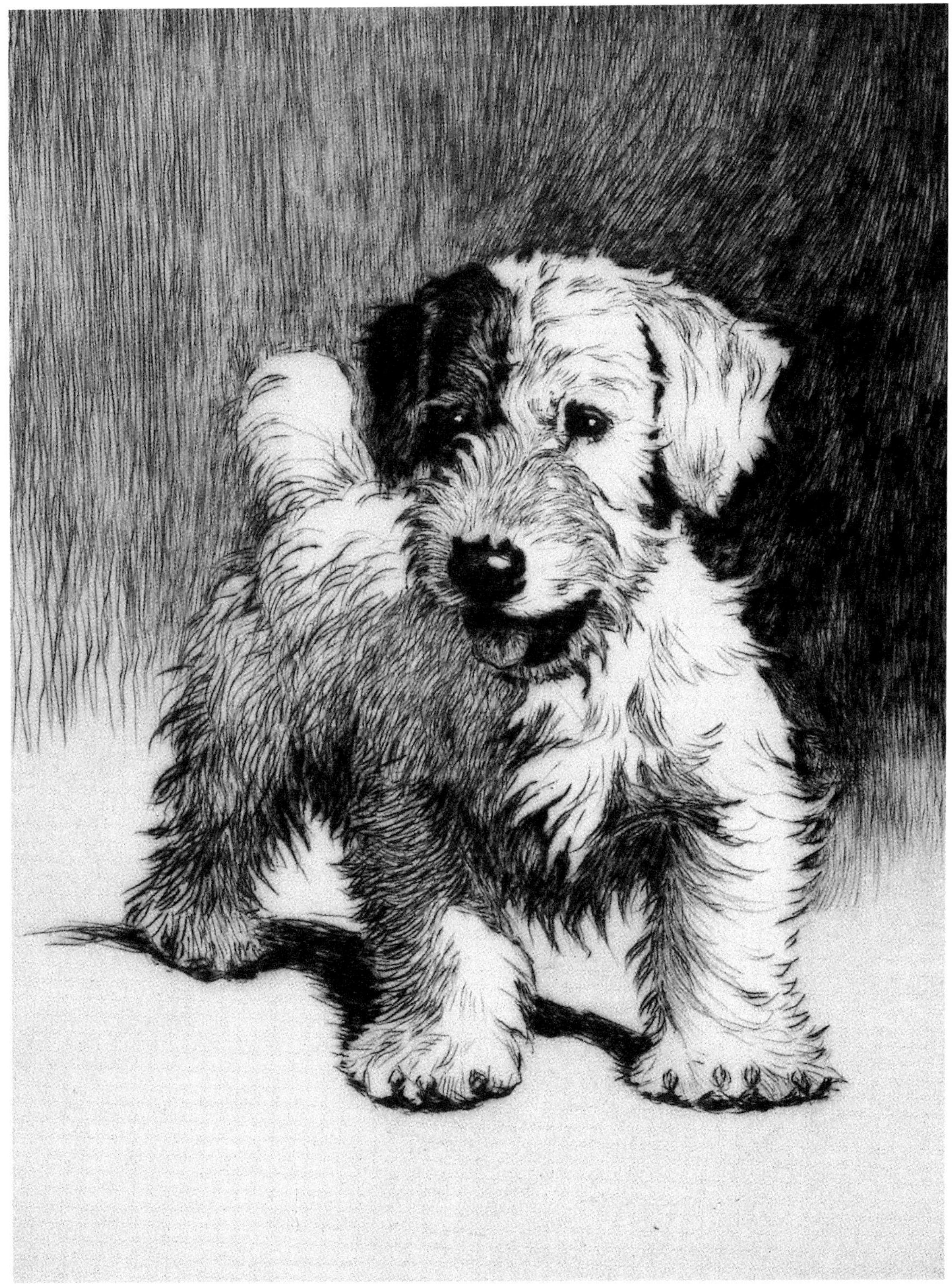

'A Bunch of Mischief'.

Aldin's dog etchings are universally recognised as some of the finest etchings of dogs ever made and one must remember that it wasn't until he was over fifty that he started to work in this difficult medium.

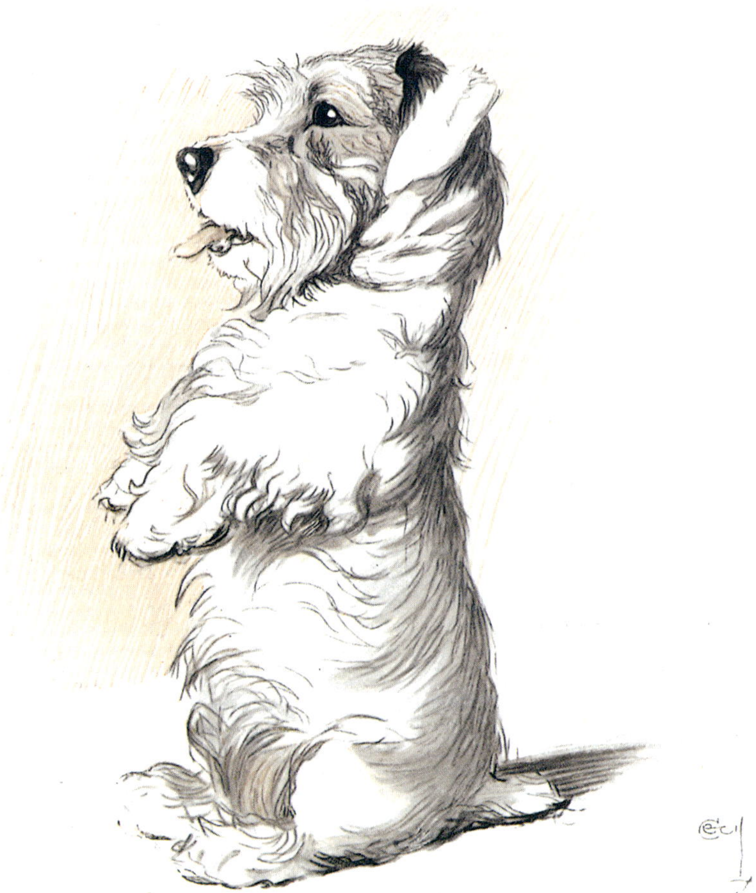

'Slickerson' and 'Good Boy', 'Bad Boy'

Slickerson, who was a neighbour of Aldin's in the 1920's when he was still living near Reading, was one of his favourite models. Aldin commented that Slickerson spent more time upright than horizontal and locked out of his house would merely sit begging by the front door until he was let in.

From the mid 1920's, right up until the time of his death, Aldin produced a number of light-hearted drawings of dogs such as 'Good Boy' and 'Bad Boy' opposite. These became regular features of Christmas Supplements of The Illustrated London News, The Sketch and other high calibre glossy magazines.

Slickerson featured regularly in these Christmas specials, mainly as he was happy to be 'dressed-up' and did not mind being laughed at.

Because pictures such as 'Good Boy' 'Bad Boy', 'Turps finds a new use for Cracker' and 'Funny Face', illustrated over the page, are humorous this does not, in my opinion, in any way detract from the greatness of the drawing.

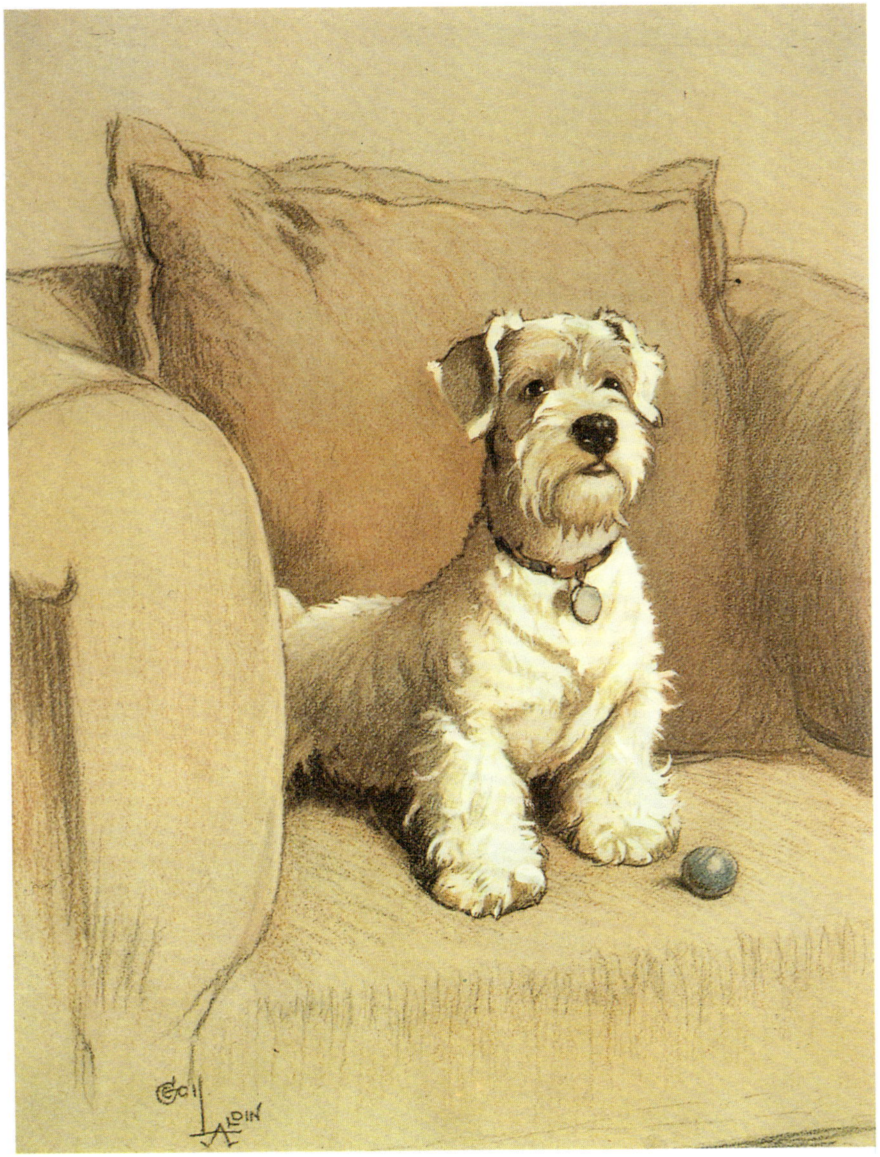

'Good Boy'.

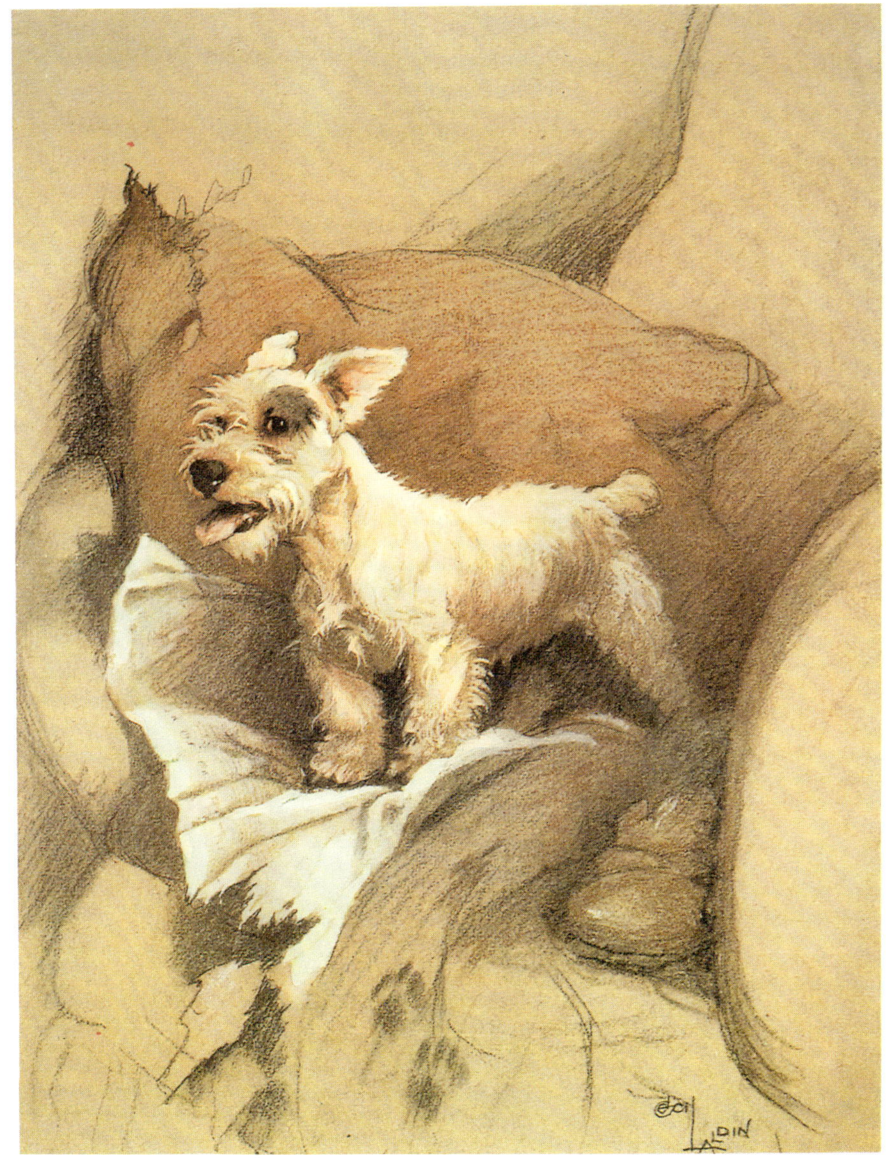

'Bad Boy'.

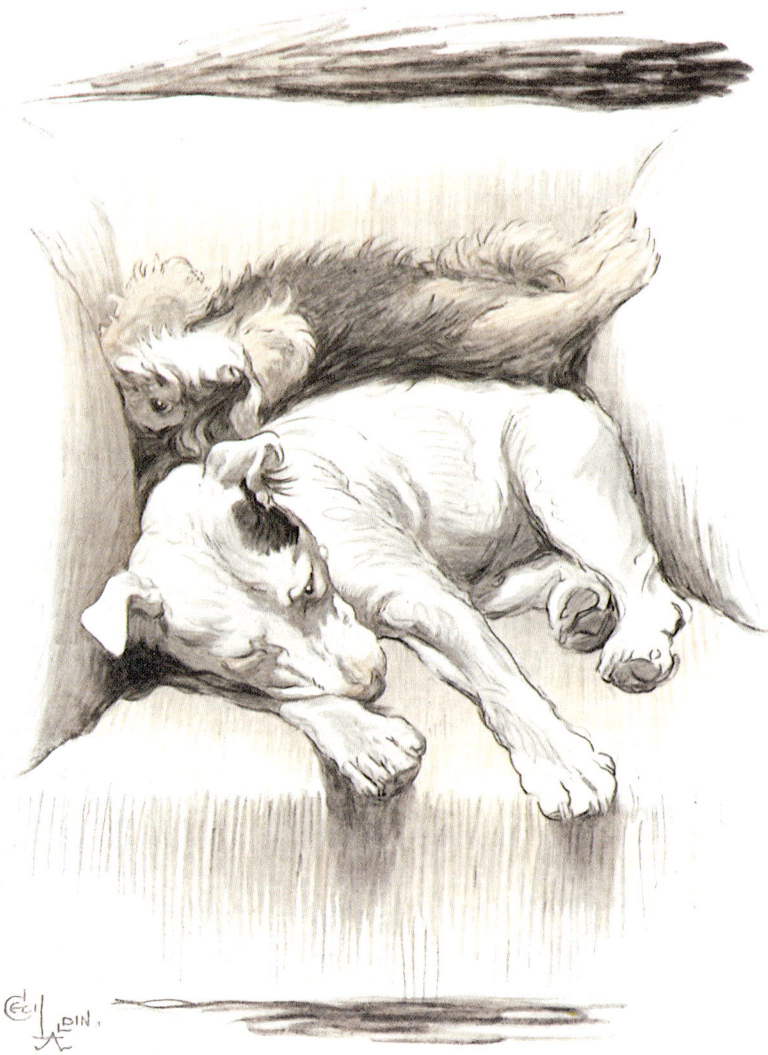

'Turps' finds a new use for bull-terriers.

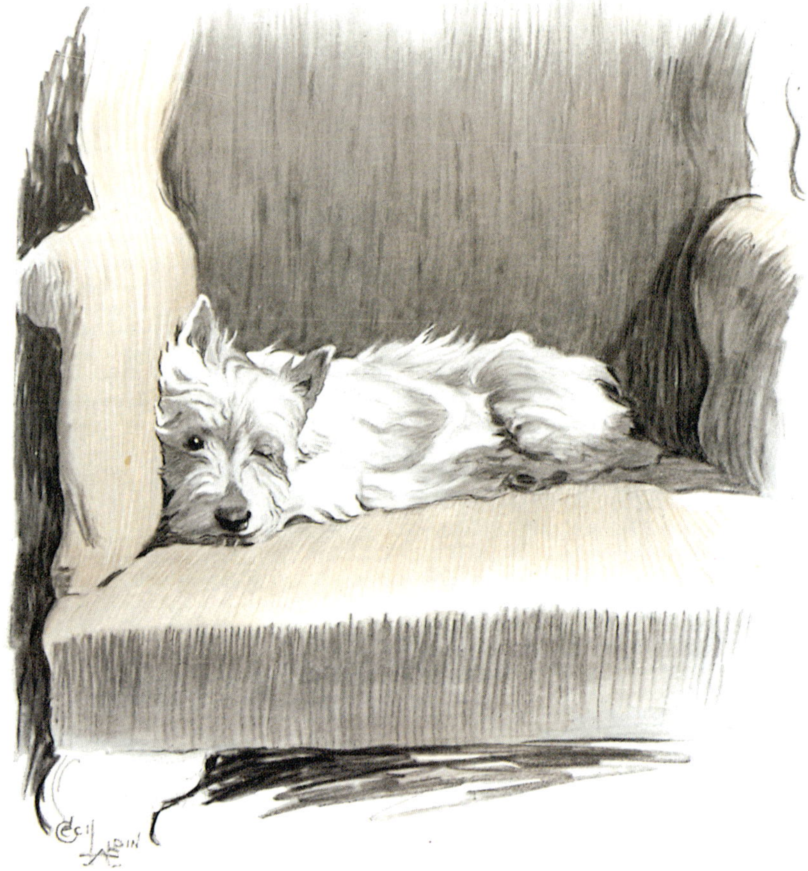

Funny-face.

Lost, Strayed and Stolen and *Flax, Police Dog*

In the last four years of his life Aldin illustrated a number of highly successful books for other people with pen and ink line drawings. Two of the most popular were *Lost, Strayed and Stolen* by Marion Ashmore and *Flax, Police Dog* written by the Danish author, Svend Fleuron which were both first published in 1931 in England.

As can be seen from the illustrations on the next few pages, Aldin's style had greatly changed from his earlier, soft line work during the 1890's. In fact, if Aldin had used these bold and decisive lines then he would probably have been very much more successful as an illustrator for *Punch* in the ten years 1904 to 1914.

Lost, Strayed and Stolen, is the story of an Aberdeen terrier by the name of Woppets, who was stolen and offered for sale in a street market (Brick Lane in the East End of London). From 1890 until the First World War, stealing pedigree dogs for re-sale was a common occurrence. While he was a student, Aldin had a pedigree dog stolen and always afterwards campaigned for the closure of markets like Brick Lane.

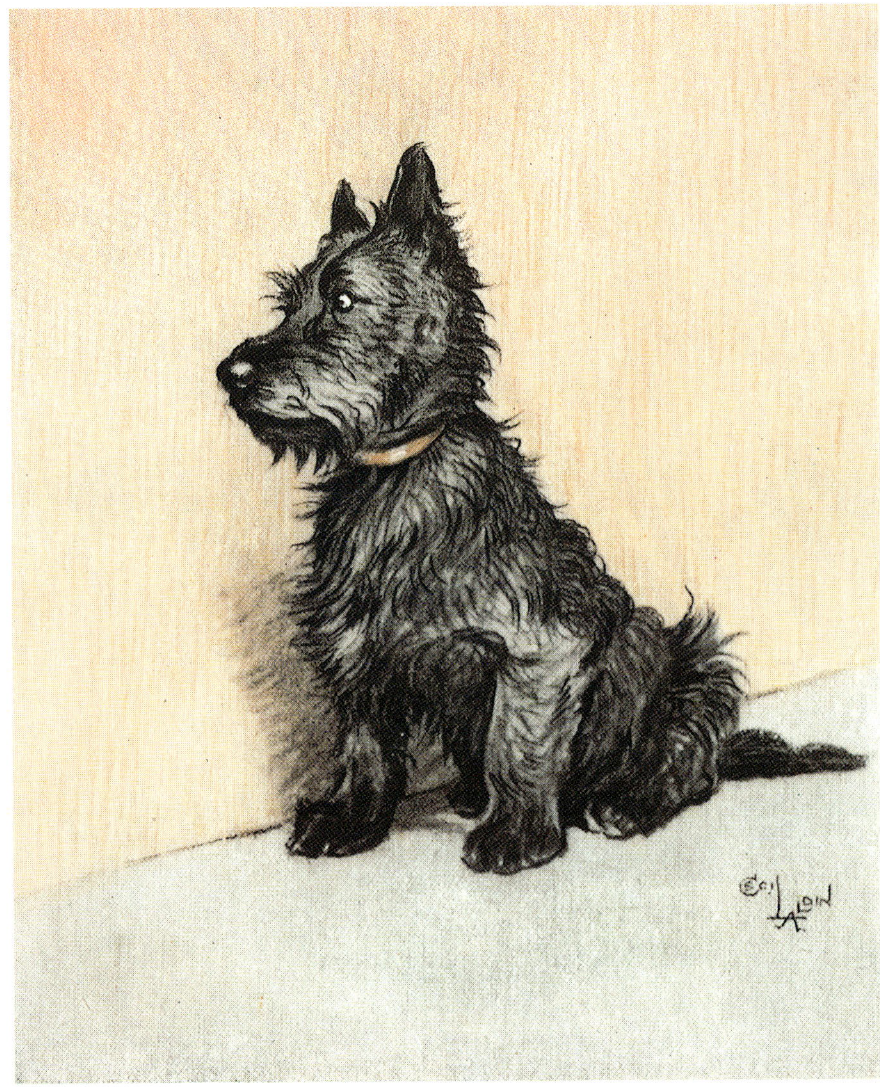

Woppets

Lost Stolen or Strayed

As long as one knows the name of the book *Lost Stolen or Strayed* for which Cecil Aldin did these drawings, one hardly needs any text. Although often very slight, these drawings virtually tell the story without words.

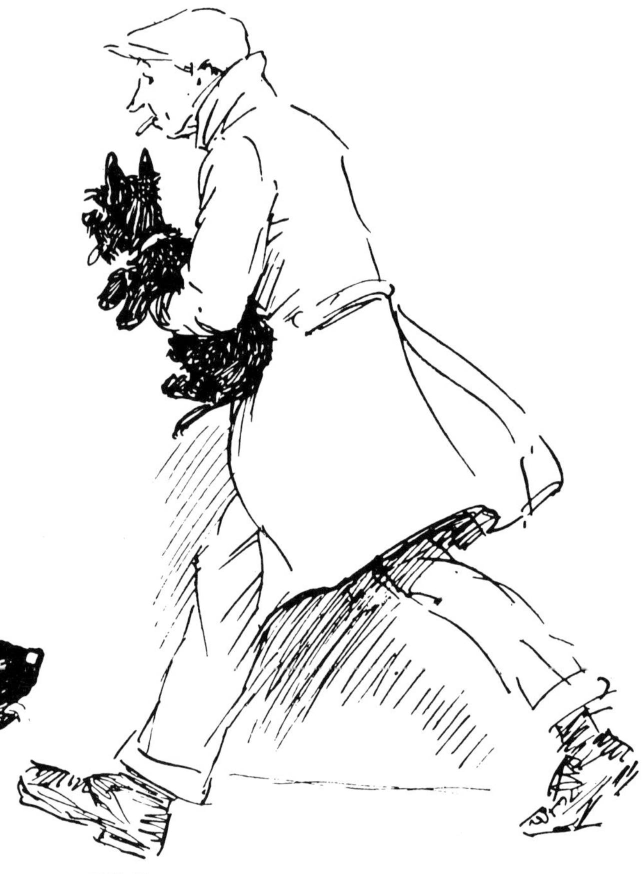

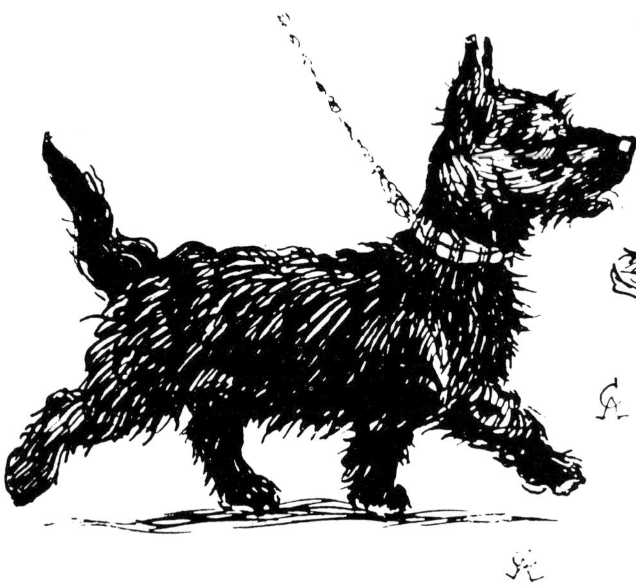

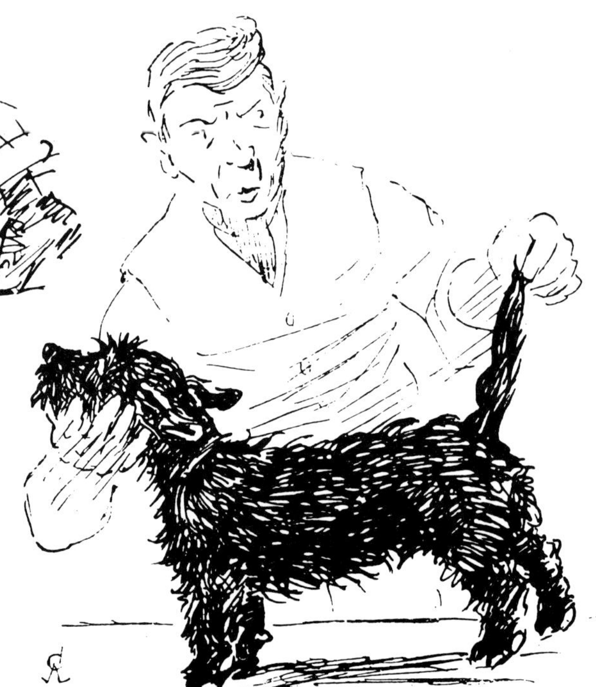

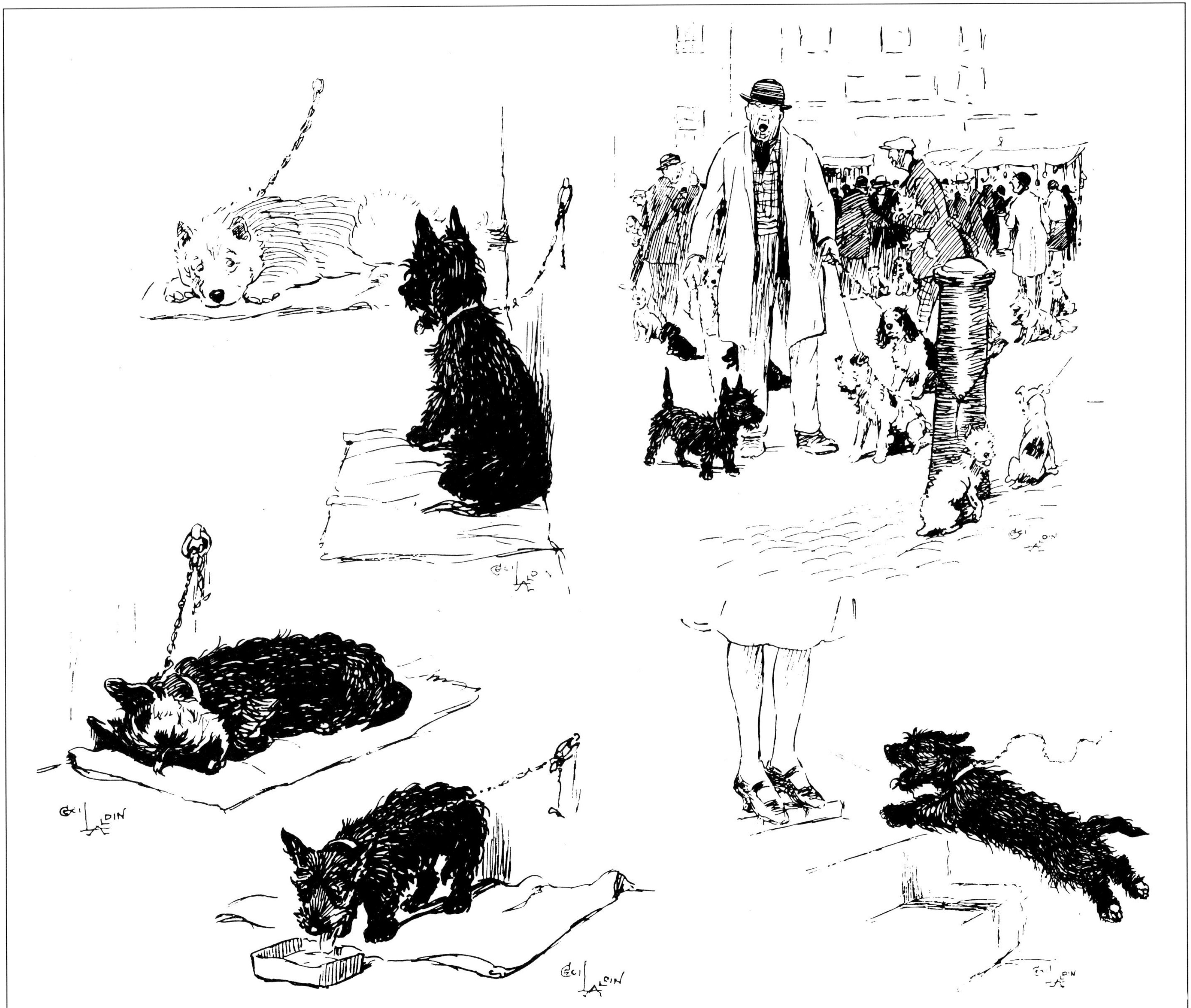

Flax, Police Dog

Cecil Aldin did these drawings in 1930 for *Flax, Police Dog,*
when he was over sixty and had been a professional artist for some forty years. However, they are fresh, boldly executed and would have done credit to a man of half his age.
Aldin's habit of changing subject, style and working medium on a regular basis stopped him going stale and no deterioration is visible in his work, even after the age of sixty.

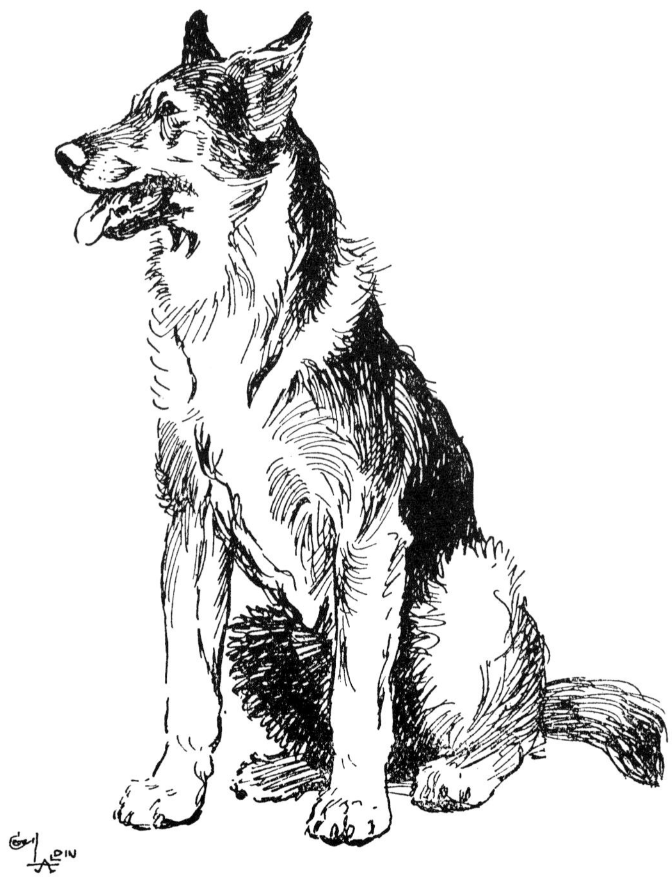

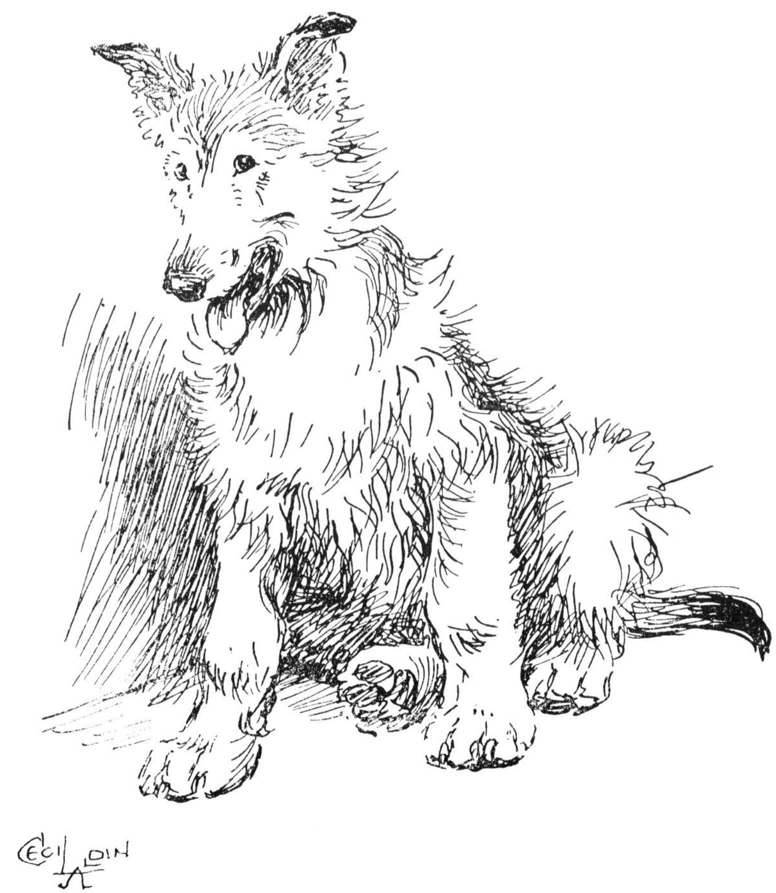

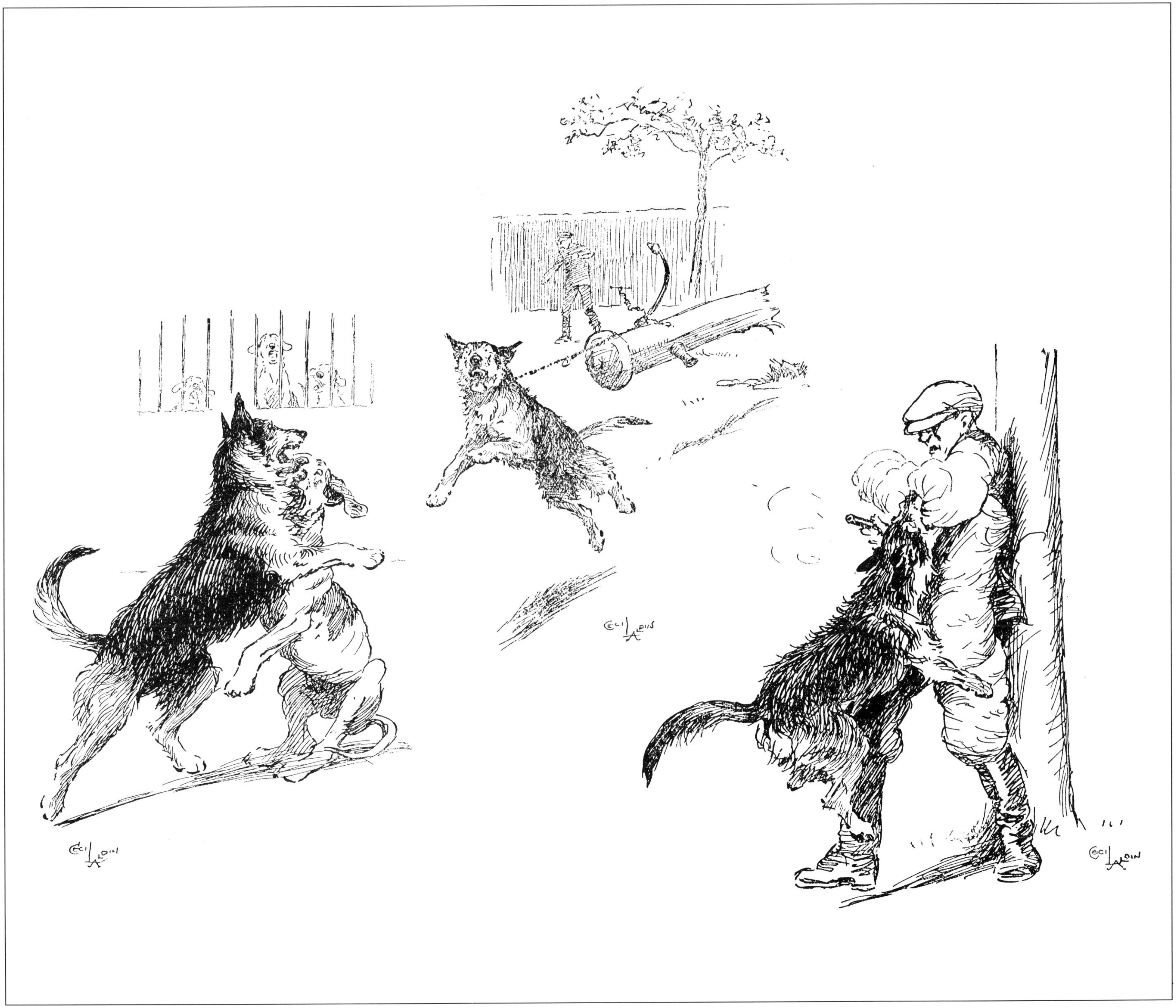

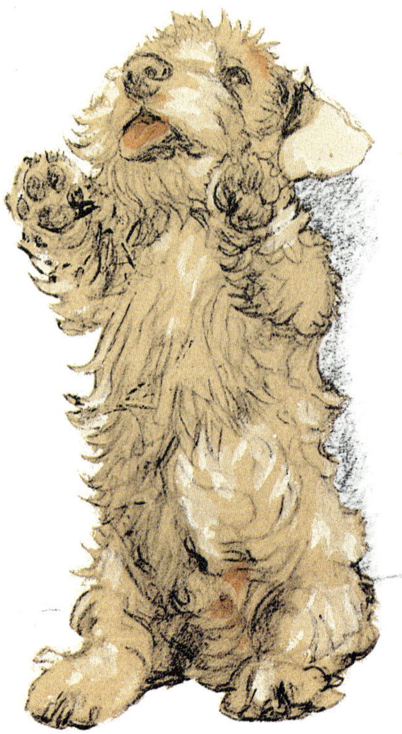

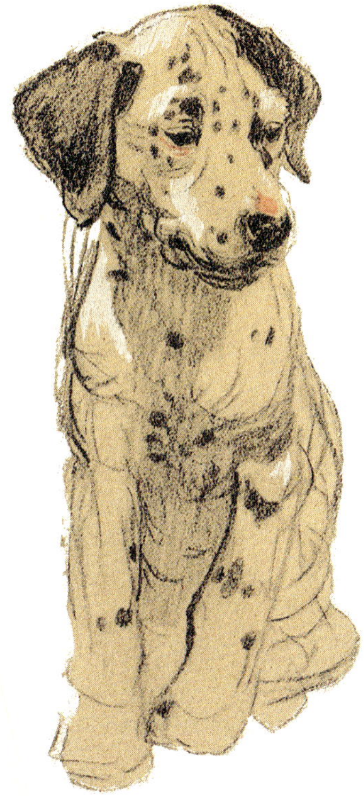

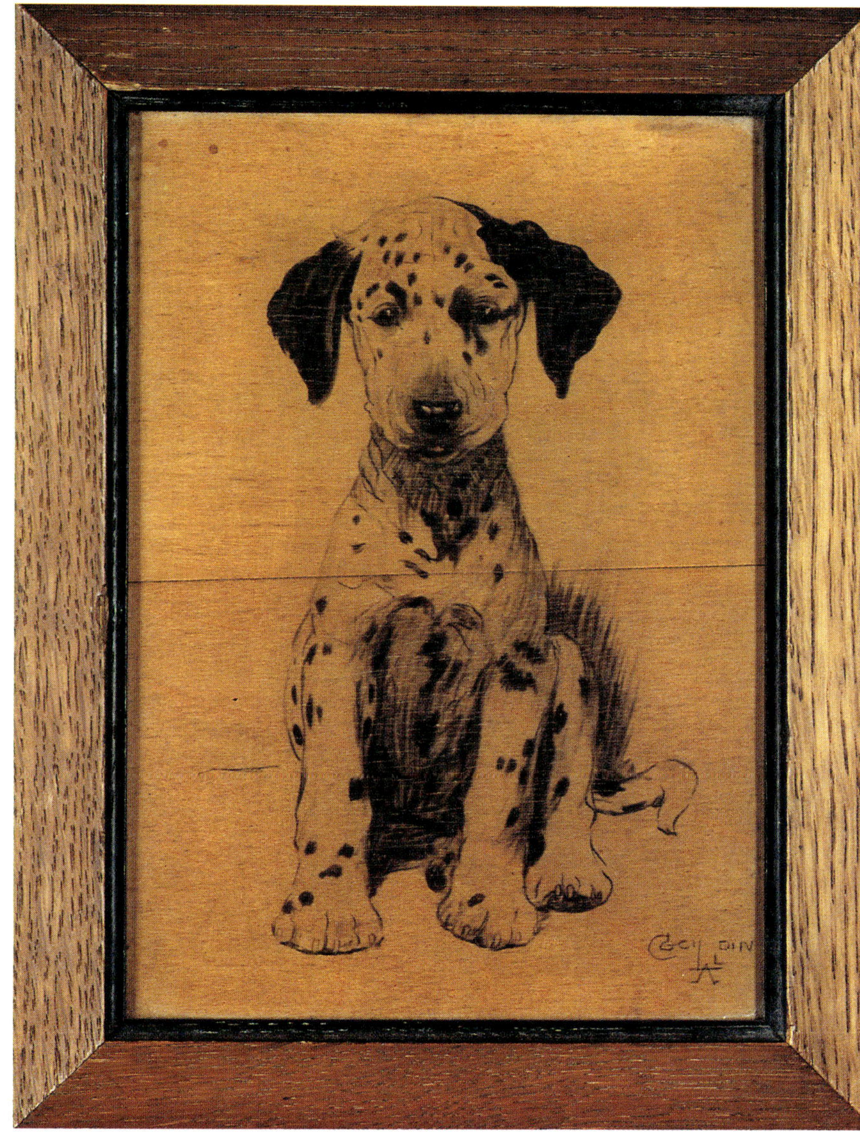

Ceramics, Toys and Ephemera

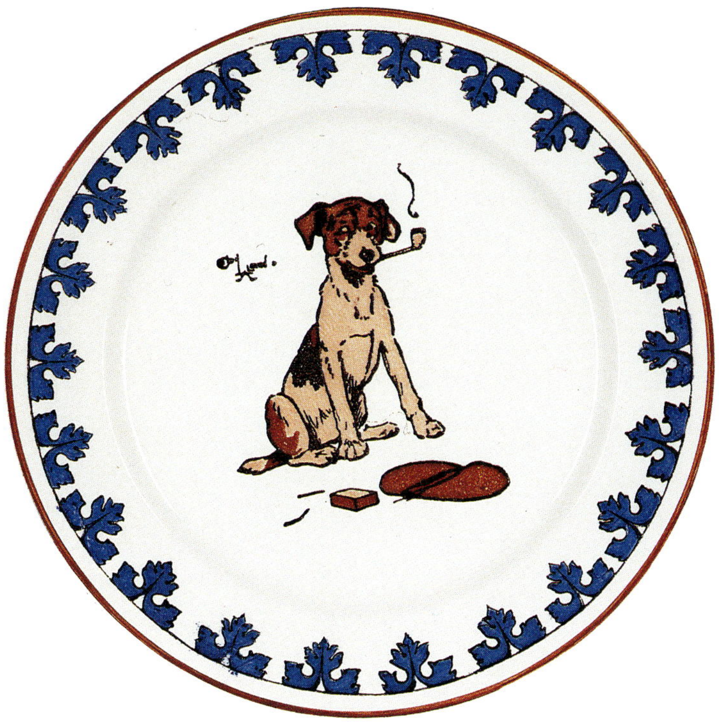

For many people one of the nicest and most exciting things about collecting 'Cecil Aldin', and for me it is certainly one of the best aspects of dealing in his work, is the great variety of material available. Naturally one has watercolours, etchings, ivorines and the other obvious artefacts of a great and successful artist.

What does make Aldin completely unique among all the great British artists of the first half of the twentieth century is the variety of ephemera associated with him. For a large number of years Aldin was responsible for designing pottery and porcelain, mainly for Royal Doulton, like the plate just to the left. Huntley & Palmer produced a large number of biscuit tins from his designs, but his best known ephemera of course came from 'The Cecil Aldin Toy Factory'. Initially, the toy factory produced hand-finished and painted toys for such upmarket shops as Liberty's, but later on, after the First World War, they diversified into producing wooden plaques (like that on page 100) and placemats. Other ephemera which can be purchased, often quite cheaply, are cut-outs, jigsaws and playing cards.

Yet another word of warning about purchasing Cecil Aldin's work. 99.9% of his work on wood is not original but stencilled onto the wood in the factory and then hand coloured and, as such, is not worth large sums of money.

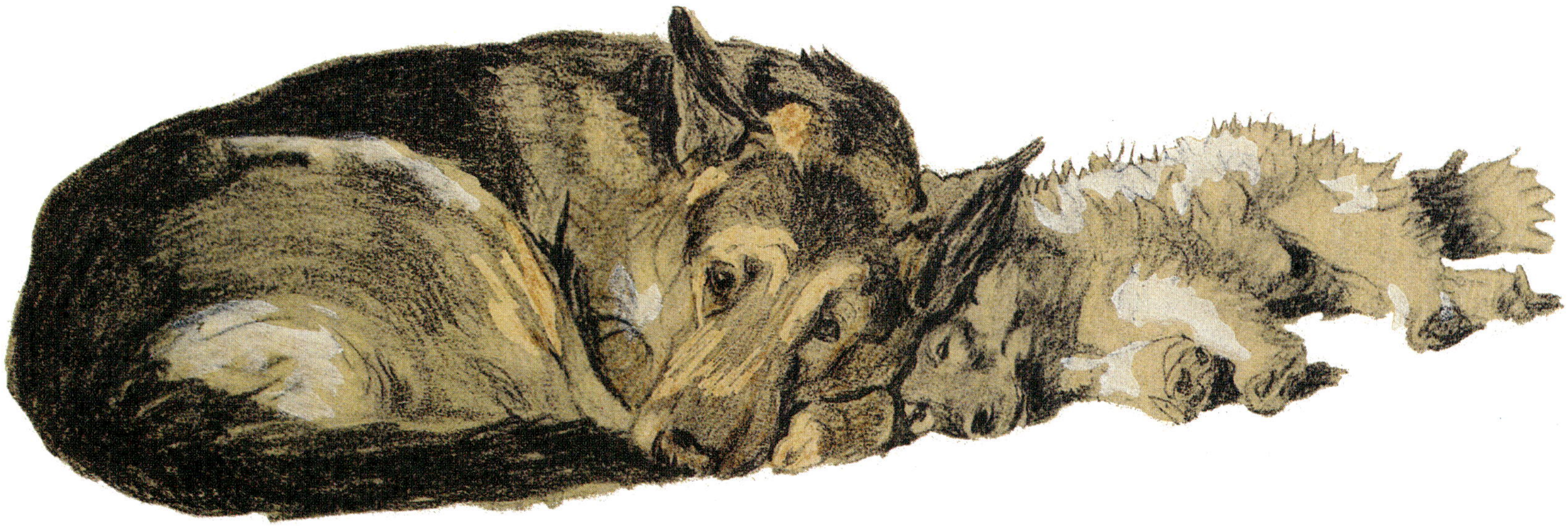

Cecil Aldin only came into close contact with two alsatians,
both in the period 1926 to 1929, and found them charming dogs. At that time alsatians were the `bogey' dogs of the press, rather like rottweilers are today.

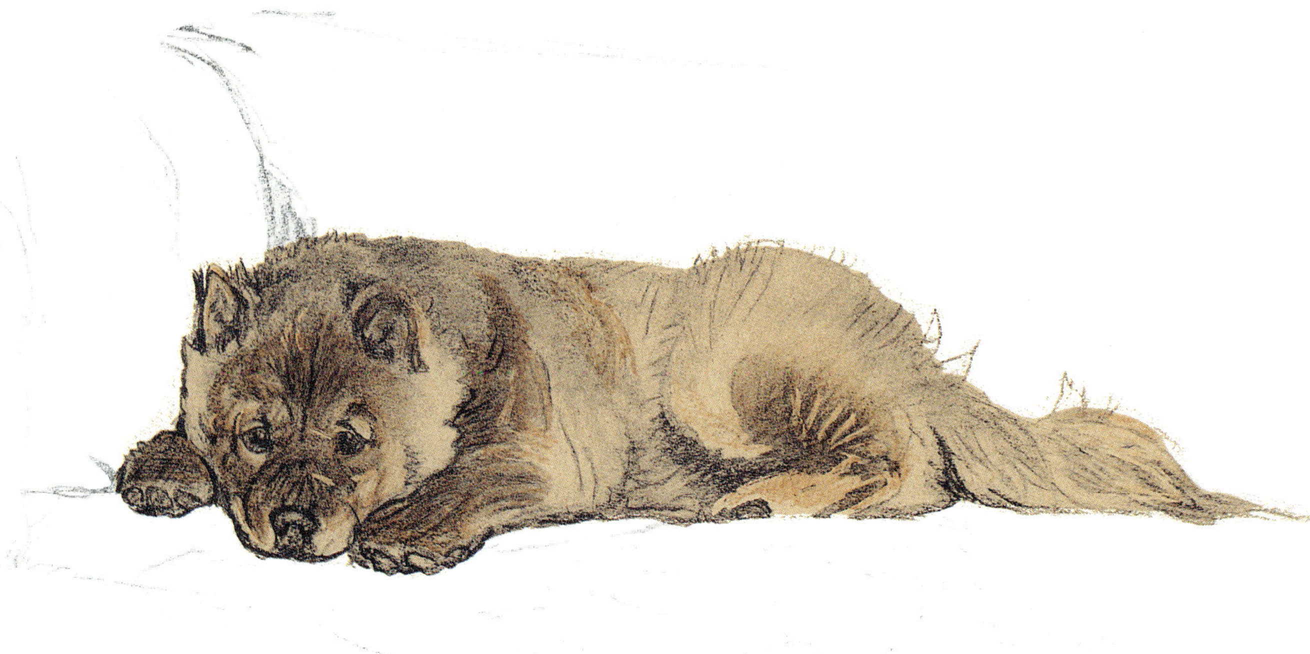

I often share an office with a chow, Mr. Charlie Chan, to whom I have dedicated this book. For me, to use a racing expression, Cecil Aldin is at least '21 lbs. ahead' of any other dog artist when it comes to painting chows. The other dog or hound he was particularly outstanding at depicting was the greyhound, although three other horse artists were also great greyhound painters, John Skeaping, Sir Alfred Munnings, P.R.A., and Gilbert Holiday.

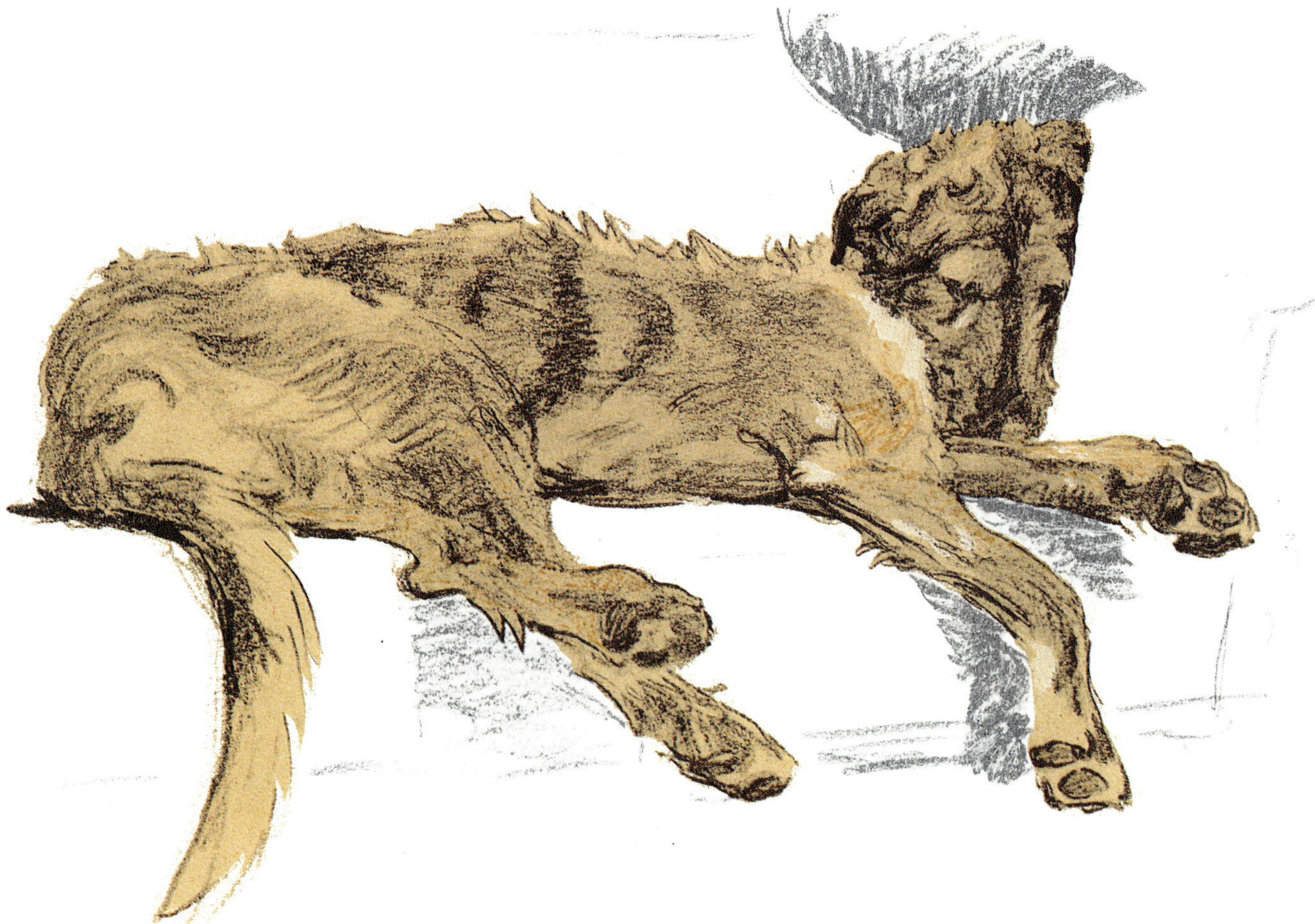

Micky, above, was not the first Irish wolfhound owned by Aldin but along with Cracker was undoubtedly one of his two favourite dogs.

LET·US·HAVE A MONGREL·DOG·SHOW!

BY
CECIL ALDIN

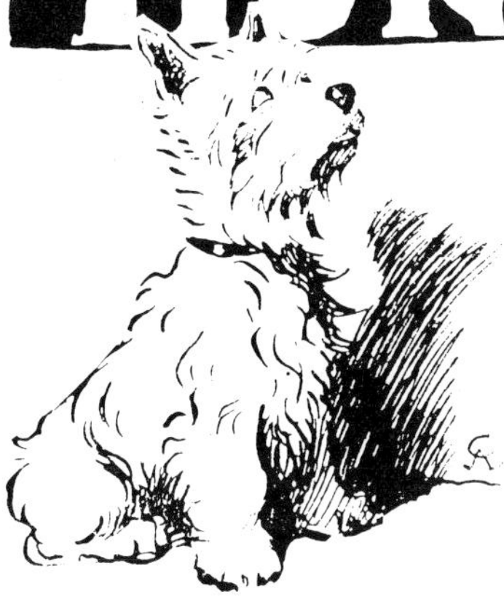

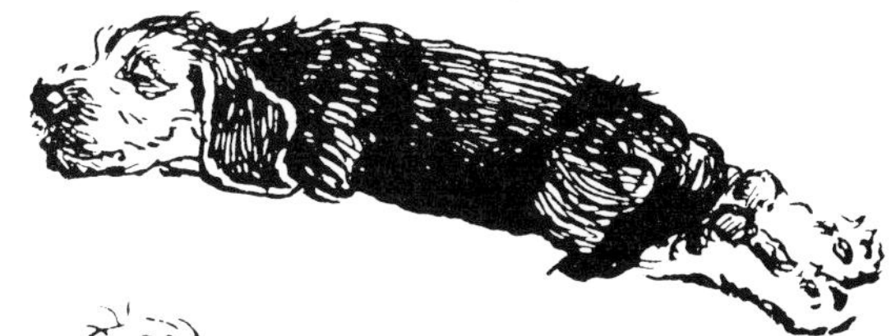

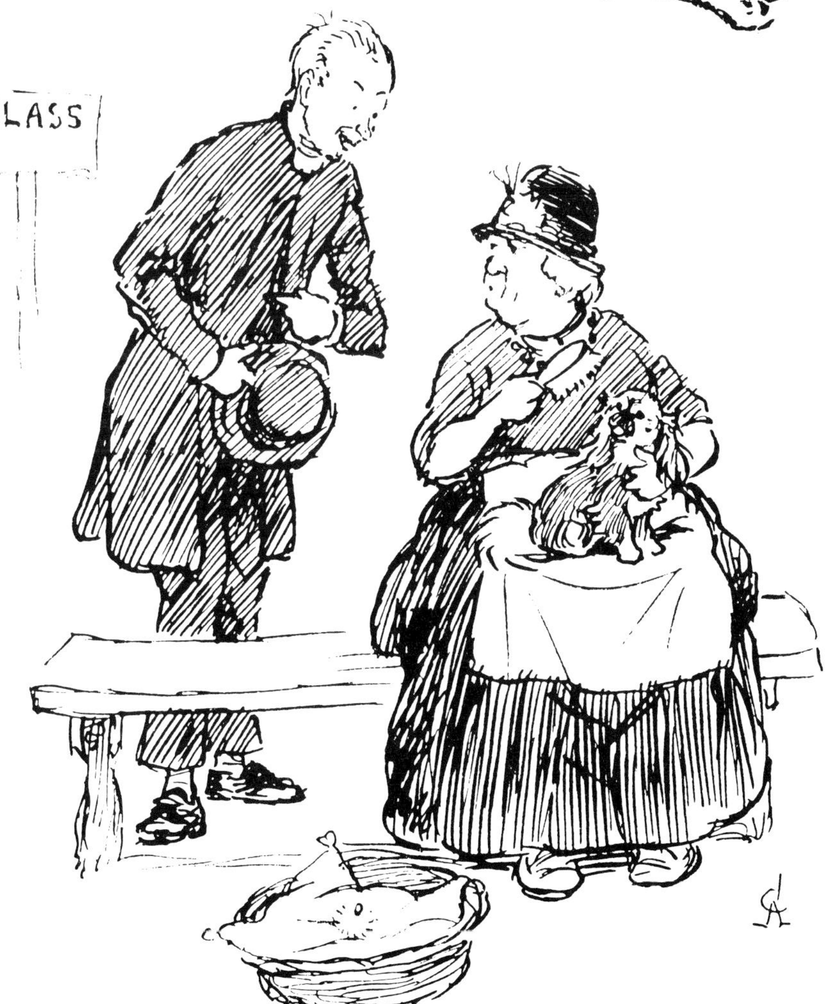

The mongrel programme should begin with some very simple class such as:

Class I	*The dog with the longest tail.*
Class II	can be for *The smallest dog (over one year)*
Class III	we have for *The worst mongrel*

Here everyone on the ground has a chance with their dog. In fact, I have known exhibitors rush out into the street and annex a dog for the occasion in the hope of winning 5s. for 6d.

The ringmaster, or collecting ring stewards, should not make the mistake of advising the owner of a pet Peke to enter for this cash on the assurance that her dog is sure to win. She will probably leave the show in high dudgeon and never speak to him again. Judges should be warned that untrimmed Sealyhams, Welsh corgi dogs, and long-haired dachshunds are not mongrels. I once saw quite a good Border terrier awarded the worst mongrel prize, much to his owner's disgust.

Next comes Class IV

The dog with the most sympathetic eyes.

Class V can be for

The dog with the most spots,

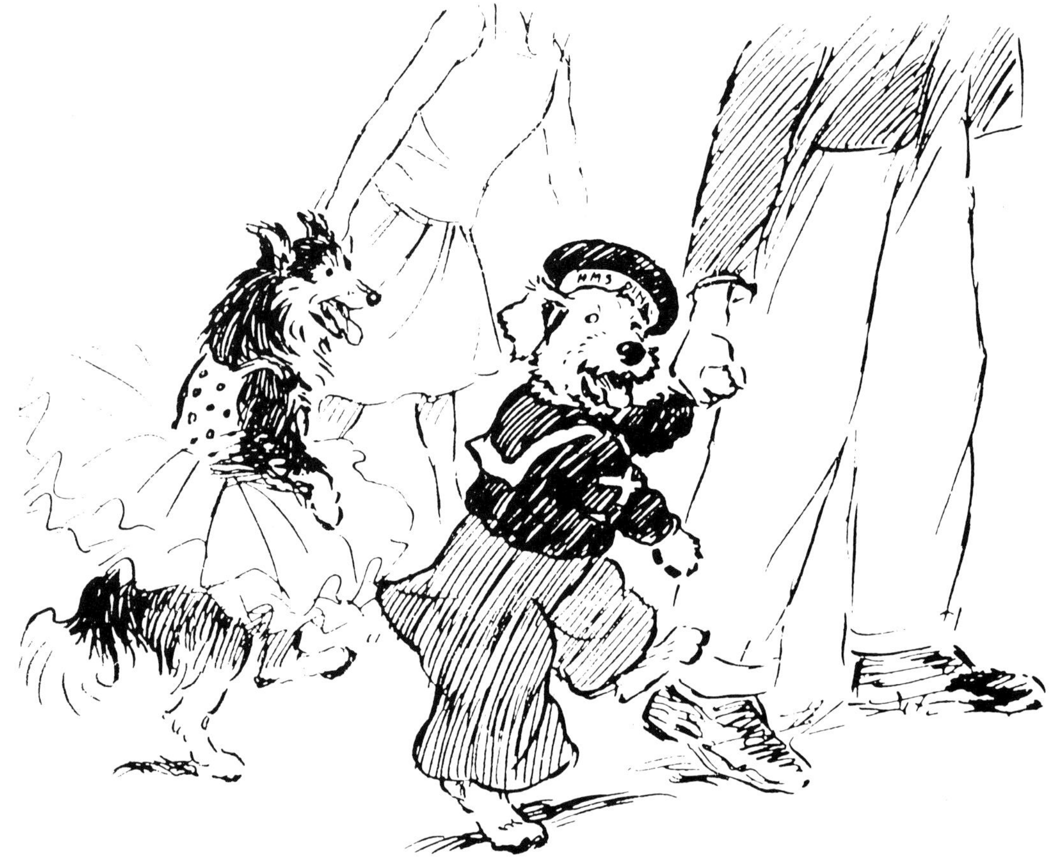

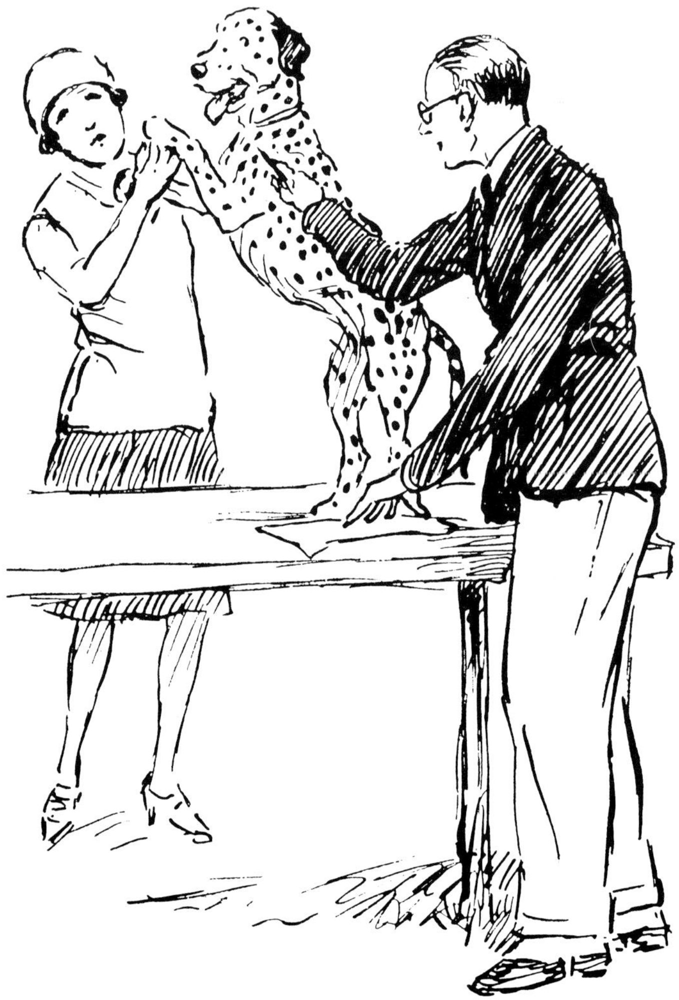

and a couple of qualified medical practitioners often make the best judges of this class.

Some people bar Dalmatians, or plum-pudding dogs, as it takes too long to count *their* spots. I think this is wrong, as the judges can always get the help of a bank clerk to assist them quickly in their addition, a bank employee being able to run his finger up the side of a Dalmatian and tell you at once the total figure.

In Class VI we can have

The dog's fancy dress competition,

and an astonishing amount of time and trouble is always taken by exhibitors on this event.

I have had between thirty and forty entries in this class, some of the costumes worn by the exhibited being well worthy of the Lord Mayor's children's fancy dress ball at the Mansion House. Pierrots, policemen, hospital nurses, columbines, babies, and bathing costumes make a variegated kaleidoscope all over the ring. The fancy dress parade is always a success.

Class VII

The dog with the bandiest legs.

The funny part about this class is that exhibitors invariably try to make their own legs as bandy as possible when showing their dogs before the judges. After a few minutes' parade in the ring even the judges themselves begin to get that "bandy feeling".

Quite knock-kneed judges get bandy-legged before their ten minutes of judging this class has expired, and even members of the audience have been known to develop sympathetic bow-legs while watching the dogs in the ring.

Although not strictly among the classes authorized by the International Mongrel Dog Show Association Incorporated, a good class to once more straighten the legs of

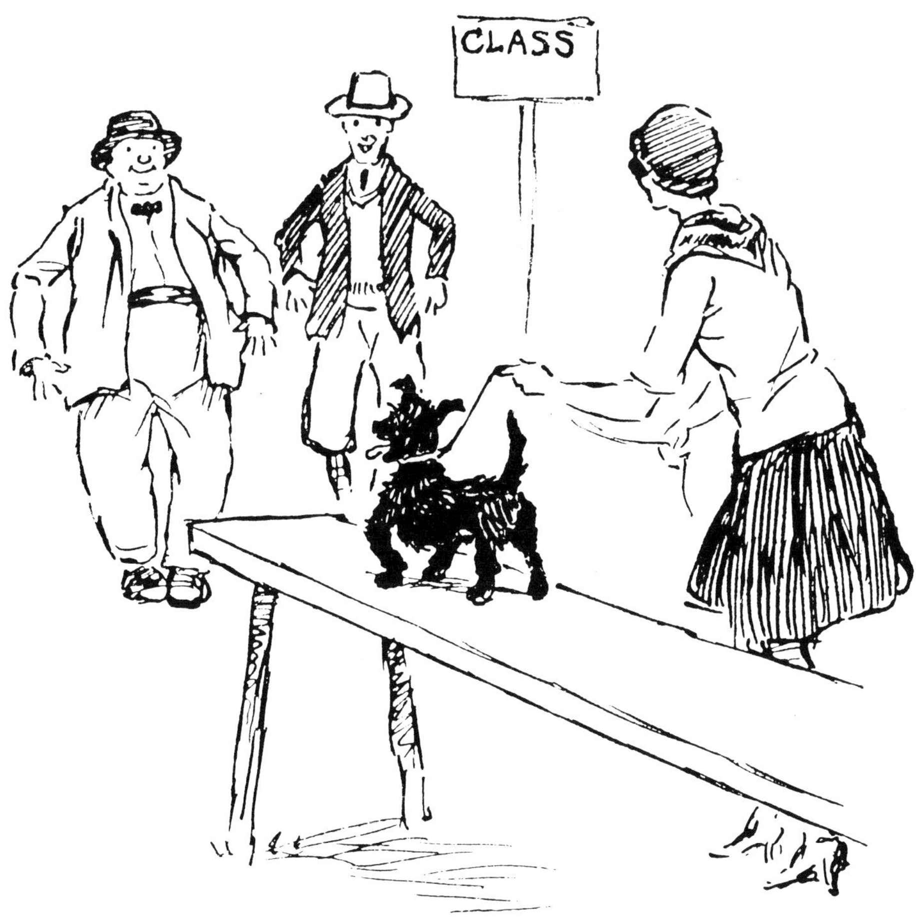

the exhibitors and audience is to insert here as Class VIII, an interval of

Mongrel dog racing

after the mechanical rabbit or cat.

This can be done under special license from the Greyhound Racing Association, Jockey Club, or some other august body, but it was originally invented by my own bull-terrier Cracker.

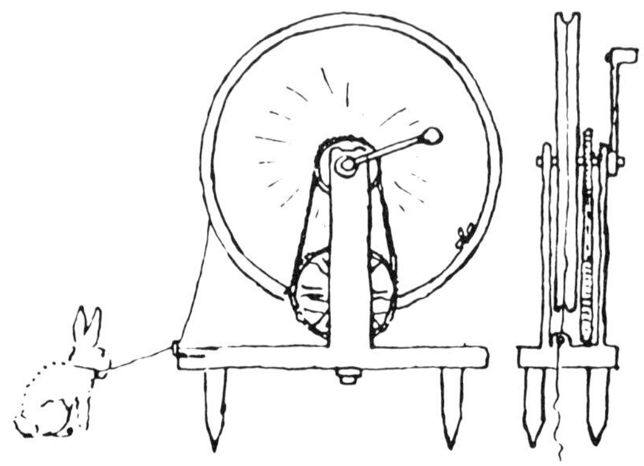

The mechanical part of this invention consists of a machine containing the stomach and hindquarters of a high-geared bicycle. As will be seen by the accompanying diagram, its mechanism is simple but effective, for when two hundred yards of strong fishing line are attached to one end and a nursery or woolly rabbit or cat attached to the other, and then rapidly wound up, no mongrel dog can possibly resist chasing it.

You can, if you are rash, allow dogs to run after it *not attached* to their owners, but my advice is **DON'T**!!! You will have quite enough to do to settle jealous canine-disputes when the quarry arrives at the winning-post with the owners attached, without asking for trouble by allowing the competitors to run loose and start their quarrels during the race. *Safety First. All dogs must be on leads* is the best watchword for these shows.

If you have large numbers of entries divide your classes into two sections, dogs over sixteen inches at the shoulder and dogs under that height.

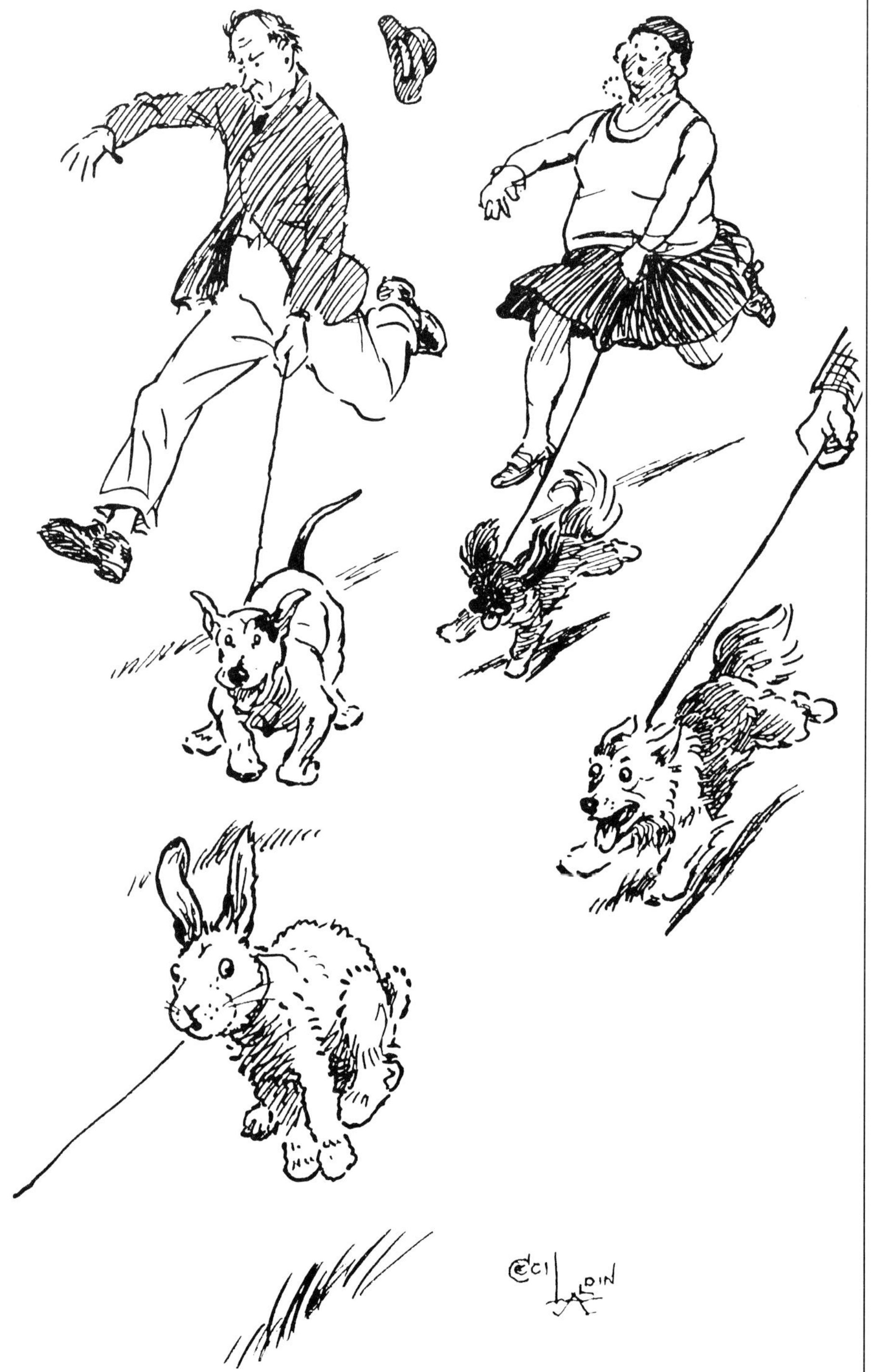

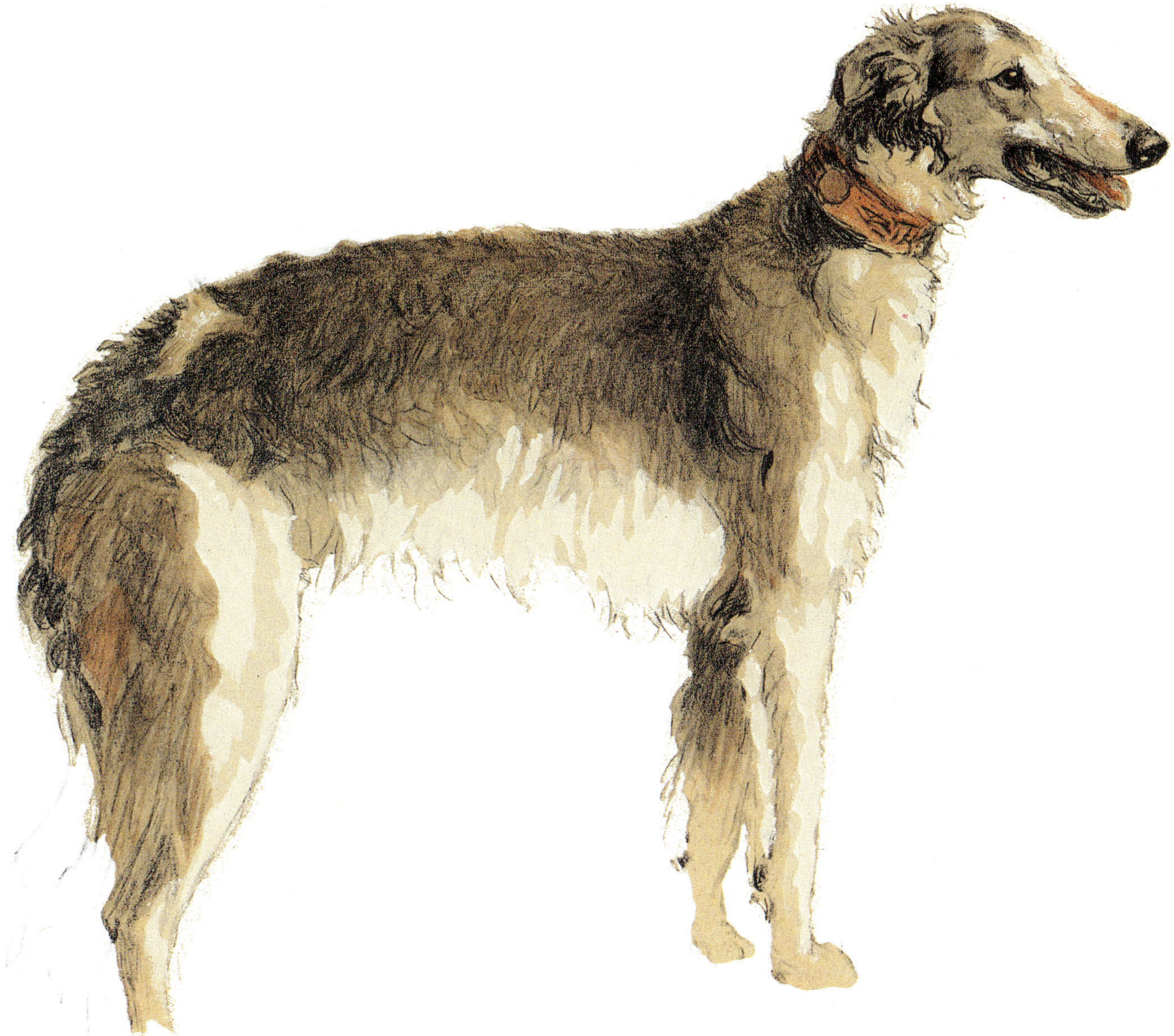

This watercolour of a borzoi is one of Cecil Aldin's most spectacular dog portraits.

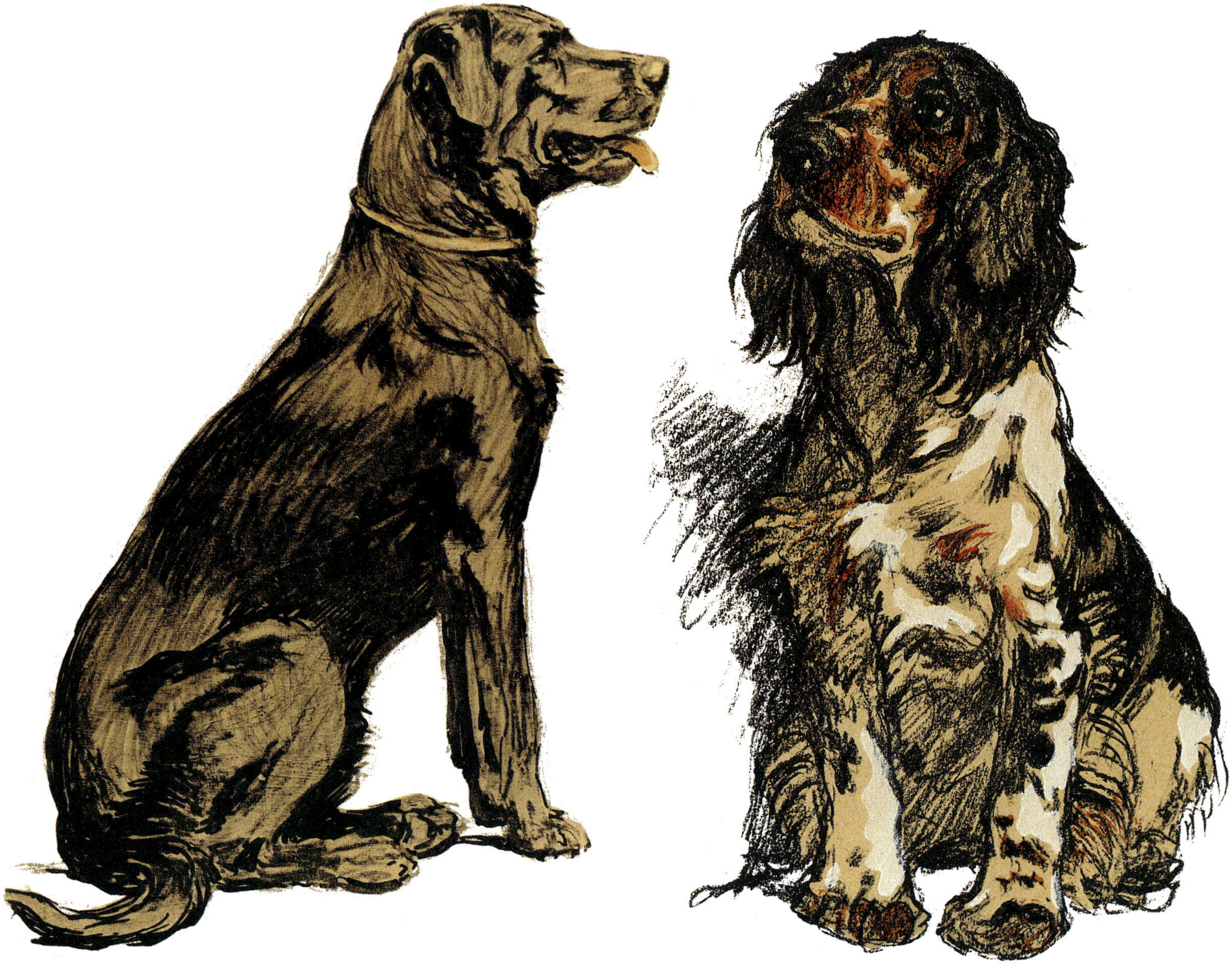

Although not known as a painter of gun dogs, these two paintings prove Cecil Aldin was as complete a master of this subject as all other canine types.

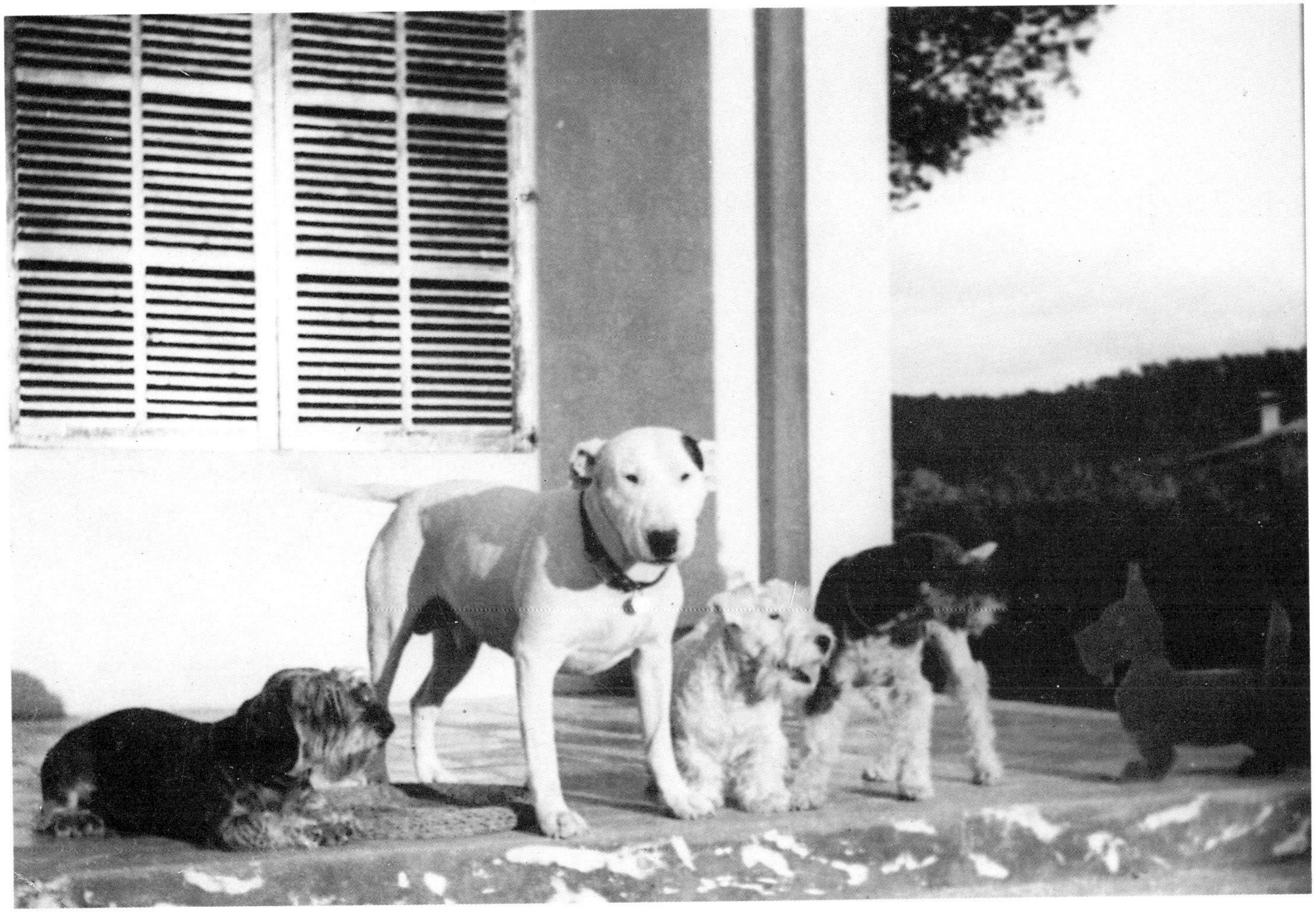

This photograph can be dated to late 1932, after the death of Micky and before the arrival of Don Quixote. Aldin was now referring to his dogs as "his family" rather than "the board of directors".

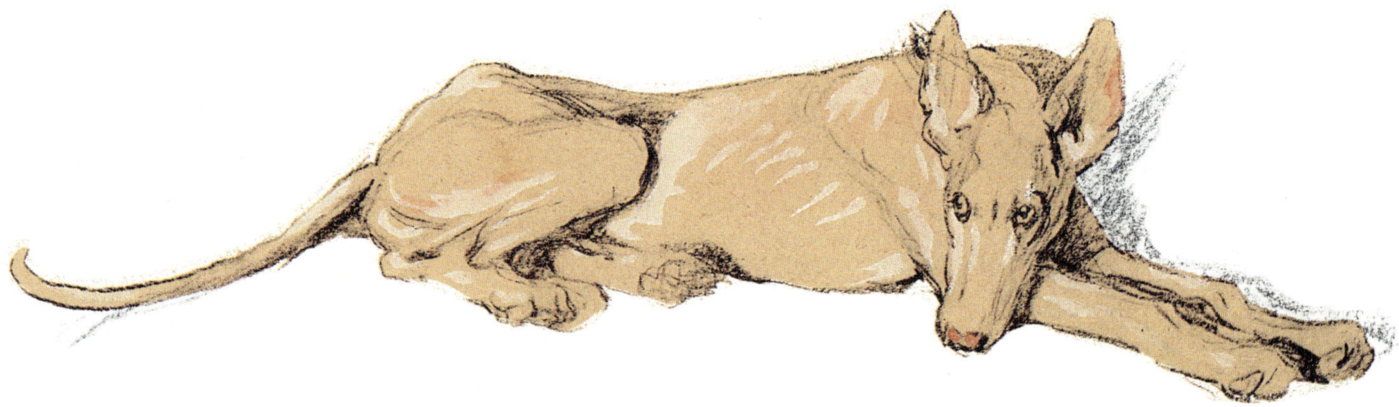

Don Quixote, above, an Ibiza hound,
was the last dog which Cecil Aldin acquired (in 1933).
He commented that Don Quixote was an interesting arrival and had more brains than a Russian wolfhound or greyhound.